M000286254

Black Transhuman Liberation Theology

Bloomsbury Studies in Black Religion and Cultures

Series Editors: Anthony B. Pinn and Monica R. Miller

Bloomsbury Studies in Black Religion and Cultures advances innovative scholarship that reimagines and animates the global study of black religions, culture, and identity across space and time. The series publishes scholarship that addresses the mutually constitutive nature of race and religion and the social, cultural, intellectual, and material effects of religio-racial formations and identities. The series welcomes projects that address and foreground the intersectional and constitutive nature of black religions and cultures and privileges work that is inter/transdisciplinary and methodologically intersectional in nature.

Forthcoming books in this series:

Black Gospel Music in Britain, Dulcie A. Dixon McKenzie
Decolonizing Contemporary Gospel Music, Robert Beckford
New Black Godz, Monica Miller

Black Transhuman Liberation Theology

Technology and Spirituality

Philip Butler

BLOOMSBURY ACADEMIC
LONDON • NEW YORK • OXFORD • NEW DELHI • SYDNEY

BLOOMSBURY ACADEMIC
Bloomsbury Publishing Plc
50 Bedford Square, London, WC1B 3DP, UK
1385 Broadway, New York, NY 10018, USA

BLOOMSBURY, BLOOMSBURY ACADEMIC and the Diana logo are trademarks of Bloomsbury Publishing Plc

First published in Great Britain 2020

Series design by Maria Rajka
Cover image: *Don't Stop the Dance* © Victoria Topping

A catalogue record for this book is available from the British Library.

Library of Congress Control Number: 2019949116

ISBN: HB: 978-1-3500-8193-2
ePDF: 978-1-3500-8194-9
eBook: 978-1-3500-8195-6

Series: Bloomsbury Studies in Black Religion and Cultures

Typeset by Deanta Global Publishing Services, Chennai, India
Printed and bound in Great Britain

To Tresse

Contents

Abbreviations

AC	Alternating Current
ACTH	Adrenocorticotropic Hormone
AVP	Arginine Vasopressin
BBB	Blood Brain Barrier
BD	Blood Draws
BLM	Black Lives Matter
BMI	Brain Machine Interface
BOLD	Blood Oxygen Level Dependent
CNS	Central Nervous System
CNT	Carbon Nanotubes
CRH	Corticotropin-Releasing Hormone
CT	Computer Tomography
DA	Dopamine
DBS	Deep Brain Stimulation
DLPFC	Dorsolateral Prefrontal Cortex
DMI	Digitally Mediated Institutions
DTI	Diffusion Tensor Imaging
EC	Entorhinal Cortex
ECoG	Electrocorticogrpahic
ECT	Electroshock Therapy
EEG	Electrocardiogram

EMG	Electromyography
ES	Electrosleep
fMRI	Functional Magnetic Resonance Imaging
GABA	Gamma-Aminobutyric acid
GPS	Global Positioning Systems
GSR	Galvanic Skin Response
HAC	Hypothalamic Arcuate Nucleus
HPC	Hippocampus
HR	Heart Rate
HRV	Heart Rate Variability
HT5	Serotonin
IoT	Internet of Things
LC	Locus Coeruleus
MALDI-MS	Matrix-Assisted Laser Desorption/Ionization Mass Spectrometry
MDMA	4-Methylenedioxymethamphetamine
MPFC	Medial Prefrontal Cortex
MPL	Modular Prosthetic Limbs
NAACP	National Association for the Advancement of Colored People
NE	Norepinephrine
NRI	Noradrenaline Reuptake Inhibitors
OT	Oxytocin
PCC	Posterior Cingulate Cortex
PET	Positron Emission Tomography
PFC	Prefrontal Cortex
PSPL	Posterior Superior Parietal Lobe
PsTs	Posterior Superior Temporal Sulcus

rs-FC	Resting State Functional Connectivity
SMA	Premotor/Supplemental Motor Area
SSRI	Selective Serotonin Reuptake Inhibitors
STEM	Science, Technology, Engineering, and Mathematics
STG	Superior Temporal Gyrus
TBI	Traumatic Brain Injury
TCC	Tai Chi Chuan
TCET	Transcerebral Electrotherapy
TES	Transcranial Electrostimulation
TPJ	Temporoparietal Junction
VMPFC	Ventromedial Prefrontal Cortex

Acknowledgments

To the village that spans two coasts. To the many who have cheered me on. To those who are able to share in this victory. To my two sons, born on this journey, Micheal and Edmund. I love you, and I thank you.

Introduction and Overview

The scholarship of Black spiritualities and Black (Christian) liberation theology has yet to offer meaningful reflection on the role of technology in the lives of Black people. A deep reflection on the role and potential of technology in the lives of Black folks in the North American context may demonstrate technology's potential to be the perfect partner for spirituality. In saying this, it means that technology helps to create and cultivate a sustained internal disposition primed for liberating the self toward a collective and physically manifested version of liberation. This project is a theological juxtaposition based on the liberation genre/theme forged through the combination of transhumanism and spirituality. This theology starts from the premise that theological anthropology is the foundation for understanding spirituality's role in the work of liberation. My goal is to bring attention to current and emergent technological advances in order to imagine what it means to begin utilizing technology's personally augmenting capabilities to enhance human spiritual experiences. I hope that this exercise will provide a physical foundation for realizing the implications of what it means to spiritually struggle against oppression, concretely. The tangible implications of Black transhuman liberation theology manifest as it melds technology and spirituality in a manner that helps individuals create an internal disposition that points toward liberation, keeping the mind clear and focused in the pursuit of the ultimate liberative goal.

I chose this project for several reasons: (1) to begin the discussion of integrating neurophysiology into the study of Black spirituality in the US context; (2) to reflect on potential practices that combine the power of technology and Black spirituality; (3) to bring to the forefront the thought that participation in the Science, Technology, Engineering and Mathematics (STEM) fields by Black folks is crucial to achieving the fullness of that compilation—as a means to direct its potential; and (4) I see the combination of these two realms as key to the materialization of liberation that Black folks seek.

With the current rate of technological expansion, it may sometimes appear that technology's reach has no end. Technology has seeped into nearly every facet of everyday life, even into the way in which governments function. As prosthetic creatures, human beings, or human animals, have and continue to coevolve alongside the technologies we create.[1] In that effect, humans have always been transhuman. Very basically, transhumanism is a cultural and philosophical movement. It asserts that any use of technology to augment human intellectual, physical, or psychological capability makes one transhuman.[2] This can be seen in the example of the cave dweller, who utilized rocks and sticks to aid her in hunting, cooking, art, and the creation of fire. It can also be seen in the basic biotechnology inherent within the body itself: the brain, neurons, cells, transmitters, etc. So, from this acknowledgment two questions arise: (1) Have we ever been just human? (2) Are we even human—if we've always been transhuman? Because if we are not human, then the guidelines for the way we engage others, the world, and ourselves change dramatically. These questions are important to Black folks because as we move into the future, the complex relationship between governing authorities, ourselves, and technology will have a large impact on the way we are then allowed to—or allow ourselves to—live in the world, which is essentially the way we are free.

This project will be the first of its kind to integrate transhumanism, biological science, Black spirituality, and liberation theology. This is important because our global society leans toward an ever-increasing integration of human life and technological advancement. Presently, transhumanism and its stance toward technology challenges classical theological notions of God and the limitations which result from necessarily upholding the sanctity of the human form. So, this project seeks to determine what a successful integration of these categories might look like by melding spirituality and transhumanism where they intersect: the Black body.

Theoretically, no Black theologian has wrestled with what it means to be as theologically in tune with technology as they would be with nature. This project views technology as an extension of nature. Furthermore, a constructive theology that engages these issues must consider not only the necessity of this convergence but also the logical and practical implications of this convergence as well. For instance, barring some global reformation toward agrarian preindustrial minimalism, transhumanism will become the means by which society operates. So, new questions will arise. This is especially true as it pertains to Black people, though this is not to exclude other people of variously marginalized experiences. So, we must ask questions such as, "How will racist social structures persist in the implementation of transhumanism?" This question is incredibly important. In the instance of the genetic modification of embryos via designed evolution, it is important to think about how this procedure is accessed (a question of socioeconomics) and to whom will the implementation of this procedure first be disseminated (a question of race), especially since it might initially be considered an elective procedure. Notions of privilege and White supremacy must be considered when determining equity in the technological progression of humanity.

I believe that Black folks need to accept that we are already transhumans. This acceptance would hopefully lead to a greater intentionality toward how Black folks identify and operate within transhumanism. When someone utilizes the benefits of a prosthesis, mechanized or otherwise, that is transhumanist. When elderly people remember to wear their hearing aids, this is an example of transhumanism. The point I am making is that since Black theology has yet to offer meaningful reflection on the ways that Black folks use technology, there remains a theological dissonance whereby Black dependency on technology is unexplored, and we fail to understand how theological dissonance relates to the historical narrative of Black bodies and Western American science. This Black theological dissonance does not permit the existence of a cohesive and theologically grounded understanding of science. This project serves as a bridge for some Black folks to see a reconciliation among science, their bodies, and their faith. For the Black community this is a big deal. If a theology arises affirming the scientific interest of Black minds, then there may be less aversion toward science and the theological self and less pushback on the inherent ability of Black children to excel in STEM-based curriculums and careers. It is time for Black communities to begin taking seriously their stake in science so that they can begin carving out their own space in the transhumanist future.

Science, even neuroscience, has not been fully integrated with spirituality as a whole, much less with Black spirituality. Theoretically, this returns to the idea of the body as a modality of universal axiom, especially since Black bodies were used in the formation of American sciences. When I say this, I am referencing the biological body, as the phenomenological experiences of bodies differ based on social context. The use of the Black body to carve out the basics of American science suggests that it is the prototypical body referenced in anatomical diagrams, even though the picture depicts someone else as normative. This project allows Black spirituality to begin the dialogue with neuroscience that begins theorizing the importance and physical effectiveness of Black spiritualities that have historically been vilified as purely emotional. However, a neurophysiological assumption of all mental and bodily states is that every human state is emotionally grounded (neutral or otherwise).[3] So, this project has the potential to undo negative ideologies that have been projected onto and internalized by Black folks about their own spiritual practices through the affirmation of scientific wisdom. This project has the lofty intention of cultivating a spiritual and scientific awakening to the possibilities of a reciprocal relationship between Black spiritualities and science. Although there are some Black scholars who actively denounce the need for objective affirmation through science, specifically due to its European roots, this would also be an opportunity to connect with the history of science and mathematics that leads back to African origins.[4] By introducing Black spiritualities to neuroscience, this project can introduce Black folks to their physical internalities that have been disconnected for generations.

Ultimately, this project is the construction of a practical approach to liberation for Black folks through the combination of technology and spirituality. So, this work is important in this space for three reasons: (1) It takes liberation theology beyond its natural scope of outlining histories and theological assumptions in lieu of their liberative meanings. (2) It does not enlist God as the salvific catalyst of liberation. And (3) it takes liberation theology into the cultural future.

Liberation theology must begin to engage current and emergent technologies. Accepting technology as integral to societal operation allows liberation to remain relevant and meaningful.

The practical portion of this project works on constructing an intentional catalog of spiritual practices that is geared toward liberation in conversation with technologies readily available, and with that which are on the horizon. This is important because the production and improvement of technology will not stop. This theology is also important to the practical effort of the liberative future. It begins the discussion of what liberation looks like in a technocentric and transhumanist society when political change and human transformation are not only the result of spiritual practices but also the result of technological breakthroughs grounded in human action.

Impending technocracy

Liberation theology as a genre has provided numerous sketches of freedom visions in relation to Black folks, Latinx, Asian, womanist, feminist, LGBTQ, and persons living with disabilities. But after almost fifty years of writing we still find ourselves in the throws of a similarly oppressive ideology, resulting from the evolution of US oppression systems in an effort to maintain power over bodies. We have witnessed this evolution before, at the end of reconstruction, with the implementation of Jim Crow laws, and again with housing laws. This same lingering oppressive ideology is present in today's voter's rights laws and "religious freedom" bills of the South. The phase changes of power have arrived under the guise of neoliberalism's attempt to keep the marginalized at hands length.[5] Yet in the midst of this, we find ourselves at the onset of a looming technocratic rule—in the form of electronic governance (e-governance) by an elite class of technical and technological experts—that might be considered the next phase change of oppressive structures. This is due to the reincarnation of subjugating principles through far-reaching technological advancements packaged in various consumer-based modalities. Access to these devices provides an almost limitless amount of information and entertainment, and this access is elevated through mobile technology. Psychological attachment to technology has developed to the point where people are now literally afraid to be away from these devices.[6] Their mass market appeal continues to expand, increasing the reach of these devices, their ability to influence communication, and their impact on how people live with/among one another in the world.

There is an ongoing conversation about whether people are actually less connected to one another with the advent of the social media communities.[7] While some suggest that social media connects humans more, others suggest that it predominantly creates an even wider chasm and a greater sense of disconnection among people. For those who prefer the virtual environment, these worlds foster experiences of augmented reality where many individuals are free to create fabricated personas that further their ability to hide from the world in anonymity. But, there is also a sedating quality associated with these spaces that distort personal perception through a psychological proposition, where people think their virtual social actions make concrete systemic change.[8] This is not to deny the importance of bringing awareness to particular causes, but it is an attempt to emphasize the fictitious sense of confidence that social media interactions tend to generate. What may be considered the worst part about personal technology is its ability to serve as a substitute world where people can mask their personal pain. As people continue to buy into the grandeur of these virtual spaces, which is a direct symptom of personal technology's nocuous effects, people find themselves steeped in the cyclical economic traps that force them to maintain socially generated standards of civilized existence.[9] This socioeconomic form of oppression, in true capitalist fashion, places technological advances just far enough ahead of consumers to perpetuate the demand cycle through planned obsolescence.

The potential for technology to be utilized as a form of governance can be seen through its roots. For instance, consumer products are often the most basic form of the actual technology used to create them. Many technological comforts taken for granted today, due to their widespread use, began as innovations of war. Global positioning systems were used by the military to track position; digital photography was used for surveillance; and the internet, especially the dark web, was used for communication by the government long before mass consumption. But the existence of these technologies as offshoots of government innovation alludes to the planned obsolescence of era-dependent forms of government. The nocuous and mesmerizing effect of consumer technology is evidenced in the ways in which systemically applied versions of these personal technologies very easily assert influence over human decision-making. Users frequently and willingly secede the luxuries of privacy, autonomy, and personal environmental awareness in order to adhere to technology's hyper-engaging allure.

The technocracy itself runs on two major components—big data and automation. Big data is the process of collating large data sets composing of user activity within a particular technological medium. These sets necessitate real-time analysis. Real-time analysis allows for greater conceptual understanding of their practical application.[10] The computational modeling of these sets can be utilized to determine behavioral trends, providing insightful information regarding user action/interaction in any given space/environment. Through computer modeling, big data can be applied as a means of surveillance, persuasion, and social engineering, geared toward steering mass consumption, public opinion, social norms, and social politics.[11]

Automation, as a governmental tool, creates avenues to complete tasks without direct observation or engagement through previously written code. It is the foundation of digitally mediated institutions (DMI) operating within the larger government apparatus. DMIs are government organizations characterized by their high degree of digital infrastructure and widespread use of digital applications and tools.[12] They rely heavily on policy feedback and the inherent longitudinal dependence of government implementation (path dependence) to allow for the installation and ensuing codification of digitally automated policies in the form of electronic systems.[13] It is important to note that the process of digitally reifying government policies is essentially the transformation of said policies into digital ontologies. As digital ontologies, added layers—in the form of technology via programming languages—create further separation between those who are governed and the actual technological components that work to automatically process governance. Meaning, the processing of government becomes a digital ontology, which adds extra layers between the laws being implemented and persons on the ground—increasing the difficulty of political action.[14]

DMIs utilize big data to streamline the governing process. The automation of computational modeling and of data sets bridges the benefits of big data with the seamlessness of automation. Since DMIs rely on path dependence to sustain their place within the e-governance model, those who initially created their infrastructure are now free to move on to something else entirely. The experts, who construct the automation of government, shrink the size of government solely for the purpose of maintaining current and past forms of order and not to make government smaller for the sake of the governed. The sinister side of automating DMIs is found in the fact that, like many other government officials, the code which runs them is simply doing its job. In this way, finding the person to blame after a policy or law is automated creates another deeply layered process.

Timing and sequence matter in the potential influence of DMIs on society. The endless automation of big data produces a compound analysis that increases the ability to decipher feedback provided by these large unrestricted data sets. This allows for more precise predictions as DMIs seek to effect "political interactions of organized interests and policy makers." The goal of DMI's is to influence public policies that affect the "beliefs, preferences, and actions of diffuse mass publics," because "public policies affect the depth of democracy, the inclusiveness of citizenship, and the degree of societal solidarity."[15] Essentially, the technocracy, or technocratic e-government, works to embed measures of behavioral surveillance in order to track actions/interactions of citizens for the purpose of determining more efficient ways to socially engineer automated methods of control. This is not unlike governing structures of the past. Governmental policies, which maintained a specific position toward certain groups, will still hold those positions. Except this time, marginalized groups can only blame the machines for their predicament. The programmers responsible for reincarnating oppressive structures through digital ontologies only come back to work if there is a glitch in the system, and that is so they can fix the glitch, not the system.

The technocratic e-government is not a novel way to oppress Black folks. In fact it could oppress anyone. It is particularly sinister for that reason, because fundamentally it is no different than the governing system already in place. So, for the American contingent who have and continue to place their faith in the current form of American government as being grounded in fairness and non-bias, an automation of the current system will not be viewed as problematic.

In fact, it will be seen as useful and adding value to everyday life. However, the technocracy's ability to simply automate the already oppressive structures of Americana (deemed normative) as outlined in Michelle Alexander's *The New Jim Crow*, is particularly dangerous for Black folks.[16] The added layers that automation creates further increases the distance between lawmakers, law enforcement, and citizens who become abstracted into statistics of criminality. Automated governance will make it harder to fight against the inherently oppressive nature of the American government, literally codifying its inherent bias for Whiteness—through computer language. Technocracy's ability to render the human element of relationality between those who govern (lawmakers and law enforcement) and those who live under laws (citizens) as opaque creates a dangerous vulnerability for those under the law who already face disproportionate discrimination from its enactment. The state of vulnerability Black folks experience will then be delineated by the preset whims of disinterested machinery running lines of code so that it may simply do its job. This is a distinctly different level of volition than officers, judges, or lawmakers who currently say they are only doing their job. The most treacherous component of technocratic e-governance can be found in how it removes the direct weight of culpability from those who govern onto the technologically embedded layers, via the esoteric logic of computer language that underlies information systems, its software, the hardware that stores it, and the data science which augments its own capabilities. In essence, the promise of new technology distracts from the fact that when it is given the chance to govern it can only generate a snapshot of governmental structures that are dependent upon the temporality in which it was created. So, as society moves into the future, which often assumes a sentiment of social progress, the laws which govern society will more than likely remain in the digital ontology connected to the temporal existence from which they emanated.

Spirituality and liberation

Historically, Black spiritualities have been presented in two distinct forms. First, via living theologies embodied by various iterations of organized and unorganized Black religious expression, although predominately manifesting as the Black Church in the United States. Second, through Black theology as outlined by Black religious scholars. It is important to note the term "Black Church" is not meant to monolithically describe the entire context of Black churches, as if all

Black churches are simplistically uniform. The Black Church exists as a complex landscape of denominations and iterations of Christianity. Kelly Brown Douglas suggests in *Black Bodies and the Black Church: A Blues Slant*, "The [B]lackness of this church depends upon its morally active commitment to advance the life, freedom, and dignity of all black bodies."[17] For the purpose of this project, I use the term "Black Church" as a means to describe the complex manifestations of Black Christian organization. This is inclusive of historically African American denominations, Black mainline Protestant congregations, Black expressions of Catholicism, etc. I ground this descriptive definition's ability to include a broad grouping of Black churches in what Anthony Pinn describes in *Black Religion and Aesthetics*, as a "mov[e] beyond strict attention to doctrinal considerations as the proper cartography of shared religiosity, without the assumption that religion within this expansive cultural arena means the proliferation of a particular religious tradition," over another.[18]

In contrast, Black theology is an academic discipline rich in its historical complexity. The term serves as an umbrella for theological discourse stemming from Black experiences. Black theology focuses on exploring theologically grounded notions of freedom and liberation. The term was coined by the National Committee of Negro Churchmen, via a full page statement that appeared in a 1966 issue of *The New York Times*, which demonstrated that Black ministers and academics were beginning to wrestle with the relationship that Christianity and Black Power might have.[19] James Cone wrote Black theology's initial book length iteration, *Black Theology, Black Power*, in roughly five weeks following the assassination of Martin Luther King, Jr.[20] While the Black power movement was considered antithetical to Christianity, in many regards, Cone's work argued for a synthesis between the two. He followed *Black Theology, Black Power*, with *A Black Theology of Liberation*. It was a more systematic approach, which *ultimately repositioned God as Black*. For Cone, God's Blackness was determined through God's ontological proximity to the poor and oppressed/marginalized. "The [B]lackness of God means that God has made the oppressed condition God's own condition," turning the preferential option for the poor to something intrinsically tied to Christ's embodiment and social status. Through these initial projects Cone grounded the liberation of Black folks from White racism in the theological affirmation of Blackness and Black humanity.

Cone's prophetic offering of Black of theology was not received without criticism. Black men who raised questions concerning the construction of Black theology were among the most prominent of Black theology's early critics. For instance, Charles Long thought it might be more helpful to consider the nature of Black religion, more broadly. He posited that religiosity was the fundamental orientation of Black folks, which might provide greater insight into understanding what it meant to be Black in the American landscape. J. Deotis Roberts proposed that racial reconciliation is a necessary component of the liberative exercise. William Jones posed one of the most pressing critiques of Cone's theological undertaking. His analysis questioned the existence of a God whose aim was to liberate Black folks. Furthermore, Jones implicated God as a culpable entity in the oppression of Black folks, suggesting God functions as a means to maintain racially stratified power dynamics. Jones suggested that a God who allows for the continuance of White racism is actually a proponent of it. Still, there remained the critiques of Cecil Cone and Gayraud Wilmore which focused on the theoretical foundation and operational utility of Black theology. Cecil questioned the very Blackness of Black theology, given its foundation in European scholarship. And Wilmore's analysis considered Black theology too otherworldly—de-radicalizing its Blackness and de-Christianizing its radicalness.[21]

While Pauli Murray was among the first to advance a gendered critique of Black theology, Jacqueline Grant's *White Women's Christ, Black Women's Jesus* became the first widely recognized demonstration of the sexism inherent within Black theology. The development of womanist theology by scholars such as Katie Cannon, Delores Williams, M. Shawn Copeland, Emilie M. Townes, Monica Coleman, Kelly Brown Douglas, and Keri Day challenged the assumptions of Black theology along with the dangers and limitations that may arise from its connection to Black male privilege. Womanist theological ethics began to recount the theologically grounded narratives which outlined what it means to be a womanist, "womanish," or woman loving under the notion of "unequivocal justice for all." It is important to note that gendering Black theology opened up the door for Black theology to deal with Black sexuality and the varying levels of dis/ability involving the Black body. These progressive strokes in Black theological discourse have worked to expand the conversation of justice and liberation. And as Black theology moves into the future more complex forms of embodiment, including the fluid nature of gender and sexuality, must be included in the conversation—giving an account of markers of biological diversity and environmental adaptation.

Although both the Black Church and Black theology engage spirituality, there still remains a disconnect between the two regarding how each engages spirituality. While Black theology has begun to wrestle with and highlight specific forms of Black spiritualities, the Black Church recognizes the inherent spiritual aspects of its heritage. But, the Black Church does not specifically engage spirituality on a grand scale. Although Black theology's influence has begun to bleed into the practices and discourse of certain Black churches, to say that these entities are one and the same is problematic. Black theology's obsession with freedom from oppression through critical theological engagement with social and political structures intended to rethink the assumptions of lived theologies, sometimes clashes with certain Black churches who emphasize personal piety or upward mobility over liberation. Furthermore, to say that these entities explicitly and overtly engage spirituality in an extensive manner is not true either. "Black spirituality," as a blanket term, has always been implied but not necessarily deeply explored. The research specific to Black spirituality marks a recent shift in scholastic focus with a little over thirty years of research having been completed. Yet, in Black churches spirituality has always been the sweet-smelling savor of Black religious practice. This is to say that in the Black Church spirituality has always been the result of Black religiosity manifesting as lived theology. It is so interwoven into the fabric of the church's existence that it might explain why spirituality has not always been the target of explicit exploration. The ramifications of Black spirituality's existence have always been implied through the embodied culmination of Black religion: its wisdoms, traditions, and physiological effect on individually and communally engaged Black bodies. My use of Black spirituality in the US Christian context is meant to serve as a material bridge between Black theology and the Black Church. Material, in this sense, is taken from natural science as being composed of matter. So, spirituality should be seen as the material effect of religious expression on the body in all of its expressions. This is not to exclude the effects of nonreligious spiritual expression on the body. Nonreligious Black spirituality does exist and is of importance to this discussion. Note, however, in the case of Black spirituality tied to the Black Church or historical notions of Black theology, spirituality should be seen in this way—tied to religion, or Christianity.

As a parallel phenomenon to the increase in scholarship focusing on spirituality, spirituality has undergone a reemergence in the United States within the last few decades. This is in opposition to traditional forms of American religion in the United States, where more individuals are beginning to dissociate from formally organized versions of religion in lieu of wider spanning versions of spiritual connection.[22] Even those who remain within a particular religious landscape are opting to practice their faith differently than generations past. Spirituality, in a broader sense (beyond US forms of Christocentric normativity), is not always explicitly defined. So, for the purposes of this project spirituality, including both religious and nonreligious spiritual expressions, will be defined as the felt and unfelt connection one has with God OR that which is beyond the self, through the physical world (both seen and unseen). I chose to incorporate the seen and unseen within the bounds of the physical world as a means to introduce the importance of the body to this spiritual proposition. The body, although visible, is the only consistent space that humans experience spirituality. The physical world is the setting that the body interacts with which helps to form the basis of any experience. The body's underlying processes (i.e., the brain or heart) are not immediately visible, but do exist. An assumption that I carry into this definition is that people with bodies are reading this, so it is important to propose a spirituality where biological aspects are the fundamental components of spiritual connection to the natural world. Ultimately, these connections that are seen and unseen carry real and traceable markers—via scientific understandings.[23]

This understanding of spirituality is in line with those who have denounced Cartesian dualism that separates body and mind. The formation of a physical spirituality results from the need for spirituality to move beyond the phenomenology of experiencing God to the biologically empirical structures that underpin phenomenology. Empirically grounding spiritual experience is something that matters deeply to more individuals who are interested in the physical outcomes of their particular spiritual experiences. These physical outcomes are also important as people continue to search for the most fitting spirituality, not just for the individual but also for communal needs as well. Today, people who seek and choose their own spirituality do so for some of the same reasons they do anything else of their own volition. This often includes making decisions for the purpose of efficacy and personal potency—potency being the power felt by the spiritual practitioner based on their perceived importance of the practice. Understanding the biology, more specifically the neurophysiology (based on the convergence of neuroscience and physiology) of different forms of spirituality, helps the reader determine what may be the most biologically and psychologically efficient spirituality with the greatest metaphysical potential for them. Although spiritualities are based on belief, essentially they must make sense to those who subscribe to their wisdom.

The move toward a spirituality that works also parallels a dramatic exodus of dissatisfied persons from mainline Protestant Christian traditions. Pew Research shows that a growing number of adults are becoming religiously unaffiliated while professing to experience a greater sense of wonder about the universe.[24] Interestingly enough, one may look at the data and determine that the same

7 percent of individuals who left Christian churches provide nearly 86 percent of the 7 percent increase of those who now identify as religiously unaffiliated. So, people are actively seeking and beginning to find spiritualities that fulfill them. Most notably, that fulfillment is no longer occurring in mainline institutional churches. This is true for the Black Church as well. The 2014 religious affiliation poll showed a 6 percent increase among Black folks who self-identified as religiously unaffiliated. This was accompanied by a roughly 5 percent decrease in Black folks who affiliated with the Christian faith.[25] This information almost forces us to question how one can experience spiritual fulfillment apart from religion. The investigators at Pew Research did not ask how important Jesus was to their participants' spiritual life. Such a question may offer a stark distinction for those who are no longer religiously affiliated and the presumptive spiritual power that may still reside in the newly unaffiliated person's perception regarding the Jesus character. Because, if Jesus is still an integral part of the unaffiliated person's spirituality, but the religious institution is not, then there might be something to say about the ecclesial success of creating an environment that is spiritually efficient and satisfying. Another issue that arises from exploring this space is asking what makes spirituality satisfying aside from a particular emotionality or sense of community. I would suggest that a spirituality that is liberating begins with being the most satisfying.

Spirituality is meant to be liberating. Joining that which is beyond the self with the self in a manner that has both spiritual and physical manifestations provides the most satisfaction. It is hard to argue with the notion that freedom is a pressing and unrelenting concern for the human. Some philosophers might oppose this view arguing that immortality, meaning, or wealth is the unrelenting concern of the human—in lieu of freedom. However, in response to that I would submit that immortality is freedom from the unknown or the limitations of corporeality. Meaning is freedom from nihilistic existentialism, and wealth is freedom to move about the physical world, free from the restrictions associated with those who cannot afford to. So, with freedom being the unrelenting concern for the human, a spirituality that is not spiritually and physically liberating of the whole person will not be able to sustain that person or foster a need for continued affiliation with any given community over a long period of time. At one point Black churches in the United States were thought to be the places that provided spiritual liberation with physical manifestations; that is to say, they were thought to be where physical deliverance from oppression would initiate. However, it is no longer seen as that place. This is not a question of whether the Black Church still has prophetic capabilities. This is however a claim on the ability of the Black Church to provide a sustainable affect of spiritual satisfaction/ spiritual connection beyond its walls that impact and influence the way its parishioners engage the world and position themselves toward acts of liberation. Furthermore, the Black Church has replaced deliverance from oppressive structures with upward mobility, and just like any hierarchical syndicate, only the chosen ones rise to the top. However, there is an implied possibility for those outside the chosen group to "make it" if they perform certain tasks. I simply believe people are beginning to want more than cycles of oppression masked as spirituality. Spirituality must liberate. Spirituality must go beyond the church and not just in an evangelical sense. Spirituality requires a type of embodiment that causes people to be free no matter where they are, with the goal of legitimate materialized freedom from oppression.

Personally, I can affirm the benefits of the Black Church. In my experience it has been a place that has helped me facilitate my own connection with God. It has also provided me with a community, linking me with others from the diaspora who may not live in close proximity to me, through faith and cultural similarities. However, for me, the generative emotional state that came from spiritual experiences I had in church was not enough to sustain me after I left its walls. The church did not give me the tools to engage the world through that same generative emotionality. Instead, I primarily had to draw from what I have come to perceive as personally damaging forms of personal piety. In one period of my life, I found myself spending a considerable amount of time reading scripture or in prayer, which had hermit like effects on my sociality. I enjoyed being by myself communing with God, but did not always enjoy the company of others. Consequently, I did not always have the skills to generatively be with others. Even more so, I found myself easily agitated when interacting with people after returning from experiences of spiritual connection. This hinted at the fleeting and volatile nature of the spiritual affect I encountered—either at church or in personal prayer times.

Spirituality and technology

The shifting landscape does not require spirituality to completely reject technology. It requires a complete acceptance of it, especially theologically. By simultaneously taking on the mantle of liberation and fully immersing one's self into the technological world, one can actually embody a constructed theology that subverts technocratic attempts to control the human body and mind through the enticing makeup of the psycho-realistic virtual world. This mind numbing force can be usurped with the utilization of spirituality in conjunction with technology as a tool in the liberative fight against oppression. This project seeks to begin a theological discourse that incorporates the technological reach of oppressed peoples in conjunction with the spirituality they embody as a practical conversation partner in the fight for liberation.

The continual progress of technology goes far beyond making human life easier. It is actually part of a collective effort to fully integrate living organisms and technology, fusing them together in hopes for a technorganic experience.[26] Implantable devices, wearable technologies, biomechanical limbs, nanobots, and gene splicing all serve as examples of the increasingly blurred line between people, nature, and machine. Although many of these concepts are seemingly far off, the majority of these concepts are present in their nascent stages. My point in saying this is that the technology we regularly carry with us; cell phones, laptops, etc., will one day have the capability of being part of our anatomy. This represents a cultural push toward transhumanist integration. The goal of transhumanism is the arrival of the posthuman.

Historically, liberation theology has been consumed with concepts and approaches to theology that deviate and oppose the oppressive dominant theological landscape/narrative.[27] Many of these theologies end with hypothetical worlds or examples of where each particular theology has taken ground in the world.[28] However, very rarely has liberation theology spoken squarely to the implementation of a particular spirituality, taking its claims to their logical ends backed by empirically quantifiable methodologies. Intentionally, I am using a hybrid methodological approach to theology that includes quantifiable empirical methods, which are what I believe to be the future of the theological discipline. Quantifiable methods have the potential to strengthen the foundation of theology, grounding it in the physical world. Theologies that can be touched and felt may potentially provide the hope of realism that materializes the world of ideas most often associated with theological pursuits. This is not to completely forget the aftermath that arose from the Enlightenment project's approach to the world, which left many theologians skeptical of the reductionist nature of quantification—equating life with numbers through abstraction. However, fusing the numbered belief system along with a theological proposition that reasserts the importance of life, nature, and equity has the potential to demonstrate the meaning/importance of accepting where the mystical and the quantifiable meet.

Furthermore, liberation theologies have yet to deal with the biological processes of the human body, let alone the Black body in ways that allow for both universal and particular claims. There are Black theologies that address the discursive body.[29] But, these theologies have not addressed the ways that the body's biological processes affect spiritual experience. This is important to me as I continue to explore spiritual embodiment beyond the limitations of phenomenology for a theology that is grounded in not just the experience, but the repercussions of said experience. I acknowledge that my perspective comes from wrestling with Black theology. My critique of Black theology comes from my deep entanglement and commitment to it. While at Emory my mentor, David Pacini, would always say that the greatest level of commitment requires the greatest level of critique. It is from that perspective that I engage Black theology and seek to push its bounds.

Blackness, spirituality, and technology

In 1995, Victor Anderson pushed the bounds of what it meant to conceive of Blackness in liberation theology. *Beyond Ontological Blackness* outlined the necessity of moving beyond the dichotomous notion of Blackness as the antecedent to whiteness. It did this through the narrative of Black monolithic solidarity and Black heroic genius that has been perpetually pitted against white heroic genius in an effort to disavow notions that justify categorical racism. In his project Anderson deconstructed Black Liberation Theology, suggesting that its mirror of white racist ideologies does not allow for it to create an idea of Blackness that is free from whiteness. This ultimately proposes that Blackness, and subsequently Black folk are not free. This concept forced the bounds of Blackness to grow, if not shatter, allowing for different forms of Blackness to not only emerge but also matter. This is important to the Black transhuman liberation theology project as it does not simply seek to effect just the Protestant Black Christian in the US North American context. Protestant Black Christianity is a type of Black representational embodiment that is not the totality of Blackness nor is it singular in its own representation. Blackness and the subsequent spiritualities that those who are Black subscribe to are increasingly broad. The spiritual practices that emerge from the wide existence of Black embodiment must be able to find space within this theologically anthropological particularity. Due to the range of Black spirituality, I must focus on more than Black Christianity. As such, I will reflect on a multiplicity of Black spiritual experiences.

Spiritual histories documented by Barbara Holmes, Diana Hayes, Akasha Hull, Angel Williams, Charles H. Long, Sherman Jackson, and a plethora of other Black scholars suggest there is a multidimensional continuum of Black spirituality. These authors go beyond what many perceive as the primarily Christian aspects of Black spirituality, delving further into the variety of ways that Black spirituality presents itself. Barbara Holmes points out the origination of the Centering Prayer from the Desert Mothers and Fathers of North Africa.[30] Holmes emphasizes the Islamic roots of West Africa as well as some of the indigenous African religions, whose practices made their way into slave religion and remain today in Black Church settings, although often undetected. Diana Hayes points out the Bantu cultural influences that were pervasive over other cultural representations in African American contexts, even though West African tribes made up the majority of the population.[31] Akasha Hull provides narrative examples of Black women who participate in Christian methodologies, sometimes in tandem with or as completely alternative to the traditionally Black North American Christian norm.[32] Angel Williams gives a Black Buddhist perspective on spirituality. She even provides practically applicable notes for the reader to follow. Charles Long looks at Black spirituality from a theoretical stance. He talks about the history and formation of spirituality in the North American context, and the implications of their implementation that can be found in societal norms and political policies.[33] Sherman Jackson provides a picture of what it is to be Black and Muslim in America. The breadth of wisdom presented by these insightful scholars help to delineate a spectrum of Black spirituality that essentially finds everything to be natural. For instance, Hull's interview of Alice Walker presents the idea that walking a dog is natural, and so is praying to the ancestors.[34] I draw from these authors to pull on the wide landscape of Black spirituality in order to show their possible integration with technology and accentuate the spiritual variety of Black bodies. The wide range of Black spiritual experiences furthers the point that spiritual liberation (as described through Black transhuman liberation theology) is open to anyone willing to travel its road.

Spirituality in the form of contemplation has had the most amicable interaction with biological sciences. Many neuroscientific studies, including one by Paul Lehrer, have looked into effects of spirituality on the brain, its subsequent nervous systems (parasympathetic and sympathetic), and their physiochemical reactions in the body.[35] Studies dedicated to meditation demonstrate through blood oxygen level dependent (BOLD) techniques that meditation activates the prefrontal cortex of the brain on both hemispheres (mostly on the right side).[36] This also happens in the right anterior cingulate as well. Brain activation within these regions signifies concentration and calm. Another key brain system that undergoes activation via the BOLD system during meditation is the limbic system. The important regions to remember are the amygdala, hippocampus, hypothalamus, and thalamus. One region that becomes less active is the parietal region. Its lack of activation is important to meditation and its relationship to personal transcendence. Their combination is often associated with a lost sense of self, unity with nature, or the divine in spiritual experience, as the parietal lobe is responsible for facilitating spatial recognition; of the self in relation to other objects. So, the lack of activation or decreased activation in this region provides important insight regarding the parietal region's role in the experience of transcendence.[37] Based on these previous neuroimaging studies, I plan to theorize how the brain and body are impacted through participation in various spiritualities.

Transhumanism, as a term, was coined by Julian Huxley. According to Nick Bostrom, it encompasses the belief that "current human nature is improvable through the use of applied science (technology) and other rational methods, which may make it possible to increase human health span, extend our intellectual and physical capacities, and give us increased control over our own mental states and moods."[38] The use of applied science to enhance human capabilities has had polarizing effects on those pondering what it means to be human. Gregory Stock, a UCLA biophysicist, deems it a necessary human responsibility to undertake all that transhumanism has to offer with our new understandings and powers via scientific discovery.[39] However, in public discourse, transhumanism has received mixed as well as ardent reactions. Leon Kass, the former chair of George W. Bush's Council on Bioethics, suggests that changes to human beings disregard the essential nature of what God intended to be considered human.[40]

A good portion of transhumanist work has focused on genetics. An example of this would be the human genome project which focuses on the mapping and understanding of the human genetic code, or genome. Transhumanist applications of transcribing the human genome are the use of directed evolution. Genetically, "directed evolution" is the intentional method of protein engineering. It is an attempt to control the process of natural selection. Directed evolution is a process widely critiqued by authors such as Maxwell Mehlman, who raise questions about the harm and potential extinction of the human race based on the inevitable setbacks and mistakes native to the scientific process, which is an inherent danger of transhumanist concepts of progress.[41] However, this is not the only method of transhumanist innovation. Implantable devices, genetic manipulation, medicine/supplementation, and even wearable technologies demonstrate the imminent convergence of technology on the body. Mehlman points out a genetic study conducted on mice that enhanced their muscular stamina by 200 percent. The result of the genetic modification was also passed onto the mice's offspring, demonstrating the selective propensity toward genetically strong traits.[42] Black transhuman liberation theology essentially advocates for incorporation of technology which emerges alongside, and potentially in conjunction with the body, Examples of this are genetic engineering, implantable tech, wearable tech, and pharmaceutical innovation. It is my hope that a further look into the transhumanist posthuman, through a Black transhuman liberation theology lens, will allow for a move toward the acceptance of directed evolution; hinting toward the **technorganisms** who may inhabit the future.

Methodology

This project does not fit into the normative scope of recent liberation theology texts. I won't be critiquing the evolution of liberation theology systemically to demonstrate the significance of my own proposition. I think that writers have successfully deconstructed liberation theology's assumptions and damaging underlying ideologies, which further engrain forms of categorical racism, white hegemonic ideologies, patriarchy, and heteronormativity.[43] Neither is this a continuation of Black theology in its historical effort to unify Blackness under a solitary concept, or through furthering established Black hierarchies and caricatures based on differing personality types.[44] In my engagement with the multiplicity of Black identity through spiritual subscription/affiliation, I will attempt to demonstrate the variety of ways in which Black folks embody spirituality, much like in Akasha Hull's *Soul Talk*. It is important to note that the term "Black folks" refers to the multitude of experiences and iterations of Blackness in the United States. There is no one particular definition of Blackness, but the amalgam of Black bodies; their biologies, discursive meanings, and subcultures accumulatively constitute the term "Black folks." However, my methodology will not be ethnographic in nature. Although this project does not follow the normative trajectory of a liberation theology, it still constitutes as liberative for three reasons:

1. Its intended telos is that of a practical form of liberation, grounded in the physical world and the tangible physiological affect of spiritual practices.

2. Its particular scope: Although technology and biology do have universal reach, for the purpose of this constructed theological perspective, I will explore their implications for Black folks in the US context.
3. The inclusion of theology as the overarching lens for an anthropological look at the intersectional approach to spirituality and transhumanism.

I plan to draw from the decolonial scholarship of Frantz Fanon, engaging his work on Black non-humanity. I use Fanon's non-humanity as the starting point for the transhumanist discussion of reconfiguring the epistemology of Black embodiment. Because if Black folks are not human, Black folks are also no longer bound to the theological claims which uphold the sanctity, or need for preservation, of the "human" form. So, deconstruction becomes the necessary avenue for exploring this strong theistically inclusive transhumanist approach to spirituality. The Black transhumanist approach is different from weak humanism and Anthony Pinn's African American non-theistic humanism, which will allow me to engage the breadth of Black spirituality, ultimately constructing a secular theology based on a biologically grounded spirituality. In *The End of God-Talk*, Pinn outlines the key distinctions between what he classifies as a weak theistic humanism and what he calls a strong or non-theistic humanism. For Pinn, weak humanism includes belief in God, a clear dependence on God's providence, a particular eschatological telos that is indicative of God's soteriology, and a belief that God acts through human muscle.[45] Human worth and responsibility are acknowledged, but ultimately there is an assertion that God is behind human action and steadfast belief that God has the capability to impact the natural world. Pinn distinguishes weak humanism from what he proposes as its stronger non-theistic African American version, with a fundamental idea that the concept of God is one that has served to limit humanity. For Pinn, the term "God" has run its course as a symbol of meaning and is devoid of value for Black folks. He further explains the African American non-theistic stance with the help of five guiding principles:

1. There is recognition that humanity is fully and solely accountable and responsible for the human condition and the correction of humanity's plight.
2. There is a general suspicion toward or rejection of supernatural explanations and claims, combined with an understanding of humanity as an evolving part of the natural environment as opposed to being a created being. This can involve disbelief in God(s).

3. There is an appreciation for African American cultural production and a perception of traditional forms of Black religiosity as having cultural importance as opposed to any type of "cosmic" authority.
4. There is a commitment to individual and societal transformation.
5. There is a controlled optimism that recognizes both human potential and human destructive activities.[46]

I do not believe that a stark distinction between the poles of humanistic manifestation is necessary. I think that the best of each humanism can be housed in an intelligently succinct theological proposition as a complex paradoxical epistemology. So, I will work to mediate a bridge between each version that will become the basis of a Black posthumanist ideology. This Black posthumanist ideology is important to Black transhumanism because it forms the soft boundaries of Black transhumanism. Black transhumanism is a juncture that leads to, and simultaneously arises out of, Black posthumanism. This is a stark difference from the teleological and ideological gaps between cultural transhumanism and critical posthumanism. Black posthumanism needs Black transhumanism to mediate the space between the current mode of human existence and futuristic existence, but Black posthumanism is the metaphysic that Black transhumanism relies upon. More plainly, Black transhumanism is the means through which Black posthumanism may become palatable (and to fruition). Nevertheless, the metaphysical lens of Black posthumanism can be understood/encapsulated within these nine principles:

1. Complex knowledge is paradoxical and nonlinear.
2. Vital energy underlies life and is nondeterministic.
3. Relativity of the subject is not unsubstantial. It is everything.
4. All matter is interconnected due to blurred interdependence.
5. Nondeterminism does not negate super nature, that is, God, gods, immateriality, and so on are substantantive value.
6. The world is constructed of uncertainty and disorder.
7. Language is the biggest technological prosthesis that humans are trying to replicate in various ways—most substantially through cyber technology.
8. The human is an animal at its core. Therefore it is no more important than nonhuman animals, and it is ultimately a part of ecology. What happens to the world also happens to human animals.
9. Everything is becoming. There is no final theory.

Although Posthumanism can be seen as an offshoot of process thought, Roland Faber and Brian G. Henning suggest in the introduction to *Beyond Metaphysics* that within process there needs to be a conversation with some of the philosophical discourses of the time, critical theory, Marxist theory, post-structuralism, etc., and posthumanism provides the framework to do that.[47]

I will also use neuroscience as a hermeneutical tool. I will use neurophysiology to correlate and make meaning of the spiritual experience. This engagement with neuroscience will require a revised understanding of the soul and what it means to neuroscientifically peer into the soul. David Hogue suggests that many of the functions of the soul can now be described as predictable outcomes of a functional central nervous system (CNS).[48] A definition of the soul akin to this understanding is paramount for moving forward to use neuroscience as a hermeneutical tool. Many neuro-philosophers would suggest that even the mention of a soul takes away from the neurological reaction that occurs through the interaction between the environment and the internal narrative. Much of the neuro-philosophical discussion revolves around materialism and monism. However, when employing this neuroscientific lens I choose to employ a physicalist lens which proposes a material correlation to abstract concepts of the soul while leaving space for meaning making. When attempting to draw meaning from the utilization of a neuroscientific lens, I will pull heavily on cognitive science and the importance of human cognitive operators. Collectively they work to help people build meaning out of life experience and the world around both individuals and the human collective. Andrew Newberg outlines seven cognitive operators in the mind, three of which are specifically important for this work:

1. Binary operator: This cognitive operator works to set up conceptual understandings of opposites.
2. Abstract operator: The abstract operator works within the individual mind to understand abstract concepts.
3. Causal operator: The causal operator works within the mind to determine objects of first cause. It is essentially the operator that helps individual minds decipher origins.[49]

The acknowledgment of cognitive operators helps posthumanistic constructs engage the mind in a productive way regarding theism. Pinn forms the foundation of his non-theistic humanism on physics and the need for symmetry. He emphasizes the need for humans to use mathematics and science, taking what each discipline provides at face value to see beauty in the natural architecture—

materialism. However, materialism proves problematic if a merely mathematical approach is taken to meaning making. Meaning is derived from the cultivation of myth, regardless of the symbol associated with the abstraction. That is to say, no matter what symbol is chosen, the meaning applied to symbol precipitates its importance. The interaction and overlap of these three operators within the individual mind are the basis of human meaning making. Historically, when a purely mathematical approach to meaning was applied, it was done with a sense of suspended disbelief, in terms of the inherent symbolism in quantifiable methods.

Chapter breakdown

So far, I have work to set the stage for this project. By introducing Nick Bostrom's basic definition of transhumanism I am suggesting that Black folks are already transhumanist. Since Black folks are already transhumanists, an acceptance of Black transhumanism provides reason to reflect on the ways that Black folks are already living in the world transhumanistically. Simultaneously, an acceptance of Black transhumanism might provide greater impetus for Black folks to consider how transhumanist realities should interact with Black spirituality. The combination of spirituality (or embodied theology) and technology is intended to create an accessible avenue for Black folks to pursue and realize the type of liberating realities we seek. The incorporation of technology and spirituality becomes integral as society continues to move toward digital automation, especially in the form of electronic governance.

This project will be broken into four chapters: (1) "Thinking of Black Transhumanism: Non-Humanity, Moving Away from Transhumanism's Roots"; (2) "Foundations of a Black Transhumanism: Blackness as the Biotechnologically Mediated Experience of Black Vitality"; (3) "The Neurophysiology of Spiritual Experience"; and (4) "Black Transhuman Liberation Theology."

"Thinking of Black Transhumanism: Non-Humanity, Moving Away from Transhumanism's Roots" explores the limits of the term "human" for Black folks and enters the transhumanist conversation with a historical exploration of transhumanist thought. This chapter begins by building upon Frantz Fanon's challenge to the space Black folks occupy within the human declension. It is meant to reflect upon the need to address undue loyalties to the term "human" while offering Black folks a way to think about a different means for identification. From there it provides an overview of transhumanist history. Beginning with current transhumanist understandings it then explores the historical evolution of humanist thinking that precluded transhumanist thought. The chapter concludes with an analysis of the racist history that is woven throughout transhumanism's origins and continues into the present.

"Foundations of a Black Transhumanism: Blackness as the Biotechnologically Mediated Experience of Black Vitality" reimagines the Black body as technology. So, in this chapter I explore biological Blackness, as Black biotechnology. While laying the foundation of Black transhumanism I first set it apart from Eurocentric transhumanism by refusing to reify mind-body dualism. This raises questions regarding the technological status of the Black body if the mind is not something that sits within it, powering it or running it. In this chapter I explore the potential of vitalist panpsychic animism to be the underlying force that energizes Black biotechnology. I critically examine African vitalism in order to determine which components ought to be maintained within Black transhumanism. From there I imagine the ways vitality might interact with Black biotechnology via Eboni Marshall Turman's womanist ethic of incarnation. This chapter sets the foundation of Black transhumanism by situating the body as a set of complex biological systems with multiple layers of features that provide vitality the opportunity to experience life on earth.

"The Neurophysiology of Spiritual Experience" outlines the neurophysiological components of spiritual experience. This is the most scientifically technical piece of the project. Essentially, it is a biological breakdown of spiritual experience in the four realms of experience: physiological, psychological, neurological, and somatic experience. I will define the neurophysiological terms necessary for understanding the remainder of the project. This chapter will include information gathered from prominent studies on spirituality and explores Black spiritualities (contemplative practices, different forms of meditation, and somatically dominated spiritual practices) biologically. This chapter will also outline various Black spiritual practices while proposing potential neurophysiological progressions associated with the intentions of each spiritual practice. The is important, because if Black folks understand the biological implications of the spiritualities we engage in then these spiritualities might be aptly applied in a proactive approach to freedom fighting.

"Black Transhuman Liberation Theology" reintroduces transhumanism along with the implications of pairing technology with Black biotechnology in everyday life. It looks at the possibility of cultivating a spirituality of revolt within the biotechnology of Black folks. That possibility for revolt spirituality to remerge is based on the ideology that once the mind or spirit is awakened and remains so, nothing exists that can stop it. The question becomes, How does one keep one's mind/spirit awake? My hope is that an awakening to the vitalist non-determinant qualities of Black transhuman liberation theology might allow for a welcoming of dynamic differences in embodiment and action to surface. An acceptance of the variance within the presentation of Black embodiment and action might shift the way "collective action" is conceived, which should have a positive impact on the way different approaches of liberative action is perceived. This chapter will explore a wider swath of biotechnology than in previous chapters to demonstrate how Black biotechnology is part of an ever-evolving environment that is being directed by intentional interactions with the environment. So, I provide a sketch of what I propose as the spiritually augmenting possibilities of pairing Black biotechnology, Black spirituality, and technology through an exploration of emergent technologies.

"Black Transhumanism as Revolt Spirituality" explores the meaning of revolt spirituality in the context of transhumanism of Black transhumanism. Since Black folks are part of a larger biotechnological environment, the use of invented technologies to enhance life and progress in the pursuit of shifting power dynamics is only a logical step. This chapter will also discuss what it means to be with the sacred and with technology. I close this chapter with an afrofuturistic short story that serves as an example of what it means to be fully immersed in the technological.

1

Thinking of Black Transhumanism: Non-Humanity, Moving Away From Transhumanism's Roots

In this chapter I work to set the stage for thinking about the Black body as technology. It will begin with a reflection on the relationship between non-humanity and Blackness. Then it will shift to a brief discussion of transhumanist thought, which will lead into an examination of the racist shortcomings of transhumanism, serving as a point of entry into the conversation of transhumanism and Blackness.

Blackness and non-humanity

I begin this discussion on non-humanity by echoing Frantz Fanon. Black folks are not human.[1] We never have been. However, respect for humanity, and its uniqueness, has been integral to the foundation of Black liberation theologies, anchoring these liberative excursions in Eurocentric epistemologies whose linguistic designation for what it means to exist, as human, continues to situate Blackness as oppositional to proto-normative means for embodiment. The problem resides in the employment of the term itself. Saying that Black folks are not human suggests that any participation in the epistemic system associated with this term, even through rebuttals of what this term ought to mean, is a subscription to the cybernetic nature of its colonial roots. Thus, this chapter serves as an invitation to unsubscribe from its declension.

The ability of the term "human" to encapsulate an evolving physical form is a clear demonstration of its technological capacity. What we have come to recognize as "the" human form has not always been. Evolutionary biology positions human materiality as something having undergone chronological changes concurrent with each passing temporal period.[2] Similarly, the technologies that humans construct and cultivate have paralleled the temporalities of each evolutionary progression. The technological apparatus of linguistics is no different. It evolves by enhancing its cybernetic capacity through broad measures (dynamic semiotics presented in dialects or technology through emojis, memes, etc.), to shorten the distance of understanding and application while either reifying regimes of power, explicating them, destabilizing them or constructing them. It is important to note that Black transhuman liberation theology defines technology as any system that can manifest itself in the natural world. These systems can be open or closed, autopoietic (self-replicating) or allopoietic (other producing), complex or simple. They may also occur with or without human intervention. Thus, as a technological system tasked with facilitating meaning, the grammar of language situates entire realities that precipitate any perception of one's own ability. So, the convergence of connotations, histories, value systems, and power dynamics connected to any word establishes language as potentially the most dangerous of weapons, given its connection to formulating the elements of existence—let alone its ability to deploy single words to pigeon hole, stymie, cut, buckle, and crush those who are shaped by them.

Linguistics functions as a dynamic technological apparatus which Black folks are capable of taking on and off, to an extent (think code switching). We put on and take off different versions of this linguistic prosthetic, recalibrating our personal epistemologies based upon our interactions within the environment we find ourselves. We use these pre-prescribed modes of meaning/understanding to safely navigate the unpredictable waters of existence. The problem is that the technological prosthetic of the term "human" can only be partially removed due to the level of investment we have in contemporary society. The problem associated with this technological prosthetic hints at the depth of our entanglement within this epistemologically delineated existence, which is so dependent upon Eurocentric codices for meaning making. It is both the matrix and the twilight zone all in one. We cannot articulate ourselves apart from the language provided, and the mere attempt to do so keeps us in conversation with that prescribed language. Attempting to distance ourselves from current linguist epistemologies places us in close relationship with them once more. It is this frightening recurrence, this thought that we will never be free, which haunts us. The idea that we cannot use the "master's tools" is faulty, mainly, because we have trudged so far down this particular time line of existence that we cannot simply make our way out. Thus the only way out is as follows: through its logical end, through an intentional bursting of its seams, or through a demolition of the tunnel we darkly feel our way around. However, demolition is scary. Because it projects to be suicide since the tunnel may fall in on us. But, what if demolition is not suicide? What if we survive? Suppose we make it out alive, and are able to construct something new? How beautiful might that be?

I do recognize that the term "human" is the primary mode of linguistic currency when referring to bi-pedal, predominantly hairless and self-aware beings with supposedly superior intellects. I also recognize that certain rights are given to those who are classified as human. But, in America, those rights and protections evaporate in disparate proportions when the recipient is Black. The utility of the term "human" also evaporates when presented as currency for liberative exchange. Similar to the offering of Anthony Pinn's reflection on the utility of the term "God," I would like to move a step further. I propose that the term "human" which has been employed as a tool for claiming one's worth has not served to produce any concrete manifestation of Black liberation.

In his book *Black Skin White Masks*, Fanon claims that "Black [folks] wants to be white. [Yet, white folks] slave to reach a human level." While Fanon was attempting to speak to the fleeting relationship that both Black and white folks have with this term, it is also an allusion to the limitations of the term "human."[3] While Fanon claims that Black folks ought to forge a new (hu)man, which I argue has transhumanist implications, the reasoning he employs creates a double-layered conundrum that highlights the depth to which Black folks are buried in the struggle to break free from the white gaze. The first layer arises through the relationship Fanon rightfully exposes. Black folks want to be white, and white folks want to be human. For Fanon, this serves as a statement of clarity, because it exposes the never-ending problem of assimilation. Assimilation into white culture does not protect Black humanity. The second, and most entangling, layer of this conundrum can be found in Fanon's use of the term "human":

> But, if we want humanity to advance a step further, if we want to bring it up to a different level than that which Europe has shown it, then we must invent and we must make discoveries. . . . We must turn over a new leaf, we must work out new concepts, and try to set afoot a new [hu]man.[4]

Fanon's declarative search for a new human hints at his recognition of the inherently problematic nature of the term. However, his maintenance of the term "human" only recycles the dilemma he highlights earlier. Trying to fit Black existence within Eurocentric codices confines the constructive potential of the chosen descriptor. So, when I say that Black folks are not human I am suggesting that the deeply racist and exclusivist history attached to the term needs to be considered. This is especially true since the use of the term continues to impose boundaries upon Black bodies regarding how we ought to live. The boundaries associated with the term stems from its weaponization. Molly Randell-Moon and Ryan Tippet call attention to the necropolitics associated with this weaponization in the introduction of *Security, Race, Biopower*, suggesting the human designation was used for the "economisation of . . . resources in favour of those who 'deserve life.'[5] Essentially, the human classification functions to protect the proto-normativity of white supremacy by upholding epistemological systems of anti-blackness, which are dependent upon the meaning disproportionately imbued upon those who bear its monicker. When we consider the role that the technological apparatus of language plays in undergirding anti-blackness, it could also be inferred that white people are not human either. White people are simply the benefactors of this technology, given their status within the cultural milieu in which it is employed. So, when Black folks insist upon participating within the supposedly protective schema of this term, Black folks are actively reifying anti-Black hierarchies inherently embedded within its cybernetic reach.

So, what is a new (hu)man? And why maintain the use of the term (hu)man at all? Why lay claim to a terminology that has been used to leave so many out of its designation, and create hierarchies of race? Why buy into a term that is part of the larger Eurocentric linguistic machinery? Most importantly, why employ a technology that was meant to subjugate the "Other" when it cannot adequately communicate the complexities of embodiment, let alone Black existence? Now, one could easily argue that the use of any European linguistic derivative maintains a connection to Eurocentric power dynamics. I would not disagree with that argument at all. This is not a departure from a term for the sake of being provocative. It is an intentional departure from the cognitive limitations associated with what it means to be human and Black. Nevertheless, until Black folks become linguistically liberated (something that I will not be able to unpack here) the very components that comprise the reality in which Black folks understand themselves will be influenced by Eurocentrism. The term "human" functions as an elusive value marker, of which Black folks have been unable to grasp due to our lack of control of the term. In this temporality, it is not a derivative of Black epistemic technology. So, in this invitation to unsubscribe to the use of the term "human," I am taking into account the tumultuous history of the term and positing a temporary marker in its place, something a bit more generative—something a bit more true to form. W. E. B. DuBois's testament to Black tenacity may be an indicator of the willingness of Black folks to combat maladaptive narratives surrounding Blackness, in order to usurp the suffocation of anti-Black power structures. It is with that in mind that Black transhuman liberation theology calls for a further deconstruction from the term "human," and ultimately a separation from it. Black folks are transhuman, flexible, and adaptable. But why transhuman? Why utilize the very term I am asking Black folks to unsubscribe from as the root of this new label? Simply put, transhumans do not carry the same boundaries as humans. They are not limited by the constraints of their form, or situation. Transhumans are transcendent, yet grounded in materiality. Nevertheless, an adoption of the designation of transhuman for Black folks is rooted in the idea that Black bodies are technology—complex auto-/allopoietic biological systems undergoing constant change. But ever more so, it is a recognition that since transhumans are always in a state of becoming, the term "transhuman" is only a placeholder for categorizing Blackness. Thus, it is an invitation not only to depart from the human designation but also to wrestle with the uneasiness and potentiality of what Black folks might be. This is also an assertion that futuristic iterations of Blackness are unbounded. So, it has yet to be determined what Black folks are. We are just not human.[6]

Pulling away from transhumanism's racist roots

Max More envisions the "transhuman" as being actively engaged in the politics of "rising above outmoded human beliefs and behaviours."[7] Being affixed in materiality, while intentionally directing one's own evolution, is the underlying component of transhumanism. I briefly provided a basic definition of transhumanism in the introduction, but the formal definition is two pronged:

1. The intellectual and cultural movement that affirms the possibility and desirability of fundamentally improving the human condition through applied reason, especially by developing and making widely available technologies to eliminate aging and to greatly enhance human intellectual, physical, and psychological capacities.
2. The study of the ramifications, promises, and potential dangers of technologies that will enable us to overcome fundamental human limitations, and the related study of the ethical matters involved in developing and using such technologies.[8]

Essentially, transhumanism is a speculative philosophical humanistic disposition that views the merger of technology and human biology as the primary means for exploring the potential of human existence. It promotes an interdisciplinary approach that draws from bioethics, speculative fiction, broad approaches to current and emergent technologies, and literature to imagine the future of human existence. Given that the transhumanist telos is to guide human evolution, its intention is to move into the next phase of existence: posthumanity.[9] The transhumanist posthuman is an entity that exists beyond humanity's current form of embodiment, psychology, intellectual capacity, morals, etc. This is not to be confused with Aristotelian forms. As an extension of Darwinian thought, transhumanism posits that the human form is merely in its nascent stages. Further, it proposes that the human form can, and ought to, undergo guided evolutionary processes to greatly enhance the ways in which humans exist within the environments they inhabit.[10] This implies that posthuman existence is grounded in the central idea that the final form of human materiality has yet to be conceived.[11]

Transhumanists primarily assert two main paths that will produce the transhumanist posthuman. The first is in line with the concept of the singularity.[12] This type of transhumanist posthuman is speculated to be uploaded into the digital plane, potentially allowing for eternal digital embodiment. Unless there happens to be a large scale crash, power outage, or loss of digitized psychological backups one could potentially live forever. Digital eternality also implies a mind-body dualism, whereby the body can be bypassed, and replaced, through the digital plane or transference into another body altogether.[13] The second transhumanist posthuman configuration would be the result of an extension of human abilities via technological enhancement. An early step toward this posthuman can be seen through the use of dietary supplements which aid in enhancing biological proficiency. This biohacking would lead to genetic enhancements, prosthetic limbs, brain computer interfaces, nanotechnology, etc., in efforts to produce a form of existence superior to the one we currently recognize.[14] Now, while transhumanism presents itself in a primarily positive light, it does not negate the reality that technological advancement has its casualties. Transhumanism recognizes that progress is not guaranteed. It also purports to acknowledge the dangerous ways in which technology has been used in the past (especially by governing authorities who emphasized eugenics) and the potential for experimental technology (particularly genetic engineering) to have catastrophic effects, that is, disease, sudden maladaptive mutations, and the possibility of extinction level population drops.

However, when transhumanists talk about embodiment, race is seen as inconsequential. For transhumanists, race refers to the totality of humanity. However, the term for racialization within transhumanist literature is human biodiversity (HBD). This term is meant to encapsulate the varying degrees of phenotypical expression, experience, and life, all while absorbing and thereby invisiblizing the complexities of racial difference. The biocultural import of histories, cultures, socioeconomic classes, genders, sexualities, etc., associated with racial difference, are shelved during transhumanist discussions. These complexities are replaced by an overarching cry for equality in embodiment and faculty, except when cartographies of contribution are concerned. This invisiblization becomes increasingly problematic when transhumanists trace their own philosophical lineage.

Enlightenment thinking, or rational humanism, is the logical foundation for transhumanist thought.[15] While notable Enlightenment figures, such as Immanuel Kant and David Hume, were pushing for daring intellectual determination to push humanity beyond its immature belief systems, these thinkers were simultaneously advocating for the dismissal, discrimination, and subjugation of Black bodies by Western civilization. For instance, it is well documented that Kant asserts that "the Negroes of Africa have by nature no feeling that rises above the ridiculous. . . . So essential is the difference between these two human kinds, and it seems to be just as great with regard to the capacities of mind as it is with respect to color." He also demonstrates his willingness to dismiss the words of a Black man, purely on the basis of his skin, arguing that "there might be something here worth considering, except for the fact that this scoundrel was completely black from head to foot, a distinct proof that what he said was stupid."[16] However, some would suggest that Kant had an evolution of perspective. In "Kant's Second Thoughts on Race," Pauline Kleingeld argues that Kant's racist views on difference were from the 1780s, and his views shifted in the 1790s. Kleingeld's focus on Kant's statements from *Toward Perpetual Peace* and *Metaphysics of Morals*, where Kant emphasized universal humanity, omitted racial hierarchies, included Black and Native Americans in juridical and contractual agreements, and rebuked the role of chattel slavery in restricting "cosmopolitan rights," were supposedly evidence that Kant's racism should not overshadow his philosophical contributions.[17] However, every construction of universality, cosmopolitanism, or reference to legal writ was sourced through a lens of white supremacy. Whereas Kant may have criticized the barbaric manner in which European countries functioned globally, his expectation still fell under the Euro-normative considerations of what universality, cosmopolitanism, and legality ought to be. This also included who was expected to take leadership. If his notions of peaceful reciprocation and law stemmed from European notions then it might be safe to suggest that he also thought Europeans ought to take the lead in these collaborations. This is especially poignant, given his thoughts on assimilation:

> Intelligence is either comparative *(ingenium comparans),* or argumentative *(ingenium argutans).* Intelligence unites (assimilates) heterogeneous ideas, which often, according to the law of the imagination (that is, association), lie apart from each other.... Intelligence is a characteristic of the understanding... which not only hampers the faculty of assimilation, but also the inclination to use this faculty.[18]

Assimilation as a mode of nature implies that the natural intermingling of biologies, or intellect, would fall under an epicenter of Eurocentrism. Here, evolution is not the coevolution of human organisms and peoples but the conforming of human biodiversity to European constructs and European biology which alludes to a shifting of racist white supremacist orientations. Kant no longer boldly proclaims racial hierarchy. He merely predicts that it is natural to produce a new amalgamation of human organization, oriented under Euro-normativity. Even though Kant concluded with a prescription that depicted a mutated racist ideology, Hume was a bit more direct:

> I am apt to suspect the Negroes to be naturally inferior to the Whites. There scarcely ever was a civilized nation of that complexion, nor even any individual, eminent either in action or speculation. No ingenious manufactures amongst them, no arts no sciences. On the other hand, the most rude and barbarous of the Whites, such as the ancient Germans, the present Tartars, have still something eminent about them, in their valour, form of government, or some other particular. Such a uniform and constant difference could not happen, in so many countries and ages, if nature had not made an original distinction between these breeds of men. . . . They [do] talk of one Negro as a man of parts and learning; but it is likely he is admired for slender accomplishments, like a parrot who speaks a few words plainly.[19]

Hume's claims are irreconcilable. Still, he is heralded for his contributions to the Enlightenment. But, it is important to be clear. As a predecessor to transhumanist thought the human he referenced in his work was very clearly not the human of African descending bodies. This mode of thought carried over into the earliest transhumanist thinkers.

The Huxley brothers led the transhumanist charge of the early to mid-twentieth century. Julian Huxley, a noted evolutionary biologist, coined the term "transhuman." Julian first mentioned transhumanism in his 1951 essay, "Knowledge, Morality, and Destiny," depicting it as "the idea of humanity attempting to overcome its limitations and to arrive at fuller fruition."[20] He is most notable for being the first Secretary General of UNESCO. His brother, Aldous Huxley, was a prominent author. Aldous's most notable work, *Brave New World*, is a dystopian novel considered one of the earliest speculative transhumanist fictions. The Huxley brothers were each liberal proponents of progress through scientific advancement, although Aldous seemed a bit more reluctant/realistic than his brother when considering the potential negative aspects of scientifically grounded progress. While these men represented liberal humanism, their racial views exposed them as perpetuators of traditional liberal notions of white supremacy, given whom they considered to be human and subhuman. Each touted a particular transhumanistic telos. However, the direction of their proposed transhumanist telos remained grounded in eugenic approaches to population control and racial hierarchies.

While Julian is lauded for his stance against the racial discrimination of Jewish folks during the holocaust, his track record when commenting on African descendants—which proceeds his efforts to combat racial discrimination in Nazi Germany—is much different. Although Julian insisted that while growing up he thought of Negro men as brothers, his experience with Negro men in the southern parts of the United States opened his mind to the differences in race.[21] In 1924 he suggested that the differences among the White and Black races in America were due to temperament, mental capacity, and lack of determination. However, since no sufficient measurable markers for difference in intelligence were validated, so he resorted to arguing against the mixing of races.

> Then there is the undoubted fact that by putting some of the white man's mind into the mulatto you not only make him more capable and more ambitious (there are no well-authenticated cases of pure blacks rising to any eminence), but you increase his discontent and create an obvious injustice if you continue to treat him like any full blooded African. The American negro is making trouble because of the American white blood that is in him.[22]

Interracial reproduction was problematic for Julian, whether, socially or biologically. He credited interracial offspring with heightening racial tensions in the United States. He remarks that "the Middle Westerner and to a lesser extent the Yankee are for the first time experiencing the [N]egro at balk and at first hand; and there is a certain grim humour in seeing their high moral principles and lovely theoretic equalitarianism dissolving under the strain."[23] It was around this time that Huxley began to acknowledge the faultiness of his own thinking. He slowly recognized that differences in intelligence could not be justified at any level. Nor could claims to egalitarianism be maintained if those of African descent were outwardly discriminated against. Yet, even with an accepted tolerance of the intellectual, physical, and aesthetic prowess of Black bodies, there remained an expectation of that prowess to continue functioning under white hegemonic forces (similar to Kant). This proves to be another example of proto-normative white supremacy, which promotes the maintenance of whiteness in positions of power, whether it is due to comfort and tradition or to a proclivity for the cultural methods of whiteness. At one point, Julian resorted to segregation. During this time he placed value in what he saw as the purity of the Nordic blood. He thought that the closest genetic, or blood, relatives to the Nordic people were Northern Europeans. Similarly, he saw Southern Europeans as having blood lines closer in relation to Africans, given their darker complexions. So, his proposed geographic solution suggested that the North be "where the [N]egro could be kept out, or at least allowed no privileges."[24] He even extended this conceptualization to be a blueprint for the United States.

Still, Julian underwent another evolution of thought concerning race. In *We Europeans*, published in 1936, he and coauthors Alfred Cort Haddon and Alexander Morris Carr-Saunders present a compelling case dispelling the myth of the Aryan race:

> The "racial" concept, as we have seen, is almost devoid of biological meaning . . . the adoption of the evolutionary standpoint in the study of language and culture has often led to rash and reckless use. . . . Language is frequently passed from one group to another. Sometimes a conquering people forces its language on the conquered. . . . Terms like "Celtic," "Jewish," "Indian," Arabic," "English," or "Irish" serve to denote a people or group of peoples bound together by tradition, or history, or language, or religion, or geographical continuity, or unity by cultural affinity or political usage (or misusage), even though the members of such a people are diverse in origin. . . . It was Sir William Jones who introduced the word *Arya* into modern European literature. He used it to . . . distinguish certain Indian language speakers from others. . . . The word itself means "noble" and is applied especially to dieties. . . . It happened that at the beginning of the nineteenth century the Romantic school in Germany became attracted to he study of Indian languages. . . . Moreover Max Muller threw another apple of discord. He introduced a proposition which is demonstrably false. He spoke not only of a definite Aryan language and its descendants, but also of a corresponding "Aryan race." The idea was rapidly taken up both in Germany and in England. . . . There is not need to trace in detail the history of the Aryan controversry. It will be enough to say that while the Germans claimed that the

> Aryans were tall, gair, and long-headed—the hypothetical ancestors of the hypothetical protoTeutons—the French, mainly on cultural grounds claimed that the langue and the civilization came into Europe with the Alpines who are of medium build, rather dark, and broad-headed.[25]

Ultimately, Julian spent a considerable amount of his time advocating for eugenics programs. His convictions as an evolutionary biologist directed his inclinations to the more empirical findings of genetics over the politicization of racial differentiation. Even though Julian chose to highlight the germinal variance demonstrated within racial groups, he still chose to employ terms such as "savage" and "hunting pygmy" in the same nomenclature as "Nordic businessman" and "Chinese sage." He was still committed to proto-normative white supremacist ideologies.[26] Now, one could suggest that he was simply utilizing the language of his time. However, just as he could explicate the social implications of Aryan propaganda, one could assert that he also knew the damaging effects of the language he employed. And as champion for eugenics programs, even though Julian began to shift his stance toward racial categorization, he remained elitist in his choice to focus upon the sterilization of the "unfit" within any particular society.[27] For him the unfit were those suffering from mental deficits or mental illness.[28] Nevertheless, Julian was unable to adequately consider the complex role of racial and cultural implications for difference which allowed for germinal variance within an ethnic group without giving into racial stratification. He simply thought that affirming there is no genetic or intellectual difference that could be determined between races, and that it was enough. It was as if a cavalier admittance of biologically situated racial equality would either gloss over the effects of colonization or render the histories of these races irrelevant, given their current status as operating under Eurocentric power structures. Hence, it could be argued that the lack of racial exploration within current transhumanist discourse persists as a result. But there is no historical engagement of African, or African diasporic, innovation (mathematically, philosophically, or technologically) that has contributed to the transhumanist narrative of progress (theoretically, or otherwise) that is so pressing to its discourse. So, it infers that while Black folks may be capable and welcome to enter into transhumanist discourse/culture, Black folks have no historical gifts to offer.

Current transhumanist discourse only engages racial issues in a cursory fashion, if at all. For instance, in one of two references to racial issues among the entire nineteen-chapter volume of the *Transhumanist Reader*, Aubrey de Grey mentions slavery as merely a bygone affinity that humans have outgrown due to moral evolution. He does so to demonstrate the capacity for social normativity to change over time. Grey referenced slavery as evidence to support his argument for the use of technology to enhance human lifespan.[29] He also adds that those who presently view aging as amoral will eventually be seen in the same light as those who once supported ethnic cleansing. This careless misuse of issues pertaining to race and ethnicity, as inconsequential tools for argumentative construction, demonstrates three things: a lack of connection to these events; a lack of empathy with those who suffered under its proceedings; and a lack of experience exploring the weight or the depth of the histories, bodies, and lineages connected to race, ethnicity, and power. Regardless, within the corpus of transhumanist literature this is actually one of the few instances where race and ethnicity are even mentioned. For transhumanists the bygone affinity of slavery has taken with it the need to address issues of human diversity. Even more so, it reads as if de Grey is pointing a finger toward the past and suggesting that current global landscapes are now different. He is implying that we, as humans, are better now and racially oppressive technologies are no longer in operation. When race is mentioned within transhumanist discourse most of the conversation ends with the holocaust. But, there is a lack of acknowledgment that Hitler's blueprint for the holocaust came from the American model of genocide and slavery.[30] Additionally, current transhumanists admit that transhumanism is built upon Enlightenment humanism's epistemological edifice to support notions of societal progress—although specifically through technology.[31] This also suggests that transhumanism is an inherent carrier (to use genetics terminology) of the pitfalls of Enlightenment humanism, which is why I highlight the histories that Enlightenment humanist philosophical thinkers had with race, particularly Blackness. Race cannot simply be a technology that Euro-descending thinkers once used to stratify the world. The fact that the linguistic apparatus of race is now so easily thrown away due to recent genetic findings, coupled with the shifting tide of social consensus demonstrates its faultiness. But, as a technology of stratification, it accomplished what it was created to; it placed value propositions upon bodies, based upon pigmentation, which manifested in social hierarchies that serve as boundaries of death for bodies that do not fit within the gauge of normative pigmentation. Furthermore, if historically vilified methods such as ethnology, craniometry, and chattel medical practices were used to categorize the differences presented through Black embodiment, liberal social evolutions and genetics are the means that current transhumanists scholars are employing to erase Blackness.

The best example of transhumanist scholarship dealing with issues of race comes from Michael Shapiro. He also contributed a chapter to the *Transhumanist Reader*, entitled "Performance Enhancement and Legal Theory." While Shapiro refers to race and ethnicity as being part of the "problematic classifications" that must not persist, he acknowledges the difficulty, and subsequent divide in access to, or reception of, newer technologies that classifications like ethnicity or race provide. He rightfully adds that these gaps in access or reception would exacerbate current disparities and create tremendously dangerous conditions for those left on the margins.[32] While this provides a realistic picture of the potential emergent technologies have for creating devastating disparities, it places the onus upon those who bear designations of problematic classifications to avoid these devastating conditions by ridding themselves of these classifications. But, to be rid of my Blackness, let alone to ask anyone to rid themselves of any lineage simply because it is classified as problematic invisibilizes all that it means to be connected to that lineage. This includes all connections of all degrees. Even more so, it creates a larger dissonance for those whose embodiment manifests as an indictment of those who are asking that these problematic classifications be done away with. To them, these classifications are a reminder of all that was necessary to get to this evolved state of civilization.[33] Because if these classifications were to end, the system which maintains the forces made visible through classifications would be rendered imperceptible—an offense with the potential to lead anyone trying to understand the foundations of their plight to madness. Therefore, any attempt to remove these classifications is an attempt to diminish, or do away with, the ontological debts and lingering effects of ancestral violence associated with the histories whose success depended upon the ability of these classifications to function. So, for Blackness to be maintained I am proposing that Black folks shed our humanity.

2

Foundations of a Black Transhumanism: Blackness as the Biotechnologically Mediated Experience of Black Vitality

Blackness stands as a loci of experience whose mere existence implicates power structures which support white supremacy. Regardless of the continued disproportionate inequities experienced by Black folks in America, our being/existence continues to counter the capitalist white supremacist neoliberal narrative that everything is just fine.[1] In "Dunham Possessed," Stephanie Batiste infers that the creation and maintenance of stock versions of Blackness signify an imperial process of identifying the native, appropriating culture, and reifying stock versions of Black identity.[2] While considerable work has been done to demonstrate how monolithic approaches to Blackness are a problematic fallacy, what Batiste is referring to further implicates Blackness, specifically stock versions of Blackness, as the result of imperial social production. That being the case, the intricate manner in which Blackness is connected to identity forces the society which constructed its stock caricaturization to wrestle with the historical outcomes, and lingering present-day consequences, of its function in society. Nevertheless, Blackness stands as an important Other in the case for the conditioning of social normativity.

Postmodernist and poststructuralist scholarship both assert the need to emphasize the multiplicity of embodied existence.[3] And, if Blackness is to operate beyond society's ontological monolith as an expression of Black individuality, then the complexity of Black embodiment will find helpful support from evolutionary biology's assertion that the greatest level of biodiversity occurs within groups.[4] This same finding concerning genetic variance is also used to support claims denying the existence of racial difference, because of its ability to be interpreted as a proposition that human beings are fundamentally the same. While genetics research has historically moved from the racism of biological determinism to neoliberal notions of genetic similitude this shift only functions as a color-blind assertion of universal biologies.

The reality is this, problematic racial differences do occur at the genetic level. In 2018, a team at Johns Hopkins University constructed an African Pan-Genome (APG) from a composite of 910 deeply sequenced African diasporic genetic samples. Samples were received from the Consortium on Asthma among African-Ancestry Populations in the Americas. The study was conducted in an effort to reenforce the call to diversify the human reference genome. The "current human reference genome derives primarily from a single individual," who so happens to be white and male.[5] After comparing the African Pan-Genome to the human reference genome the team discovered 296.5 Mega-basepairs (296,485,284 basepairs to be exact) that were unique to the APG.[6] The reference genome consists of 3235.84 Mega-basepairs. This study suggests that African descending genetics contain nearly 10 percent more genetic information than the reference genome. Furthermore, genetic structural testing reveals that African descending genetics aligns much more closely with Korean and Chinese genomes. Out of the 296.5 Mega-base pairs that were unique to the APG, 204.9 (204,928,334) were distinctly novel from the human reference genome! To this point the research team was clear in stating that "a better idea would be to create reference genomes for all distinct human populations."[7] The team who constructed this study also made it clear that the 910 genomes which comprised the APG did not fit within the scope of current human reference genome. One may assert that these issues are not very significant. But the sheer amount of base pair possibilities suggests otherwise. On a practical level, precision medicine is a burgeoning field which is examining the possibility of catering therapeutic medicine to individual genetic profiles. If the reference genome is primarily made from one white male, and doctors attempt to create genetically significant pharmaceutics for individuals of African descent the probability of success seems highly unlikely. Medicine applied to people whose genetic profile consists of regionally defined genetic variables that have not been rigorously explored could prove extremely deleterious. Until genetically oriented medicine addresses these issues more thoroughly precision medicine could function as biochemical warfare against Black bodies—given the unintended consequences of genetic research. While it may not be shocking that, even scientifically, "human" still means white male the extent to which this study may teach us about genetic difference has yet to be determined. So, any continued mention of a human "sameness" is essentially insisting on a universal human experience through the lens of a genetic framework. And the majority of those who assert a universal human experience adamantly disregard the role race, culture, or ethnicity play in influencing human needs. Given new directions in genetic research it is important to recognize that racial embodiment is also an embodiment of history's impingement upon biology. So, I think that in order to take race seriously an acknowledgment of the relational impact historical temporalities have had on biological systems is required. Specifically, in the case of Black biologies that originate from the African continent, the reality is that these bodies carry the amalgamative biological response to various temporally dependent elements. The convergence of lands, animals, sociocultural contexts, preexisting embodiments, etc., on Black biological systems is important. These dynamic interactions result in a perpetual state of becoming. Similarities among Black biologies that share a history of slavery in the United States also stem from a history of Blackness originating out of the infinitely complex environments of both the geo-specific and bio-reflective markers, which are related to ancestral lineage on the African continent and the migration patterns of genealogical family members after entering the United States.[8] The African diaspora into the United States connects biologically Black folks via physiological markers stemming from that historical connection. Still, this does not lump the experience of all Black folks in America into one biological cartography. It merely opens the discussion through an acknowledgment of the infinitely complex components that construct biological Blackness.

But what is biological Blackness? Biological Blackness is the Black body. And what is the body if not a set of complex systems, such as the central nervous system, cardiovascular system, respiratory system, digestive system, endocrine system, etc., which collectively converge upon the intricacies which undergird and promote Black life? Now, one could insert any race or ethnicity into the last sentence, which points to the fact that all bodies function as sets of complex systems. And, in connection with the definition of technology for Black transhuman liberation theology, a biological understanding of the body as an open set of complex systems would situate the body as a technology. Even more to the point, Black transhuman liberation theology is constructed for the transhumanist liberation of Black bodies, which further centers Black bodies in this conversation as technology. Black bodies are technology, and as technology Black bodies function as the means through which those who embody Blackness experience life. All experience happens within the bounds of the body. Even experiences thought to be had out of the body are mediated through the neurophysiology of the body. If the body is technology, where does this line of thought end? Can technology have a soul? Does technology embody a spirit? Are concepts such as the soul or spirit even relevant anymore? If the body is technology then what determines cognition or personality? If there is not a significant amount of genetic variance between Black and non-Black bodies then what makes Black bodies Black?

Since Black bodies are capable of manifesting through a wide spectrum of melanated hues one cannot always preclude, with certainty, whose body is Black. But, as the above description maintains, a stance of racialized derivatives suggests that there is more to determining inclusion within the sphere of Blackness than phenotypical expression. In this sense biological literature provides a space to critique critical race theory, supplying evidence (at the genetic level) to support racial difference. Hence, it is important to consider the role of one's historical lineage. This is of particular import. The manner in which direct ancestral lineage was or is entangled with various sociocultures, both intrapersonal (internally) and interpersonal (at various levels), the environmental factors that actively converge upon embodiment are expressed through individual neurochemistries and **genetics**.

For Black transhuman liberation theology genetic evolutions, generationally passed down through both genetic inheritance and nongenetic inheritance, situates each body's basic functionality as technological structures equipped to provide increasingly amenable access to life on earth. But if Black bodies are technology, then how does Black transhuman liberation theology avoid the continuance of transhumanism's mind-body dualism? Furthermore, where is the soul? Black transhuman liberation theology is grounded in the material lens of nonreductive physicalism, which asserts that the multiple levels of existence are deeply connected to the complexity of the material world.[9] So, within this framework an assertion of the body as technology—particularly the Black body—locates the Black body as the gateway for experiencing life on earth. This includes the entirety of the human body, including the mind. While some argue that the mind is not a physical entity, much like the soul, Black transhuman liberation theology's nonreductive physicalist approach recognizes that there is not a 1:1 correlation between matter and mind, such that one could point to the mind in an x-ray or functional magnetic resonance imaging device (fMRI). Nonreductive physicalism would assert that the mind is housed within the body and therefore is a part of the body.[10] It can be said that either the mind is in a localized place within the body, or it is present through a synchronized gradient of physiological activations which implicate the entire body as housing the mind, or minds, of the body.[11] So, what we understand to be the mind appears to be the output of biological systems configurations. Also, if the mind and body are singular that would also suggest that the once intangible element of the mind has become a bit more tangible through human materiality. And, if the body in its entirety can be thought of as singular, in terms of incorporating the intangibility of the mind, then it might also hold that the other intangible elements which historically were connected to the body, but were not one with the body (i.e., soul and spirit), may find immanence through embodied materiality. Still, this line of thought might raise an important question: If the body is technology and there is no dualistic premise undermining the connection between body and mind, then what does the Black body carry? What is given access to the material world through the Black body? The short answer is vitality.

Vitalist panpsychic animism

Black transhuman liberation theology's understanding of vitality is a decolonial synthesis. Specifically, it builds off African vitalisms and Womanist notions of incarnation. This section will begin with a brief outline of the African vitalist tradition introduced by Placide Tempels. It will then explore the work of scholars such as Alexis Kagame, and Wilfred Lajul who have contributed to vitalistic discourse. This section will also explore the limitations of Tempels' vitalism. From there I will introduce Black transhuman liberation theology's vitalism and the connection it has to Eboni Marshall Turman's *Womanist Ethic of Incarnation*.

Placide Tempels' *Bantu Philosophy* provides the earliest account of African vitalism. Spending time with Bantu people Tempels observed that they understand existence to be an eternal entity infused with a vital force that can be traced through both material and immaterial realities. Everything that exists is considered a force. Being denotes force. And while this force is present throughout all existence it has gradations of expression. Aside from God, Tempels implies that vital force is most prevalent in people since people have the ability to create and manipulate the environment through their imagination, extremities, and will. He also emphasizes a hierarchy of vital force. This hierarchy begins with God, who is "the Greatest person."[12] God is followed by the clan founders, then the ancestors who are ranked after them—forming a chain of vital force that links people to God. People are ranked below the ancestors, and below people are "lesser" forces, which Tempels infers are animals, plants, minerals, etc. According to Tempels, Bantu notions of life force can also be strengthened or diminished. For him, all that exists is meant to strengthen the vital force of people while they are on earth. This strengthening or diminishing can occur under a variety of factors. However, the actions that people take are considered the most important influences on the strength of vital force. In terms of language, Bantu refer to people as "muntu," or "vital force, endowed with intelligence and will." He then immediately juxtaposes "muntu" with "bintu,"which are inanimate objects or things. According to Tempels, the Bantu view things as "beings . . . [that are] forces not endowed with reason, [they are] not living."[13] The way he sets up muntu and bintu highlights his inability to actually grasp the metaphysical framework of the Bantu culture he came in contact with. Furthermore, it implicates him as a proponent of proto-normative white supremacy through a reinforcement of European subject object dualism. Subject object dualism is not a dilemma in African epistemologies.[14] But more importantly, in reconstructing a worldview that centers the entanglement of relational existence, Tempels misses the most fundament component of Bantu vitalism—"ntu."

Ntu is the vital force that runs through all of existence. It is the foundation of Bantu metaphysics. One could argue that it is what allows intelligence and will to become muntu. Valentin-Yves Mudimbe suggests that within the Kinyarwanda language there are ten classes of ntu.[15] Alexis Kagame outlines what has become the most widely accepted understanding of ntu. He highlights four essential categories equipped with specific functional capacities. Kagame's presentation of muntu does confirm Tempels' muntu, referenceing beings imbued with intelligence and will. Yet, he extends muntu to both the living and the living-dead (the ancestors).[16] Kintu, (what Tempels referred to as bintu) gives rise to beings without intelligence. These are inanimate things and objects. Hantu is the third iteration of the ntu. It refers to the relationship between time and space. Kuntu is the fourth iteration. It refers to quality and quantity. Mudimbe famously captures Alexis Kagame's depiction of the "ntu":

> In sum, the ntu is somehow a sign of a universal similitude. Its presence in beings brings them to life and attests to both their individual value and to the measure of their integration and dialectic of vital energy . . . "Ntu" is both a uniting and a differentiating vital norm which explains the powers of vital inequality in terms of difference between beings. It is a sign that God, father of all beings . . . has put a stamp on the universe, thus making it transparent in a hierarchy of sympathy. Upwards one would read the vitality which, from minerals through vegetables, animals and humans, links stones to the departed and God [her] self. Downwards, it is a genealogical filiation of forms of beings, engendering or relating to one another, all of them witnessing to the original source that made them possible.[17]

As part of the intellectual lineage of Tempels and Kagame, E. N. C. Mujynya adds to the expository, submitting that ntu also contains a four-part dynamism:

1. all elements of the universe, that is each created ntu, is a force and an active force;
2. everything being force, each ntu is thus always part of a multitude of other forces and all of them influence each other;
3. every ntu can always, under the influence of other ntu, increase or decrease in its being;
4. because each created being can weaken inferior beings or can be weakened by superior beings, each ntu is always and simultaneously an active and fragile force.[18]

Mujynya's dynamism succinctly synchronizes the fragility and inherent interdependent nature of ntu. In affirmation of the dynamic nature of this hierarchical thesis, V. Mulago asserts that Bantu metaphysics might be better understood as a metadynamic.[19]

Wilfred Lajul utilizes a regional analysis to demonstrate the differences present in East African, West African, and South African personhood. He does this in efforts to provide critical analysis of monolithic Pan-African caricatures that stem from a broad acceptance of Tempels work. In doing so, Lajul affirms the nuanced nature of African culture in his representations of African vitalisms. First, Lajul highlights the basic differences in East African and West African understandings of personhood. The East African emphasis is on the dynamic constitution of the person. In contrast, the West African emphasis is on the constitutive elements of the human person. Scholars agree, the West African person is composed of three elements: the body (nipaudua), life giving entity (okán), and the personality (sumsum). However, there is disagreement as to what the okán might actually be. Kwasi Wiredu thinks it is the innermost portion of the human or the "essence of an individual, the living soul, transmitter of individual destiny, spark of the Supreme Being" that takes on quasi-material form after death.[20] Conversely, Kwame Gyekye asserts that the okán is a divine element that goes to the world of spirits after death. There is a similar debate over the place of the sumsum, and whether it is maintained after death or not.

In addition to Lajul's West African structure alluded to above, the Yoruba have another configuration of the person. The Yoruba have four elements: the body (ora), the heart which is the center of human emotions (okán), the divine element in an individual (emi), and the head or bearer of destiny (ori). Yet, there is still some discrepancy regarding the total number of elements. Leke Adeofe, a philosopher of Yoruba origin, says there are only three elements; "the tripartite conceptions of persons." Within this system are the body (ara), mind/soul (emi), and inner head (ori). Adeofe adds, "ara . . . is physical, both the emi and ori are mental (or spiritual). This dichotomy might induce us to think of the African view as dualistic . . . Ori is conceived [as] ontologically independent of the other two elements. Thus, the African view is properly thought of as triadic."[21] This distinction is important, because Adeofe's description of the spiritual as existing in the mind places the spiritual in an indeterminate space. Unless the mind itself is a spiritual notion, then the mind is in the body, or at least a part of it. In this way, the spiritual occurs as a layer of the body, yet distinct from the body. Regardless, the differences described broader fracturing. Are the constitutive elements of the West African person compartmentalizing? Or, do they provide a smooth landscape that allows for fluidity and singularity of personhood? While no concrete answer has been determined, the Yoruba believe that the parts of the human person are created by different deities. The "Ara, the body, is constructed by Orisa-nla, the arch deity; Olodumare (God or 'Supreme Deity') brings forth the emi; while another deity, Ajala, is responsible for creating ori."[22] But what undergirds this existence of the person in Yoruba tradition? Áse. Áse is the energy, or vital force, that Oludumare uses to create. It is "the vital power or energy that animates and brings forth phenomena in the universe."[23] Wielded by Esu, áse has primordial capacities that scholars argue can be described as life itself. Furthermore áse posits a level of fundamental connectivity as an "energy of cosmic origin that permeates and lives within all that is—human beings, animals, plants, minerals, and objects, as well as event."[24] Similar to Bantu notions of ntu, áse is what ties all of existence together.

Returning to Lajul's analysis, he places South African and East African personhood together. He engages Didier Kaphagawani, who in dialogue with John Mbiti and Alexis Kagame, critiques Tempels' concepts of the person through three thesis: the force thesis, the communal thesis, and the shadow thesis. The force thesis is comparable to Tempels' understanding of life force. Mbiti sees dynamism being played out through the community, and Kagame sees force through relationality between intelligence and the heart. However, Kaphagawani goes a bit further. In a critique of Tempels, Kaphagawani asserts that when Tempels mentions the Bantu people, he is more specifically referring to the Luba people. In addition Kaphagawani points out Tempels goes on to assume that all Bantu languages "contains words or phrases denoting a force, which constitutes 'the integrity of our whole being.'"[25] Still, Lajul turns to the Acholi people from Uganda where the word for being is *bedo*, and the word for becoming, or force, is *doko*. It is important to note that Kaphagawani's understanding of force is more in line with the quasi-materiality of the okán and sumsum.

The communal thesis is a critique of Tempels' romantic notion that the African is inherently communal and anti-individualistic. Lajul points to the problematic nature of Tempels' communalism thesis.

> While the communalism thesis is highly esteemed in Africa, it would be wrong to reduce individuality to the communal. This understanding comes from misinterpreting the Mbitian phrase, which reads as quoted earlier; I am, because we are; and since we are therefore I am. It is interpreted from a Chewa proverb which says, Kalikokhanikanyama; tulituwilinituwanthu. According to the proverb, "what is alone is a brute animal; whatever or whoever has a partner/neighbor is a human being." This is similar to the Aristotelian saying that "anyone who cannot live in society is a god or an animal." Communalism does not deny individualism.[26]

Lajul is essentially communicating that both the community and the individual are equally important. Neither would exist without the other. Even more so, the individual cannot survive without the community, and the community cannot survive without the individual.

Kagame adds the shadow thesis. The shadow thesis proposes that the human is both fully animal and fully intelligent being. The vital (animal) component of the human is material, and therefore perishing, or the shadow. The intelligent component is immortal. Kagame adds that among the immaterial parts that the person possesses are intelligence and heart. Intelligence makes people reflective and meditative animals. The creative nature of persons stems from the ability to reflect. And, the heart, in the shadow thesis, binds all the internal components of the person through the will of the heart.[27] Here the heart becomes a sign of determination through a mixture of reflective creativity and intelligence.

While recent scholarship has worked to elucidate the subtle differences among the varieties of African vitalism, the utility of the concept of vitalism has come under scrutiny. Emmanuel Bueya issues a critical warning concerning the misappropriation of vitalism. In *Stability in Postcolonial African States,* Bueya suggests that vitality's misappropriation by the state has made victims of those who exist outside the ranks of the governing elite. For him, "[Vitalitism] is about religiosity, brotherhood (sisterhood), community and metaphysical life without its material conditions." So, vitalism's connection to the immaterial renders it socially ineffective since it, "ignores its conditions of production and constraints of the current situation."[28] Here Bueya proposes that the ontological nature of the vitalism confines it to idealistic imaginations of perfectionism. And so, once the phenomenological aspect of being becomes part of the linguistic millieu of oppressive structures, vitality loses the actual force it attempts to communicate when mentioned. Bueya goes onto say:

> The violence of the state prevails under African harmony and pacifism. The ethnophilosophy used by the Catholic bishops in their theological statements and pastoral letters is a lure. Today that discourse has lost its critical charge and its truth. Yesterday, it was the language of the oppressed; today, the elite holds the real power and still use the same language of liberation. Initially a romantic protest against European pride, it is now an ideological placebo on the victims's mind-set.[29]

Bueya draws attention to the power of governing structures. The state can simply attach indigenous language to its assemblages of power, enhancing its cybernetic reach by weaponizing culturally significant factors against the very people who created them. Essentially, the state uses indigenous concepts to reify its power. Vitality has been taken, and used to shape local understandings of social normativity and identity. But, this is not entirely surprising. The first account of African vitality (Tempels) was part of a larger missionary/colonial reconnaissance project. Tempels was explicit; His work was to improve catechism so that it may be "adapted [for] primitive mentality."[30] While some suggest his work proved that Africans already thought philosophically, his goal was, in fact, to synthesize Bantu wisdom into a philosophy legible enough for European consumption. The combined use of the term vitality and his need to prepare Bantu philosophical thought for Europe, as part of a colonial and missionary endeavor, is part of a larger supposition that Tempels was familiar with Henri Bergson's *Creating Evolution.* Tempel's familiarity with the élan vital or vital force supplied the language to communicatively link Bantu epistemological frameworks with Eurocentric affinities.[31] Not only did Henri Bergson, the French philosopher who popularized modern vitalism, coin the term life force or élan vital, Bergson also maintained a Eurocentric stance, as seen through his denigrating description of those who possess "primitive minds."

In *The Racial Discourses of Life Philosophy,* Donna Jones does an excellent job parsing out the racialized notes in Bergson's work. She highlights that although Bergson may appear empathetic toward primitive mentalities, he implores his readers not to forget that primitives, having lived as long as moderns, "have had plenty of time to exaggerate and aggravate" the irrationalities of the once more humane, primitive mind. But for Bergson, "the irrational [of primitivity] passes into the realm of the absurd, and the strange into the realm of the monstrous," which does not need "intellectual superiority to invent, or to accept the invention. [Essentially, t]he logic of absurdity was enough."[32] This is how Bergson and, in many respects, Tempels (who was not ashamed to utilize the term "primitive" in *Bantu* Philosophy), perceived Africans! Nevertheless, Tempels' depiction of Bantu vitalism is still an extension of Bergson's underlying racist epistemology, framing African thought in light of what Jones describes as a comparison between the childish primitive mind—that is unwilling to look beyond mysticism to explain phenomenological existence—and the modern mind. One of Jones' primary critiques of vitalism is that it still ends in mysticism. The foundational premise of Bergson's élan vital is that life cannot be reduced to mechanistic biology, which is an unfruitful precursor to emergence.[33] Still, vitalism is a central component to Black transhuman liberation theology. It is the foundation of what allows the full body to become technology. It powers the body as life itself. So, what does vitalism have to give to Black transhuman liberation theology?

The vitalism of Black transhuman liberation theology is not the vitalism of old. It calls for a radical extension of what can qualify as life force through an incorporation of mechanistic processes that were once denounced. It is a both and. It is mystical in the sense that it refers to immaterial phenomena not readily accessible. It functions as the thread of existence (ntu) which gives power to be (áse). But it is also mechanistic in that it relies on the materiality of the body; be it a person, animal, plant, or inanimate object to experience and possess the life force manifest within all existence. So, within Black transhuman liberation theology vitality is defined as the underlying force that enlivens and permeates all existence. More specifically, in humans it can be imagined as the electric current that powers the involuntary dialogue between sodium and potassium which sparks the human biological system, energizes it, and allows it to persist. In inanimate objects, vitality is the atomic and subatomic configuration that allows for each structure to take shape. In a more acute sense, within inanimate objects vitality has more atomic/subatomic significance. Atoms move. But atoms are also electromagnetic on top of their constant motion. Quarks, or subatomic particles, are constantly in motion as well. Powerful computers are constructed just to capture glimpses of particles moving to determine their existence. Every systemic formation presents itself differently at the level of people, however, for Black transhuman liberation theology, agency does not denote significance. Value is placed upon the realization that vitality is present within everything, and at all levels of scale. Now, this may be problematic for some as it does not deal directly with concepts such as sentience/consciousness or cognition. Furthermore, it raises questions concerning the force itself.

These varying structures, whether biological formations or not, share the capacity for a particular kind of psychology, which is dependent upon the system they construct. But, if the problem is with sentience/consciousness Whitehead's notion of prehensive sentience provides a solid foundation for this conjecture.

> All relatedness has its foundation in the relatedness of actualities; and such relatedness is wholly concerned with the appropriation of the dead by the living-that is to say, with objective immortality whereby what is divested of its own living immediacy becomes a real component in other living immediacies of becoming.[34]

This is to say that we live in a moment-to-moment existence where infinite potentiality and indeterminacy are the primary assertions. Effectively, we are changing with every passing moment, and what we have come to recognize as memory is merely a recognition of a past measure of embodiment that no longer exists.

> The actual world is a manifold of prehensions; and a "prehension" is a "prehensive occasion"; and a prehensive occasion is the most concrete finite entity, conceived as what it is in itself and for itself, and not as from its aspect in the essence of another such occasion. (Whitehead 2011, 61–62)[35]

Whitehead's assertion is particularly important. It stands on the immediacy of each moment and the dynamics of atomic, subatomic, and quantum personhood; even though much of what goes into preserving something such as personal psychology (mentality) is the preservation of prehensive occasions—notions of the self from previous moments.[36] I will summarize them thusly: Drawing from Whiteheadean terminology, each moment that passes gives rise to another version of an entity; each new momentary entity carries with it a memory of its prior self; however, each new moment provides a new molecular self. So, prehensive sentience is the continuation of a previous self with an acknowledgment that the previous self is not the current self, which supposes limitless possibility/potential for the most current self. This leads to the animistic quality of the vitalistic notion of energy which inhabits the body. It speaks to the transitional quality of the molecular self, which is nondeterminant in nature, but also very much alive. One could even propose that congruent prehensions are an important component of avoiding entropy, and each molecular formation of a system is alive according to the formation of the system. This allows for a greater sense of complexity as it pertains to being alive and what qualifies as a systemic recognition of existence. Just because a system is not anthropomorphic does not negate its life force. Fault lies with anthropomorphic beings since we have yet to place significant value upon non-anthropomorphic life. For instance, something like a rock has genetic expression given its texture, color, shape, erosion formulation, etc. But because it does not present itself in the same manner as maybe a dog (which is a form of embodiment that some circles of futurists are beginning to accept as sentient) then people may be less likely to respect its vitality.[37]

Vitality, or life force, in everything implies that everything is alive. This basic animism infers a type of sentience—panpsychic. So, when Black transhuman liberation theology declares that vitality fills bodies, it is essentially suggesting that every body, no matter its configuration, embodies vitality. This notion allows for infinite vitalistic configurations, and gives space for vitality and embodiment to take shape in whatever form it presents itself. This is not what Léopold Sédar Senghor describes as a "[Negro- African] animism . . . [where] all of Nature is animated by a human presence."[38] It is important to note that the sentience accompanying vitality is not sentience in terms of emotionality, awareness, or cognition. This sentience is merely a recognition that as an entity that precipitates involuntary movement, or prevents entropy, it knows to keep moving until the system it enlivens is no longer operational. Given the scalar qualities of vitality within Black transhuman liberation theology, it does align with what Senghor posits as part of African ontology. It suggests "there is no such thing as dead matter: every being, everything—be it only a grain of sand—radiates a life force, a sort of wave-particle . . . [all bodies are] therefore a composition of mobile forces which interlock: a world of solidarities that seek to knit themselves together."[39] Senghor's notion of solidarities could be used to justify a meta presence more profuse than the soul or spirit, since all of existence is infused with this force. Still, operational forms carry vitality which gives life to their form in a reciprocal manner. For example, in the case of the body, vitality gives life to the body and simultaneously the body gives vitality the chance to experience life. As previously mentioned, African vitality's greatest manifestation of life force is God, but that life force is most prevalent in people. In Black transhuman liberation theology there is no gradation of God, or that which is beyond the self. The dispensation of the metaphysical entity which becomes the thrust for existence is ever present. That is it. Hierarchies are dismembered and destroyed. Vitality as vitalistic panpsychic animism presupposes the immanence of God, or that which is beyond the perceptive self. Furthermore, life presupposes an incarnate manifestation of that metaphysical entity; the sacred in the body. In this case, the Black body. Hence, we are talking about Black vitality.

Black vitality is Black because of the Black body. Earlier iterations of Black vitality, often arising from or in conversation with the Négritude movement, proposed that there is something particular about the vital impulse that energizes the Black body, in contrast to white bodies. These binary vitalistic depictions argued for Black superiority via ontology (strong vitalism) or sociology (weak vitalism).[40] Aside from the weakness of merely addressing existence in a binary fashion, all that we now know (through critical race theory and evolutionary biology) continues to demonstrate the lack of difference among racialized forms of embodiment. Black vitality, as part of vitalist panpsychic animism, functions within a complex and dynamic system whereby operations such as cognition, exertion, extension, emotion, and form function within a broader multiplanar landscape that is often described as an infinitely complex environment. These layers of indeterminate complexity are in constant conversation with vitality through the body. Vitality itself is not Black. The Black body is Black. Vitality only becomes Black once it engages in the cell division process of fertilization which produces Black bodies. The Blackness ascribed to Black folks—soul, culture, swagger, funk, magic, etc.—can all be seen as the result of genetic expression, cultural evolution, and environmental factors. All of these are housed in the body, communal narratives (larger collective Black narratives, familial narratives, regional narratives, etc.), artifacts, and socialities that Black folks maintain, which add to the collective identity associated with Blackness. However, vitality itself is the very isness of life. The body along with culture and the various dimensions of relationality it is entangled with are all technologies that allow for vitality to experience the world. The body is the conduit for life force; for God, or that which is beyond the perceptible self, to see the world through the unique iteration of individual physicalities.

Incarnating Blackness: Vitality interacting with technology

In *Toward a Womanist Ethic of Incarnation* Eboni Marshall Turman constructs a three pronged framework of divine incarnation. For Turman, incarnation requires renunciation, inclusivity, and responsibility. Her premise of the incarnation is connected to a brokenness of binary forms of identification so "that the divine converges with the human and, through this [performative] event, bequeaths a vindication that results in parousia."[41] As a dancer Turman leans on performative narratives to outline her notion of incarnation:

> The primary state of chaos into which the dancer's body is propelled requires that the body renounce the privilege of difference that obstructs the unity of the moment . . . (renunciation). It must simultaneously employ the body in a way that tells a story that is inconceivable as its own, and yet is made real in her body (inclusivity). That is, the narrative that the dancing body tells by way of renouncing the privilege of difference and carrying a foreign story on its body (inclusivity) converges with an external gaze that recognizes the power of the in-itself that is organically (or at least apparently so) negotiating a narrative that has been projected onto her body. It is only in this mediative moment where the en sarki of the dancer's body and the kata sarka of the choreographed narrative meet, that the body secondarily moves into the range of performing its limitless possibilities (responsibility).

In centering Black women Turman specifically focuses on Black churchwomen who struggle with being excluded from the normative hierarchy of embodiment. For Turman, normative body ethics in Black churches create boundaries around who may readily access, or be accessed by, the divine without a disruptive "reach, stand, or sway" that announces the performative moment of vindicating incarnation.[42] Turman's ethic of incarnation speaks to the capacity of everybody to experience "God in us," especially if the "oppressed of the oppressed" encounters a subversive experience of the divine amid multidimensional socially constructed gender injustice and anti-Black oppression. Black transhuman liberation theology draws from Turman's womanist ethic of renunciation, inclusivity, and responsibility.

For Black transhuman liberation theology, renunciation takes on the form of renouncing Eurocentric epistemologies that negatively situate Blackness or tries to erase its existence. In addition, it renounces the necessity of vindication. The vitalistic panpsychic animism which undergirds existence, that is, God, or that which is beyond the perceptive self, is already imminent in one's existence. There is no need to seek out recognition or prove one's worth in some affirmative move to be recognized, or have one's vitalist incarnation recognized. There is nothing that can remove this vital force from one's body. Death is the only way out, and even in death the physics of a system no longer in operation are required to release the energy that once made it run through heat (thermodynamics). So, vitality itself moves into another mode of existence. God, energy, the connective fabric of the universe, which undergirds existence passes through states of existence through the various forms it inhabits over time, and only in that way is vitality transhistorical. The systems that vitality enlivens are confined to the temporality of their existence. But as long as there is life, or breath, in an enlivened system, vitality is there.

Inclusivity becomes the radical acceptance of the complex ways in which Black vitality presents itself through embodiment. This is where various factors that compose personal existence come into play for a layered and intersectional approach to existence. A focus on the four layers of connection that vitality has to Black biology will help explore the various ways in which the body functions as technology. From this perspective the body's biological systems provide the most basic features of existence. Those four layers of connection function as features that accompany the body. These layers include its biological systems; its senses; the emergent properties layer; and its identity. I use biological language to demonstrate the systematic, and therefore technological, manner in which the body operates as an autopoietic system of entropic regeneration. It is important to know that the biological overview I provide is not meant to reduce life to mechanistic forces, nor is it technically exhaustive. However, it is meant to serve as a "look under the hood" at the machinery that undergirds the body as an entry point for thinking about the ways vitality interacts with biotechnology.

I will begin the outline of the biological systems layer with the respiratory system. The respiratory system fulfills the basic requirements for a symbiotic relationship with earth's atmosphere. Without the respiratory system the body would not be able to sustain itself as an autopoietic system based upon its need for aerobic distribution of oxygen to muscles, vessels, and organs via the circulatory system. The circulatory system allows oxygenated blood to travel through the body for several reasons. Here are the ones I'll highlight: Cellular regeneration helps stave off entropy via fresh blood; Organs require blood to function; and given the nature of energy usage and depletion, oxygen depleted blood is cycled out of the body, via the respiratory system, into the atmosphere which contributes to photosynthesis—an example of larger modes of entanglement. The renal system filters blood. It helps maintain homeostasis within the blood, and removes waste from the body much like the digestive system. The digestive system metabolizes food so that it can be sent through the circulatory system, providing nutrients to the entire body. It also removes waste from the body, and impacts mental states. For instance, serotonergic (serotonin) centers in the digestive system help regulate mood and cognition.[43] The endocrine system releases hormones into the body that align with sex, environmental factors (i.e., stress or food), life stages, and other factors. Hormones secreted through the endocrine system are state dependent, meaning their response to certain situations require they are only active for the duration of the time they are needed. The exocrine system releases secretions through epithelial cells, such as sweat, breast milk, or semen. It aids in the release of toxins, and helps the body cool, but it also supports the initialization and maintenance of germ line reproduction. The musculoskeletal system consists of all the muscles and bones of the body that support and protect the body's organs and nerves, while providing the capacity for willful, remembered, and instinctive movement. The nervous system supports the entire system, precipitating movement or activation of skeletal muscles, organs, or components of other neurological systems, via signals sent through neurons, synapses, and transmitters. The nervous system provides the connecting tissue that links the brain to the rest of the body assisting with all five senses. And it transmits information at speeds up to 120 meters/second! Finally, the reproductive system functions as the center for biological replication. The immune system is also connected to all the others, fighting off infectious diseases. Together the biological systems support life, and promote new life, at the most basic level. Now, the degree of functionality which each system provides varies which also leads to differing levels of physical ability. Regardless, vitality sits at the seat of propulsion for the body, which is allowed to continue running based on the combined minimum requirement for the preservation of a unit of life. Current and emergent technologies can bridge the gap in functionality that preserves life. But as always, the degree to which augmentations are made to biological systems ought to be left up to the individual in question so that people are not forced to fit within social perceptions of physical normativity and concepts of ablism.

The five senses of touch, taste, olfactory (smell), auditory (hearing), and sight comprise the second layer of features that accompany bodily existence for biological Blackness. These senses provide the basis for interaction with the earth's myriad environments. Their primary task is survival, which is the natural state of any system. However, the senses also provide feedback for pleasure as well. The senses help to facilitate neurophysiological (electrical responses that release chemicals, such as transmitters and hormones in the body) responses that make interactions with the environment instantaneous, with effects that can last for quite some time. Touch functions as a haptic system, equipped with not only the ability to touch, but to feel and manipulate objects as well.[44] And as a haptic system touch is recorded through the combination of "kinesthetic ([muscular] force [and body] position) and cutaneous (tactile) receptors."[45] Taste is thought to be "a combination of five sensations: sweet, sour (acid), salty, bitter, and umami."[46] Umami is another word for savory or delicious. Taste not only helps in deciphering which foods are enjoyable, but also helps to inform when something is spoiled or rotten as part of an attempt to protect the health of the biological system. Taste and smell are complementary. A considerable amount of what is tasted has to do with smell. Similar to taste, smell helps decipher between what is potentially harmful or helpful to the body. Smell is also connected to emotion and memory. Hearing is the body's perception of sound. The position of the ears helps to determine sounds in relation to the body's position in space. The auditory system also helps to determine the speed and direction a body is moving in at any given moment. Sight helps the body determine objects in space. Visual stimuli received through the eyes helps to categorize differences in form, patterns in the environment, and whether something is a potential danger or not. Sight also provides depth perception, the ability to differentiate between colors (with exceptions for colorblindness), and adjusts for visual acuity in the dark.

The emergent properties layer encompasses technological features supporting bodily existence. They are consciousness as awareness, cognition, memory, emotion, and perception. "Emergent properties are complex processes . . . that cannot be predicted from what we know about the properties of individual nerve cells and their specific connections."[47] Conscious awareness can be thought of in three plains: interoception, proprioception, and nociception. Interoception is the ability to be aware of what is happening internally. It can range from an awareness of thoughts to an awareness of stomach growlings. Proprioception is the ability to understand the body's position in space and time. An example of proprioception is the awareness of being next to someone or behind something. Nociception is the ability to perceive pain. Cognition refers to thinking. It can be seen as a five-component loop that includes the sensory system (five senses and awareness), basic cognition, temporal conditions of the central nervous system (hormones and transmitters present in the blood), musculoskeletal output (action), and physiological responses to present stimuli.[48] While awareness may let you know what you are eating, and that you taste it, cognition lets you determine whether, or not, you like it. Cognition is also different from intelligence. Thinking (cognition) does not always lead to aptitude. But that does not mean aptitude is not a derivative of cognition.

Memory is the emergent property that fuses momentary iterations of the biological systems, which helps to maintain a coherent sense of self in relation to temporal factors. Memory has three dimensions: Time (immediate, working, short term, and long term), declarative (episodic and semantic), and procedural.

Time series memory storage is gradually encoded in the brain and body, depending upon factors such as arousal, repetition, and attention. Declarative memory allows the body to recall and retrieve information regarding the self, other people, places, events, etc., at will. Procedural memory applies to motor skills, associations, primings, and problem/puzzle solving. In many cases procedural memory can be considered somatic memory, or memory stored in the muscles. Memory is also more deeply encoded based upon the body's level of arousal (physiological states of excitation/intensity vs. inhibition/low interest). As a result, memory associated with high-arousal states are more bioavailable than memory associated with lower states of arousal.[49]

Emotion is another set of complex neurophysiological responses. Current emotion theory has been a long-standing conversation concerning biological order of operations. The earliest theories revolved around whether physiology (James-Lange) or cognition (Cannon-Bard) activates first.[50] These theories began to shift, placing emphasis on the interpretation of the physiological and cognitive activations of the person (Schachter and Singer).[51] Recent theories now focus on appraisal, or mental evaluations of stimuli, which incorporates subconscious interpretations that occur prior to an emotional occurrence which is attributed to preconceived value propositions regarding the stimuli being presented. So, cognitive interpretation of emotional experience occurs after unconscious appraisal takes place.[52] This means that emotion is one large entanglement of physiological de-/activations, chemical secretions, and cognitive assessments (unconscious and conscious).

The perception overlay can be broken into three components: physiological response, cognition, and behavior. Perception shapes the manner in which bodies understand the natural world and subregions of existence. It functions within an ongoing and drifting scope of homeostatic relationship to the memory of the system. Perception is the product of every new encounter with the outside world. The physiological response occurs in tandem with the presentation of new subjects or objects in space. Similar to the emotional overlay, implicit memory is weighed against present moment stimuli—influencing the unconscious response of the perceiver. From here, cognition is employed to re/interpret environmental stimuli that adds to a growing internal catalog of similar situations, external subjects, internal subjects, and objects.[53] The perception cycle is a biotech survival mechanism that combines memory with real-time assessment.

The identity overlay functions as the fourth layer of features present within personal biotechnology. They are classified under race, gender and its relation to birth sex, and sexuality. They are prosthetic extensions of emergent properties, because they aid bodies in navigating the social environment. Until this juncture, all previous features have had to do with individual physiology, physical capability, and mind. This has not been a move away from vitality or a diminishment of Blackness. It is first a recognition that vitality is in constant conversation with all the aforementioned biological systems, senses, and emergent properties; helping to facilitate the temporal dependence of each interwoven connection whose potential can invoke any point along the entire biotechnologically mediated plane. It is from this foundational understanding of embodiment that we can now discuss the relationship between the rise, valence, and meaning of Blackness, gender, and sexuality. Physical Blackness, or shades of Black skin and the veritable differences present within the Black biotechnological form, arise from phenotypical expression, and nongenetic inheritance (epigenetic or environmentally impacted genetic factors). So, we can think of physical Blackness in those two categories: phenotypical expression (directly inherited genetic expressions), and epigenetic factors. Phenotypical expression presents itself in the milieu of what we have come to recognize as traits such as eye color, height, bone structure, hair color and texture, or skin color (melanin). These are passed down through the contributing alleles of each parent, which through the use of their reproductive organs inseminate, incubate, and birth/produce offspring with half of their genetic makeup coming from each parent (indeterminately produced during gametic meiosis).[54] The space of heritable genetic expression facilitates battles over dominance (dominant genetics) and recessiveness (nondominant genetics) based upon the variance in heritable genetic donations from parent alleles. From the complex composition of variable genetic transcription bodies materialize, actualizing in an array of possibilities. But melanin is the most distinct.[55]

Nongenetic inheritance demonstrates the relational influence of a wider swath of internal and external factors. Maternal prenatal food intake, food from birth through adulthood, socialization, cultural influences, personal narratives, communal narratives, stress factors, climate, etc. These are factors that influence genetic expression. Recent epigenetic literature has explored how implicit memory housed in the brains memory, emotion, and survival center (limbic system) carries familial memories.[56] While epigenetics as a field has struggled to gain a foothold due to its nascence, difficulty in gaining consensus among its contributors as to what it is, and the breadth of its scope, there is no doubt regarding the impact of the environment on transgenerational genetic expression.[57] That being said, when we talk about the convergence of genetic and nongenetic inheritance upon biotechnology, we are essentially exploring the many ways that Mamma, Pops, Grandma, Popop, our brothers, and sisters (biological and otherwise), the homies, the neighborhood, our city, the stories we are told, the stories we tell ourselves, our history in America, the food we eat, the things we let stress us, Black twitter, our pets, other people's pets, and the myriad other parts of the infinitely complex environment that continues to impact us consciously, or not, and how they, and continue to, impact our genetic expression. All of these factors contribute to the unique manner in which individuals encounter, ingest, wrestle with, and reflect Blackness onto the world. So, through the onset of phenotypical genetic expression Blackness enters the world—as the offspring of Blackness. Whether generatively or maladaptively, Blackness colors vitality and shapes the biological space of gender and sexuality. The tension between reflecting Blackness amid what it means to be gendered and sexualized bodies arises when gender and sexuality meet modes of culturally assigned essentializations of Blackness.

Within Black transhuman liberation theology gender functions as a biologically mediated technology. Gender theories such as Sylvia Wynter's might assert that gender is another socially constructed technology (as part of the larger genealogical cartography of the human) whose affiliation must be abandoned as a prerequisite for what it means to be liberated from the reverberating epistemologies of "man."[58] Since the primary fixture of un/gendered discourse has been the site of the body, an exploration of biology in this discourse raises the question, "what role might biology play when juxtaposed to Hortense Spillers's notion of flesh and body?[59]" Even the materiality of the body—its flesh—has been engaged through meta-metaphorical criticism. This meta-metaphorical criticism deconstructs how its phenotype is read (or understood) in the larger social epistemology.[60] But the question I have posed simultaneously leads to the statement I am about to make. Biological aspects of the body respond to the sociogenic factors presented to it, and, in doing so, respond according to the converging factors specific to the individual body. How then can we explain why individuals decide to move into spaces beyond social conditioning and respectability, if not through the composite of existence? The body exists as somaticized mentalities in relationship to the infinitely complex natural and social environments. Wynters' work provides a strong case for moving away from genres of "man." In *Habeas Viscus,* Alexander Weheliye points to Hall and Spivak as an example of Anglo-American scholarship which rejects poststructuralist tenets due to the "high stakes" associated with evacuating seemingly outdated concepts whose flavorful notes are baked into "societies structured in dominance."[61]

But which societies aren't structured in dominance? And, can we ever successfully construct a society which is not structured in dominance? Above that, the weight of Wynter's call is too compelling. Projecting beyond "man" includes discourse that stems from unraveling "its" ways of knowing. Unraveling as a praxis theoretically creates space for a Freirian-like critical consciousness to appear. Wynter's utilization of Fanon's sociogenic category in her mode of unraveling was an exercise demonstrating that people cannot be understood through culture (sociogeny) or biology (ontogeny) independent of one another. She chose to bypass phylogeny because of her goal to connect coloniality with the biology of being. But I think phylogeny presents a key opportunity for analysis when thinking about being. What I assert hereafter is what I believe to be valid in the context/genre of gender. In the discourse of biotechnology epigenetics functions to create an even clearer picture of the role personal history, familial history, genetic expression, and environment(s) play in the context of being. This is why I introduced the concepts of epigenetics earlier in this chapter. It merges ontogeny, phylogeny, and sociogeny through the vitalist notion of time and space—hantu. Ontogeny supposes a genetic history of individuals in their process of becoming. However, emphasizing individual genetic history apart from important genealogical and environmental factors implies that individuals genetically emerge in isolation. Sociogeny supposes that culture's impingement upon existence is relegated to the temporality in which an organism (in this case, the body) exists. So, to further this decolonial exercise I think that phylogeny needs to be given a more important role. This biocultural argument supposes that the individual (ontogeny) and its culture (sociogeny) are not the only factors to be considered. The history of genetic expression (phylogeny) in terms of heritable and nonheritable responses to physical and psychological environments leads to unique individual expressions. This is not a discussion on genetic difference and race. However, it is one that thinks of the complex factors that go into making individuals while undergirding what it is to be—as biotechnology. So, when phylogeny, as epigenetics, is placed in conversation with ontogeny and sociogeny the tension of individuality and communality arise from the nexus of these three factors—at the site of the body. This is why familial histories (genetic dispositions, regional genetic markers, shared ancestry, context-dependent expressions or inhibitions, etc.), the infinitely variable factors of the natural environment (climate, temperature, dew point, regional insects, regional animals, terrain, etc.), play just as significant a role as culture (social factors, art, literature, oration, language, semiotics, etc.) in genetic and behavioral expressions. It suggests that there were biotechnologically stored iterations of our individual selves that predate our current individual selves. Here, individuals undergo processes of becoming alongside other individuals (who presently inhabit materiality, who used to inhabit materiality, and whose myth inhabits materiality in varying degrees). Simultaneously, previous versions of personal biotechnology give birth to current versions of selves, and others, while among each other. So, temporality (in terms of moments, contexts, eras, life spans, people, and epistemologies are grounded in vitality—hantu) also impacts biology and subsequently identifiers, such as gender, arise out of this convoluted matrix.

As alluded to above, gender and birth sex engage in an intricate dance with enculturation and individual neurochemistry to arrive at individual gendered identity. In "Sexual Identity and Neurosexism" Fabrício Pontin, Laura Dick Guerim, Camila Palhares Barbosa, and Bruna Fernandes Ternus argue against the male-dominated lenses that impose male heteronormativity as the standard of biological formation.[62] They suggest that neuroscience researchers actively look for gendered difference to substantiate socially constructed gender norms. Furthermore, Pontin et al. call upon Cordelia Fine, who states, "scientific claims reinforce and legitimate gender roles in ways that are not scientifically justified," which is to say the work presented to reify gender difference is not strong enough to maintain gender difference.[63] Instead, they propose that culture and neuroplasticity play a much larger role in forming individual gender identity, and should be given much more credit than *in utero* development. Pontin el al. acknowledge the importance of neurobiology in gender identity, but assert that the process toward gender identity, which includes neurobiology, is much more complex and nuanced due to the social factors that are part of the process. This serves to lay a foundation for the biocultural perspective of gender formation. In addition, gender incorporates personally distributed cognitive systems, the dependence of cognition upon interpersonal interaction, the arc of personal perception (including physiological valuations of environments and variables within environments), and internal dialogue to situate one's self in response to socialized dimensions of gender. All of this, operate as an extension of the body's emergent property feature.

Due to the overwhelming amount of variables that go into the formation of one's identity, it is no surprise that people cannot be bound to the binary structures of heteronormativity. This has even less to do with the history of non-binary existence within various indigenous cultures before the European colonial project. While we try to classify gender and gender-nonconforming individuals to make sense of the ever-increasing unpredictability of our world, let alone the sphere of genetic and social expression, we simply cannot contain what it means to associate in a gendered manner because the spectrum is ever widening. Any attempt to narrow the scope of individual presentations of embodiment is essentially an attempt to define others for our own sense of comfort. And any insistence on this mode of performative demand becomes an extension of the violence that reifies the colonial desire to control/determine/subjugate the other. However, life is uncomfortable. Vitality cannot be controlled. Thus, it is important to remember how the feature of gender situates itself as a biotechnological reply to social paradigms—even if its production and replication are not immediately generative for the individual biotechnology instantiating it.

Racialized people, specifically Black people, find themselves at the crossroads of being racialized, gendered, and sexualized. The trouble of navigating this space not only stems from the psychology of anticipating behavioral responses to one's mode of biotechnological existence. It also stems from the subsequent valuations associated with the degrees of distance individual variations of Black biotechnology are from proto-normative notions of existence. Gender and sexuality theorists have argued that capitalism serves to reify racist notions of gender and sexuality. Through its valuation process, it creates economic situations that have hindered Black participation in this system. The final step in the capitalist grinder stigmatizes Blackness and penalizes Black biotechnology for being outside of its system of valuation. Given the assumptive role of the dopaminergic (dopamine) reward system in decision-making, one could argue that living within environments that prize social conformity would discourage rebellious modes of existence. But vitality cannot be contained. Frances Beal outlines a socially infecting method which outlines the perspective one takes while placing one's body in the way of danger

> We must begin to understand that a revolution entails not only the willingness to lay our lives on the firing line and get killed. In some ways, this is an easy commitment to make. To die for the revolution is a oneshot deal; to live for the revolution means taking on the more difficult commitment of changing our day-to-day life patterns. This will mean changing the traditional routines that we have established as a result of living in a totally corrupting society.[64]

The difficulty that Beal stresses is the choice one must embark upon in deciding to live as one's vitalistically grounded self. It could be argued that choosing daily danger goes against one's dopaminergic reward system. Simultaneously, the decision to live dangerously for the cause of a different world places dopaminergic value in the goal of new world. While some might find pleasure in living dangerously, one might hypothesize that this type of pleasure is difficult to maintain over long periods of time (given the bell-curve comparing stress to optimal performance).[65] Still, if the ultimate goal is valued over the weight of daily stress one could argue that there is a reward being communicated through biotechnology because each day one places one's self under stress is theoretically one day closer to a new world. Even if one is skeptical about making an impact on the world one could argue that placing one's self in harm's way still aligns one's self with the validation internal vitality provides.

If we take the work of Pontin et al. seriously, then gender is the amalgamative biocultural process through which one determines to live out their lives in response to the world in which they live, in a body that does not precipitate specific actions or roles for that individual. And to be clear, gender is not sex.[66] Nevertheless, Black gender identity results from vitality's indeterminate operation within Black biotechnology. Vitality does not predetermine gender. At best vitality initiates the process of attraction that eventually leads to competition among sperm cells which carry sex determining markers. Gender selection, or self-identification, arises as the product of being with one another. The tension one experiences in this selection process bears the mark of conformity which is simply a necropolitical means of determining who ought to be protected.[67] And as I mentioned earlier, Black folks are not human. America has shown us that. By the same token, humanness is a technology that implicates white folks, or anyone for that matter, as nonhuman. Still, the human declension continues to protect those it was initially intended to. But, the transition into a transhuman reality where Black folks divorce negative nomenclature and move into spaces of fluid enhancements/biotech upgrades requires us to normalize the fluid and complex spectrum of existence without demonizing that which does not fit into a necropolitic that is not meant for our benefit. And if one is to embark upon Beal's prescription for removing one's self from a totally corrupting society it requires an acceptance of bodies as biotechnology; constantly undergoing an upgrading process. In theory, this Black transhuman perspective might precipitate decisions that shift traditional routines and notions around Black bodies, their role in the vitalistic cosmos, and the relationship Black biotechnology has with other modes of technology. It aligns with Kara Keeling's addition to Deleuze's I = I concept, where I = Another.[68] In this way it is the work of inclusivity to see every iteration or combination of embodied biology and culture as normal, because variance is normal. This may lead to questions of deviance, for some, but this also assumes we ought to know the difference between variance in presentation and deviance in behavior where vulnerable parties—such as children—are concerned. All of this is to suggest that vitality, as God (life itself) or that which is beyond the self in the body, justifies embodiment. Justification also extends to sexuality.

James G. Pfaus and Sherri L. Jones acknowledge that "sexual desire is a difficult concept to grasp." It's difficult conceptualization normally resides within the configuration of its components, which "entails objective physiological, subjective psychological, and behavioral variables that reflect conscious recognition of its own state."[69] In line with appraisal theory of emotion, sexual excitement occurs at the intersection of biological flow, cognition, and interpretation of stimuli—perception. Individual perception helps in determining what is conditionally attractive or unattractive via physical characteristics and contexts that are deemed suitable for sexual activity.[70] Now, as a technology, that is an extension of emergent factors such as cognition, emotion, perception, etc., each are separate yet entangled with other emergent extensions such as race and gender. The emergent extensions of race and gender may influence performative notions of sexually appropriate appraisals and behavior. However, sexuality is separate from race and gender. For example, someone who is born Black and female, yet identifies as gender nonconforming, can still have heterosexual attractions. Similarly, someone who is born Black and phenotypically male, identifies as female, and is transitioning into a woman can still have bisexual attraction. Likewise, someone who is a male and identifies as genderqueer can also be pansexual. The variations of sexual attraction and excitation function as a lens and director of experience for vitality, which presents a multidimensional approach to who one can be once overlays of existence are presented atop the base layers of biological maintenance. Vitality's nondeterministic nature does not squelch the potentiality of these biological iterations. Vitality welcomes it. Individual neurochemistry, as a mechanistic means in relationship with its complex environment, helps to facilitate this vast spectrum of difference.

Overall, these features actively evolve, or update, along with their environment. Updating occurs within a dynamic context, such as an environment, which infers that these features are amenable to the spaces they inhabit as protocols for survival. Survival protocols take place even if the body's version of survival places the biological system at risk. This suggests survival is more than living another day. It is the ability to live from the force of the vitalistic entity as a singular, yet fluid, biological system, true to itself—the amalgamative entanglement of individualized embodiment. Biotech features allow the body to interact with the world in a way that gives vitality unique insight into what it means to be, in a particular manner. I explore the body's systems as technological apparatuses converging upon life to open the discussion for enhancement of the Black body.

Because an understanding of the body's systems as part of a larger technological instrument might preclude a wider acceptance and an eventual move toward enhancement of the Black body's physical capabilities.[71]

To conclude this chapter I would like to continue with Turman's womanist ethic of incarnation, by focusing on the third component of responsibility. Black transhuman liberation theology's vitalist and biotechnological approach places the responsibility of liberation solely onto the bodies of Black folk. If Black biotech is vitality incarnate, then an appeal to God, or that which is beyond the self, for an intervention against systemic oppression becomes problematic. Black bodies have material agential potentiality in the physical world in a way that vitality outside the body does not. Being located in the midst of temporal biocultural entanglements provides particular insight into the dynamics of the temporalities Black bodies inhabit. These particular insights become necessarily useful, because the responsibility of Black biotechnological incarnation is to draw from the wisdom arising out of individual and collective biocultural perspectives for the active deconstruction and reimagining of the worlds we live in. The constructive move is the opportunity to create a new world calibrated by the radical centering of Blackness. Deconstructing worlds is a decolonial commitment to ontological, epistemological, and material exercises. It requires individuals and communities to face their entanglement with coloniality via their commitments to suspended disbelief. This is essentially a call to deconstruct individual and communal realities. It is a call for the violence associated with the critical turn.[72] Everything within the present reality ought to be challenged and treated as myth, even the sacred.

In "Jumpstarting the Decolonial Engine" George Ciccariello-Maher summarizes Fanon's theory of symbolic ontological violence as "making oneself known."[73] This requires dealing with the ontological nature of one's own existence. Lewis Gordon refers to the social space where Black folks exist as a "hellish zone" which oscillates between appearance and disappearance, and "to change things is to appear, but to appear is to be violent. . . . Violence, in this sense, need not be a physical imposition."[74] So, together with Beal's prescription for shifting behavior, the decolonial act of unraveling dominant worldviews that entangle Black folks is essentially a violent act, because it "constitutes a challenge to the prevailing structures of symbolic ontological violence."[75] It situates challenges as violent, due to the consequential nature of a challenge. Challenges connote wins and losses. Historically, theological discourse has likened this challenge to wrestling, and in the act of ontological violence, wrestling with concepts of being alter initial notions regardless of the outcome. Much like any biological event, interactions between ontologies preempt shifts in symbolic meaning. Even more so, symbolic ontological violence leads Black bodies to appear as un-mummified, yet re-entangled bodies, entangled in shifted ontologies grounded in the realit(ies) of our own bodies, centered in our beings. Because, symbolic ontological violence is the shedding of one technological apparatus for another. It becomes the technology capable of slicing through previous ontologies, revealing the vitalistic nature of Black individual and communal biotechnological existence.

The epistemological responsibility is an internal challenge. As vitality incarnate within Black biotechnology, individuals and communities are tasked to wrestle with the epistemological gaps in their own understandings. It is both an exercise which seeks out and rejects knowledge uncritically accumulated as a means to test the mettle which constitutes pillars of personal and communal knowledge systems. Being a component of symbolic violence, the epistemological exercise requires bravery from individual and communal expressions of Black biotechnology due to their relationship with vitality. The nondeterministic nature of vitality implies it already functions within a space of bravery. If bravery can be perceived as a willingness to relinquish control then indeterminacy bolsters an argument for the innate capacity of vitality to be brave since it allows for an infinite amount of biotechnological iterations. So, the epistemological exercise places individual and communal iterations of Black vitality in a space where each must face prehensive notions of themselves in relation to how they perceive the world. Viewed this way, the epistemological exercise is a regenerative act, forcing the self to face previous narratives with enough bravery to deconstruct them and rebuild anew. The epistemological exercise is also an act of bravery because it asks Black biotechnology to trust itself to rebuild the edifice of reality. This act implicates biotechnology, because it is the technology which creates other technologies—perpetuating acts of transhumanism. It simultaneously has the ability to reformulate the technology it creates. Lastly, the epistemological act of bravery requires self-compassion. Challenging the narratives of prehensive selves, and the realities that house these narratives, poses a potential danger to individual and communal understandings.[76] Self-compassion has shown promise in reconstructing personal and communal narratives, and might prove to be a useful tool in helping cope with the changes in narrative that may arise.[77]

The material exercise is the ongoing process of trial and error associated with living from the vitalistic entity and the critical space. The material exercise of vitalistic incarnation implicates biotechnological embodiment as responsible for the vitality it has been granted. We, Black biotechnology, are responsible for our own lives. We are responsible for God, or that which is beyond the self. We are responsible because the sacred travels in us and in those we encounter. Through the recreation of the present self, and through compassionate critical reflection of our prehensive selves, we become closer to the indeterminate complexity that situates our embodiment. Ultimately, the foundation of Black transhuman liberation theology places divine capacity within the complex manifestation of individual and communal biotechnology. In the move toward materializing liberation it emphasizes Black vitalistic worth, which decentralizes stratification, in efforts toward accumulating power. However, it remains that our current social structure functions to maintain, and thrive from, racialized stratification. As a result, the incarnation process must consider what it means to compete within this social framework so that Black folks may not only affirm our own vitalistic worth but navigate shifting power dynamics to eventually arrive at a place of intentionally derived measures of freedom. This responsibility is not the task of God, or that which is beyond the self, but ours, because we embody the sacred.

3

The Neurophysiology of Spiritual Experience

The hyper-subjectivity of spiritual experiences can be attributed to the deep relationship between personal physiology and the external environment. The definition of spirituality provided in the introduction references the felt and unfelt connection to God or "something" that is beyond the self.[1] This implication is coherent with Ann Taves's suggestion that "spirituality" is a much farther reaching term than historically thought.[2] Moreover, it recognizes that spiritual encounters do not start and stop with prayer, meditation, or worship services tied to one particular tradition. The projection of spiritual experience presented in this theological proposal is understood as felt and unfelt because it is an ongoing, never-ending process. It shares in Elaine Pagels's conception of being "beyond belief" and Jeffrey Kripal's "beyond reason." It is beyond belief in that it cannot be housed within any one tradition, which is why it must be broad. Still, as a theological proposal it accepts that is does not fit squarely within one religious tradition.[3] It is beyond reason, because "former rationalisms are simply incapable of dealing adequately with th[e] immense swath of non-rational, altered states of consciousness and energy that constitute so much of the history of religions," but I depart from Kripal in his analysis of postmodern thought which he says "[too] easily devolve[s] into an effective denial of reason in which truth has collapsed into identity."[4] Given the problematic history of the concept of truth, its history, and its progenitors, there should be no move to adhere to something holding the whole perceptive universe together given the manner in which subjectivity permeates all notions of reason. It is not a denial of reason but a denial of reason grounded in stratified notions of epistemological normativity that posit one form of existence over another (i.e., racist white supremacist epistemologies). Identity should not be dismissed, because all conjectures (whether grounded in faith or not) stem from a particular vantage point, and the limitations therein. Thought that openly announces its derivation from a particular identity participates in the act of scholastic honesty, which names the locations of emergent thinking so that scholarship cannot be mistaken for universality, timelessness, or objectivity—historical characteristics of God. The intellectual humility that is required to participate in the grandiose practice of scholarship/reason should not begin with the courage to know, but the recognition that one's ability to know anything is limited by the epistemology one employs and the blind spots which arise from one's own subjectivity. And so, scholars like Kripal fall short in their analysis of postmodern, specifically postcolonial, thinking through their insistence upon grounding conceptual foundations on the inherently racist, exclusivist, and colonial notions of enlightenment based thinking. What appears to be the issue here is the dilemma that scholars who maintain a Eurocentric framework are faced with. Since the foundation of their vantage point is exposed as inherently limited by the tumultuous colonial past it perpetuates, then what is the utility of its application? One may contend that since the methodology of enlightenment based thinking has very little to say regarding the intersections of race, ethnicity, gender, sexuality, and class that they are only codifying its colonial past. This codification takes them further down the rabbit hole and indicts them along with their predecessors. But, in abandoning Eurocentricity these scholars would theoretically be left to rebuild the infrastructure of their mythos for reality. This extends to questions regarding spiritual experience given that individual experiences are mediated through a considerable amount of factors that are in constant flux. The compounding nature of these factors in the social environment further highlight how Courtney Bender sees spirituality as "entangled in social life, in history, and in our academic and nonacademic imaginations . . . as processes of secularization . . . [which are] complex and unfinalized traditions."[5] Charles H. Long, in referencing Black religion, puts in this way:

> The religion of any people is more than a structure of thought; it is experience, expression, motivations, intentions, behaviors, styles, and rhythms. Its first and fundamental expression is not on the level of thought. It gives rise to thought, but a form of thought that embodies the precision and nuances of its source. This is especially true of Afro-American religion.[6]

As a theistic transhumanism, Black transhuman liberation theology acknowledges that spiritual experience covers more than Christian spirituality. It draws from the mystical tradition which states that life is a spiritual experience.[7] It is grounded in what we have come to recognize as human physiology.

It places importance on the biological components of spiritual experience. And in building upon the supposition that Black folks are not human, or at least not bound by the limitations of humanity, the physiology highlighted within this project more readily refers to the physiology of the biotechnology of people. One might suggest that there is no difference between humans and people, that this is a semantically grounded supposition. Some may even question whether I am suggesting that people are physiologically different from humans. I'll restate my logic. No one is human. Human terminology is part of the colonial cybernetic linguistic epistemology. So, this nominal declaration over physiology is part of the practice of changing day-to-day patterns as an act of moving toward more liberating realities. Beyond that, Harriet Washington's historical exploration of modern medicine demonstrates that Black bodies are the archetype of human biology. Here, designating Black folks as people functions as a reclamation of Black biotechnology, whose material organization operates as the very foundation of biological wisdom. With that in mind it is also important to note that as I delineate spiritual experience, specifically focusing on spiritual practices, these practices will be placed into two categories: stationary practices and somatically dominant/movement-based practices. This delineation allows for the inclusion of every type of spiritual practice, because practices will primarily fall somewhere between each end of the spectrum, as a combination of being still or moving.

This chapter will outline the neurophysiological components of spiritual experience and will be the most scientifically technical piece of this project. Essentially, it will begin with a biological breakdown of spiritual embodiment in the four realms of experience: physiological, psychological, neurological, and somatic (felt) experience. It will compare stationary spiritual practices to somatically dominated spiritual practices. Then, it will explore Black spiritual practices within the North American context. Finally, it will explore the proposed neurophysiological progressions of these practices. I do so in an attempt to decipher what these practices might mean for the practitioner, based upon the physiology that correlates with the components of each practice. The effects of neurochemistry and blood oxygen level dependent (BOLD) signals in response to activated neural regions related to these practices are an important aspect of determining the most effective spiritual practice for a practitioner. It is important to note that I am not attempting to construct directionality of causation. This is not a discussion on the causation of spiritual experience. My emphasis is on intentionality.

Four realms of spiritual embodiment

Embodying spiritual practices occurs at four distinct levels: psychologically, physiologically, neurologically, and somatosensory. Scholars such as Chris Boyatzis have argued that the connection that these levels share with empiricism are problematic. The methodology of these disciplines routinely investigates abnormal or peak examples to create knowledge concerning mundane versions of experience. So, problems arise when the abnormal or peak experience become the fodder for spiritual materiality.[8] In this case it furthers the idea that spirituality is reserved for the select few. Moreover, scholars such as Bender might emphasize that what we gain from physical information regarding these experiences is only explicated through the narratives that follow.[9] Here, the elements of exploration function as objects for interpreting the experience associated with spiritual practices.[10] So, in alignment with my earlier conjectures, the narrative that I will outline about each level of the spiritual practices will be done in conversation with previous studies that have explored the effects of spiritual practices. To expound upon the nature of these four levels of embodiment, I will begin with an outline of the body's physiological response. I will accompany that with some basic brain anatomy.

The physiological response grounds all emotional responses. The first part of the physiological response is a stimulus from some combination of the external or internal environment. This hints at the interdependence bodies and the environment share. Next, an electrical impulse is sent down an axon. Research teams, such as Marshall et al., Zampin et al., or Yang, Jennings, and Friedman, have categorized the body's appraisal sites by their location. The origin of a stimulus influences the body's valuation of the stimulus.[11] For instance, stimuli originating from an exteroceptor (think of these as the five senses) will be treated differently, or at the very least exhibit greater influence over appraisal centers of information received interoceptively (i.e., a tummy ache or muscle soreness) or proprioceptively (stimuli in relation to where your body is situated in space). Now, there are times where interoceptors may override exteroceptors (think subconscious or unconscious appraisals).

Once the impulse arrives at the end of the axon (which is called a synapse), it fires another electrical signal. Depending upon the axon's level of activation and channel type (ion or other) an action potential may occur which, if it does, releases neurotransmitters. Those neurotransmitters release their subsequent neurohormones or peptides into the brain and bloodstream. The release of neurohormones or peptides creates a cascade of emotions.[12] This cascade is determined by the appraisal of said stimulus.[13]

Many appraisal theories exist regarding the underlying frameworks which guide appraisal networks. Ann Taves references Owen Flanagan who posited that emotional appraisal stems from people's natural disposition to make sense of the world. He then suggests that making sense of the world stems from the evolution of moral emotions.[14] I don't find resonance with Flanagan's logic for this claim. This implies that appraisal evolved out of deciding what was "right." I would argue that appraisal is fundamentally a decision of survival, which is hardly ever about what is right. And spiritually grounded appraisals work to remove individuals from survival mode. In a critical move, appraisal theorists have renamed emotions as emotional episodes.[15] This reiterates emotion's status as an emergent property feature of biotechnology that arises from the composite nature of emotionality. Many affirm the five dimensions of appraising stimulus: (1) personal significance of stimuli; (2) motivation—think, attack and avoid; (3) physiological changes in autonomic responses—such as sweating, increases in heart rate, or changes in blood pressure; (4) facial expression—for example, smiling, grimacing, or frowning; and (5) feeling.[16] The appraisal process leads to a determination of what is being experienced. Essentially, as descendants of Schachter and Singer, appraisal theories of emotion propose that bodily sensations lead to an awareness of representations that are interpreted as emotion.[17] So, emotions become the result of interpreting representations that result from biochemical reactions occurring in the body. Each biochemical is equipped with a half-life. Once released into the bloodstream the half-life associated with a particular biochemical allows it to be readily bioavailable for the instance when the biological system needs to reenter that biochemical state. Even outside of the need to reproduce a specific biochemical, a particular thought or another outside stimulus can re-trigger this physiological response. This would rerelease that chemical into the body once more. For instance, cortisol, a neurotransmitter associated often with anger, has a half-life of 12 hours. An overt expression of cortisol in the prefrontal cortex during a bout of anger often makes it hard for people to think clearly. Any recollection or a similarly triggering experience within the 12-hour time period, after cortisol's initial release, restarts the internal process associated with cortisol and anger. These emotionally repetitious encounters also make it difficult to experience other emotions, unless those other emotions are more strongly coded in the body. Coded, in this case, refers to the body's preference for a specific state based on the amount of time previously spent in that state. Bodily reactions that synchronize the totality of human biology are known as the congruity of moods.[18]

Brain anatomy is essential to understanding the neurological embodiment of spiritual practices. Imagine looking at the brain from the side view, with the front (rostral) being on the left and the back (caudal) being on the right. The leftmost part of the brain is the prefrontal cortex (PFC). It takes up about the first quarter of the brain. From there is the frontal lobe. It houses the somatosensory and motor regions of the brain. Behind the frontal lobe is the parietal region of the brain. It is roughly a quarter of the brain. The parietal region is responsible for proprioception, which is the sense of self in relation to other objects in space. The last quarter is the occipital lobe. The lower middle region of the brain from the side view is the temporal lobe, which is most associated with emotion. The regions mentioned above are part of the cortical regions of the brain (its surface). Lastly, from the outside you will see the cerebellum. The cerebellum is located under the occipital lobe. It is the most neuron dense portion of the brain. If you visualize the brain being sliced down the middle the subcortical regions appear. They are the brain regions closest to the stem under the corpus callosum. The corpus collosum is a white strip separating the cortical and subcortical brain regions. Important to our topic, I will only talk about the limbic system housed within the subcortical regions. This system is home to the oldest portions of the brain—evolutionarily speaking. It is also referred to as "the emotional brain."[19] The most important parts to remember in the limbic system are the hippocampus, hypothalamus, thalamus, and amygdala. Each has important connections to the neocortex (PFC), sympathetic (excitatory), and parasympathetic (relaxation) autonomic systems.

The physiological embodiment of any spiritual practice is grounded in the metabolic process of the body's cells. Lodish et al. reminds us that the body's cells have more than 10,000 receptor sites which respond to different hormones.[20] Genetic expression or inhibition occurs in response to interactions with hormones in the body. The proliferation of maladaptive emotions can create a toxic internal environment within the body, if experienced over extended amounts of time. Maladaptive emotions have the ability to inhibit certain generative genetic markers from activating.[21] Generative emotions are defined as positively regenerating, life-giving, or beneficial to one's health. And conversely, generative emotions have the ability to allow generative genes to activate while inhibiting genes that could prove harmful to the body. This is important as the physiological response happens whether an individual practitioner wants it to or not. Physiological responses are an ever-repeating cycle occurring within an individual. Throughout an individual's life, their body engages in an ongoing series of responses to both internal and external stimuli. The key part to remember is that through a spiritual practice, individuals are training themselves to experience emotions and spiritual states which impact them at the cellular level. The impact that biochemistry has on genetic expression becomes even clearer with a realization that the body has 37.2 trillion cells;[22] that means spiritual practices have the potential to express generative biochemistry 37.2 trillion cells with over 10,000 receptor sites! The intention of one's awareness is the stimulus I credit with sparking the spiritual practice of becoming aware of God, the self, or something beyond the self. So, as the spiritual practice is embodied, the physiology of the response to one's intention bathes the practitioner's cells in her own biochemicals which have the capacity for healing and overall health and well-being. I am not saying that outside factors which may distract from the cultivation of intentional awareness do not have the potential to impact the spiritual experience. However, I am saying that the physiology of people is actively creating an internal space with the capacity to foster transformation and spiritual sustainability.

Andrew Newberg talks about the psychological embodiment of the spiritual practice. He juxtaposes cognitive operators with notions of self-transcendence. Cognitive operators allow the human mind to comprehend its experience. The cognitive operators that Newberg identifies are as follows:

1. holistic
2. reductionist
3. causal
4. abstractive
5. binary
6. quantitative, and
7. emotional valuation.[23]

He places these operators in conversation with what he claims are the six markers of self-transcendence, which are:

1. mystical union
2. cessation of thought
3. high experience of emotion or combination of emotions
4. felt paradox
5. strong sense of confidence, and
6. strong sense of ineffability.[24]

Each cognitive operator has a distinct role in the psychological embodiment of the individual; however, for the purposes of this exercise, I will focus on the abstractive, binary, and causal operators in conjunction with the six markers of self-transcendence. The abstractive operator is tied to the verbal-conceptual associations of the brain. It forms concepts into categories of relationality. In the state of self-transcendence the abstractive operator works to allow for the fluid reconstructive concept of self.[25] It also deals with the subsequent felt sense of paradox that occurs from that fluidity. The binary operator works to create myth for the mind. It operates in black and white, hard and fast. Newberg points out that in conjunction with the causal operator, humans create myths and their conceptions of God, gods, or beings of causality (first movers). The creation of these beings of causality produces internal contracts that help facilitate the felt sense of confidence, emotion, union, and ineffability. A great example of an internal myth is the thought, "If I act in a way that pleases God, then I will be blessed." These internal myths are mentioned by Kristen Brown in her book *Nietzche and Embodiment*.[26] She argues that the language of myth is the strongest way to structure identity. It helps to form theories of the past which can negatively, positively, or neutrally impact the way in which the human practitioner makes sense of their spiritual practice experience. These operators also have the same effect on personal narratives regarding internality that form who individuals become. Newberg also mentions that the experience of self-transcendence fundamentally changes the individual on a structural level in what he refers to as an emotionally corrective experience.[27]

The neurological embodiment of the spiritual practice is a direct reflection of the spiritual practice's physical effects on the brain. Hollingsworth, in her article entitled "Implications of Interpersonal Neurobiology for a Spirituality of Compassion," states that through neural integration—a process that the brain undergoes which rearranges energy divestments and synaptic connectivity—the brain changes for the better.[28] Neural integration incorporates synaptogenesis and neurogenesis, both components of the brain's neuroplastic capabilities. Synaptogenesis is the rewiring of the brain synapses. Neurogenesis is the process that creates new brain cells, which occurs in the olfactory and hippocampus.[29] Hollingsworth's suggestion is that an interpersonal neurobiology—dependent upon the brain's mirror neurons, located in the visual, emotional, and motor portions of the brain—can positively transform human biotechnology. This would suggest that spiritual practices have both an internal solitary component and a communal interpersonal component.

The somatosensory elements of spiritual practices are the key to individual embodiment beyond traditional spaces of spiritual application. The felt component of the spiritual practice is where the practitioner may step back and say, "This practice made me feel this way." It is also the most concrete version of the practice's experience. Making experience concrete shifts the locus of spiritual experience from fixed sites (mosques, temples, churches, etc.) to the body. Realistically, a spiritual experience can happen anywhere. So, the body becomes the conduit and common denominator. This speaks to the felt/somatic component's ability to aid the practitioner's spiritual experience in any geographic location. Whenever the individual feels an impending maladaptive emotional state rising, which can take them from the bodily/spiritual state they would rather be in, the opportunity arises for spiritual practice. Daugherty prescribes heartfulness.

Shailesh M. Varu defines heartfulness as a contemplative practice that emphasizes the inner wisdom that arises from the heart, and recognizes it as a place of connection with sacred reality.[30] The practice begins by noticing the internal emotionality of the body. Heartfulness then moves to invite the practitioner to create a nonjudgmental stance toward those feelings, creating a safe enough distance where the individual is not overtaken by impending maladaptive emotion. This suggests a "re-appraisal during the anticipation phase" of emotional reactivity which signals an interruption of the physiological process. This is intended to help individuals better cope with stressful situations before they are overcome with a maladaptive emotional episode.[31] It is important to note that reappraisal strategies have shown most beneficial for individuals who already have low levels of negative internal dialogue. This is not to say that reappraisal practices are only for certain people. Compassion-based spiritual practices have been shown to help lessen negative internal dialogue.[32] So, reappraisal strategies such as the heartfulness practice might be best coupled with one's fundamental spiritual practice to increases its efficacy. A fundamental practice is one that grounds an individual and is most likely connected to a particular space or tradition. This is not to go back on the idea that biotechnology is the site of spiritual experience. It is to suggest that are moments in time when it is important to reconnect with sites larger than one's self to ground one's self—like a battery. And much like a battery charging, fundamental practices can be done in solitude or in a communal setting. Examples of fundamental practices might include prayer, singing, chanting, or meditation. These fundamental practices are often used to set the physiology of the practitioner in a generative trajectory. It might be safe to suggest that individual practitioners feel better having participated in their fundamental practices. "Theirs" is key. Nevertheless, reappraisal is a call for refocusing. Refocusing asks the practitioner to place her awareness on a moment or thought of something that promotes an internality of either gratefulness or an acceptance that one embodies sacred reality. Lastly, the practice invites the individual to intentionally nurture that feeling of gratitude or sacred reality.[33] The intentional nurturing of the desired somatic state nurtures the generative emotionality that gratitude provides. Daugherty asserts that somatosensory states of gratefulness create a type of clarity and compassion for self and others, while simultaneously extending the life of one's fundamental practice. I assert that an acceptance of one's internal sacred reality has similar capacities, because it requires an acceptance of one's self as worthy of holding sacred reality. Heartfulness helps to reset and realign the individual when outside the intended space of their fundamental practice. It simultaneously affirms the individual as the site of spiritual experience because vitality lives in them. Extending the life of the practice extends one's felt connection to life itself. This is important because it is based on the wisdom of physiological half-lives. Ultimately, intentionally setting one's attention provides greater opportunity for the continuation of spiritual practices, fundamental or not. And as long as there is a body, there is room for a spiritual practice. So, the key is nurturing biotechnology as the space of the practice through authenticity and intentionality.

Neural correlates of stationary contemplative practices

Stationary spiritual practices provide an opportunity for spiritual retreat. Retreat often leads to spiritual renewal. For the purposes of this project, renewal is the repositioning of human physiology toward a generative emotional physiology. The very nature of retreat is its ability to remove practitioners from the noise of everyday life. The intention of stationary practices is to relieve stress by reconnecting practitioners with the practitioner's spiritually grounding entity. Contemplative practices are the most rigorously studied stationary spiritual practices. Researchers have been able to use empirical methodologies to begin uncovering their neurological impact on practitioners. Contemplative practices come in the form of various guided meditations, breathing practices, mindfulness practices, or volitional practices. In order to understand the biological power of these practices I will spend the rest of this section delineating the neural correlates of stationary contemplative practices.

Contemplative spiritual experiences do not follow a linear biological process. To that end, there are multiple spiritual practices that may elicit slightly different neural correlates depending on the demands or requirements of the practice. In 2003, Andrew Newberg outlined three different types of meditation. In 2006, he went on to look at the neural correlates of glossolalia, the act of speaking in different tongues (a Christian tradition).[34] In that same year, Mario Beauregard conducted his famous study of the mystical union of Carmelite nuns. In 2008, Lutz et al. conducted a study on the compassion practice and outlined its neural components.[35] Carhart-Harris et al. even conducted a study on the possible therapeutic effects of psilocybin based on its ability to mimic mystical experiences.[36] The main thing to remember is that the PFC and parietal regions of the brain play a significant role in spiritual experience. This has been a primary finding in almost every spiritual iteration studied so far. In my attempt to address the neural correlates of contemplative spiritual practices, I will outline the composite data gathered from various studies, while providing a neurochemical breakdown of volitional meditation as described by Newberg in 2003.

Beauregard's study on mystical union is important as it was one of the early neuroscientific studies of Christian spiritual experience. In the study, nuns were asked to remember and relive a time where they felt the most mystically unified with God. That study showed ten active regions via functional magnetic resonance imaging (fMRI). fMRI imaging is the current gold standard of brain imaging based on its ability to determine approximate regional activation based on BOLD signals in the brain. BOLD signals demonstrate brain activity in a time series as regions of the brain are innervated as a result of either external (environmental) or internal (thoughts and emotions) stimuli. Beauregard identified four right active regions in the brain and six active regions in the left. Those regions in the right of the brain were the medial orbitofrontal cortex (directly behind the eyes), medial temporal cortex, right inferior, and superior parietal lobules. On the left of the brain were the medial prefrontal cortex (MPFC), anterior cingulate cortex, inferior parietal lobule, insula, caudate, and brainstem.[37] This bilateral activity in multiple regions, in conjunction with reported mystical union, might play an important role in the cognitive science of connectionism. Connectionism is a theory that suggests multiple brain regions are at work for any given physical phenomena.[38] This is in contrast to the computational approach which views the brain as a properly segmented machine with components that have specified functions. Each has distinct implications for spiritual experience. In the case of emotion, it would suggest that there is not just one region responsible for a neurochemical reaction. This theory speaks to the idea that the brain, and subsequently the body, is connected in the way that bodies experience and interact with the environment. It also suggests that multiple brain regions are integral to facilitating spiritual experience. However, the fact remains that these nuns were asked to remember and relive their experience. As a result, the researcher's inability to construct a firsthand experience of the nun's experience of God's presence becomes the major weakness of this study. Large amounts of skepticism begin to arise regarding the neurological images captured from these nuns since it can be argued that remembering an experience with God and actively experiencing God are not the same thing.

Newberg's study of glossolalia is one that actually contradicts most literature on contemplative meditation. Participants in his glossolalia study demonstrated via fMRI that there was a decrease in activation of the dorsal lateral prefrontal cortex (DLPFC), but a maintenance of parietal region activations.[39] This was contradictory as most studies on meditation, while notably a different spiritual practice all together, usually shows the opposite effect. In most forms of meditation activations occur in the PFC and decreased in the parietal regions. In fact, the parietal region is normally expected to play a large role in spiritual experience because it is postulated that decreased activation of the parietal lobes is responsible for a decreased sense of self and an increase in union with nature. Johnstone et al., in 2012, conducted a study to determine the role and potential causality of self-transcendence from the parietal region.[40] They utilized neuropsychological task-based testing in participants with traumatic brain injuries (TBI) to their parietal lobe in conjunction with their ability to experience transcendence. Participants with TBIs in the parietal region provided evidence via self-report which supported researcher's hypothesis. Their injuries to the parietal regions of the brain were determined to be a key component of their propensity for transcendent experience.

In 2008, Lutz's study on compassion meditation demonstrated another example of spiritual experience in the brain. Compassion practice meditators showed greater activation in the right temporoparietal junction (TPJ), amygdala, and posterior superior temporal sulcus (PsTs) when compared to the control group. Lutz's 2014 study, along with Short's 2015 and Harris's 2008 study, also showed that meditators required less regulatory brain regions to attenuate negative emotion. This means that persistent meditators actually experience greater ease trying to calm down than those who do not meditate regularly.[41]

In 2003, Newberg did something very important for the study of spiritual experience. He provided an outline (albeit nonlinear) of the neurochemical underpinnings of volitional meditation. He differentiated volitional mediation from apophatic meditation (clearing the mind of all thought and imagery) and guided meditation (being guided by the words and promptings of another person). Volitional meditation is a self-led practice. It is important to note that this neurochemical outline comes from animal models. It would be pretty tough with current regulations for human models to achieve this kind of neural accuracy.

Volitional meditation begins in the brain with an activation in the MPFC (bilaterally, but mostly in the right) and right anterior cingulate. The MPFC then activates both the reticular nucleus of the thalamus via glutamate (an excitatory neurotransmitter).[42] Normally, the thalamus would activate the lateral posterior and geniculate nucleus via glutamate, which sends visual and somaesthetic information to the posterior superior parietal lobe (PSPL). This normal neuronal pathway aids the PSPL in determining personal proprioception. However, during meditation the activation of the geniculate nucleus releases GABA (an inhibitory neurotransmitter), which stops the lateral posterior and geniculate nucleus from relaying information to the PSPL. Newberg explains that this could be a significant factor in the loss of self that many meditation practitioners experience. As the hippocampus is activated during meditation, it begins a two lane process based on its rich and extensive connections with the PFC, other neocortex regions, amygdala, and hypothalamus. The hippocampus simultaneously activates the amygdala, and this is the second lane that I will explicate shortly. However, the activation of the hippocampus has an inverse correlation with decreased cortical activity. Meaning, the hippocampus can potentially augment cortical activity, but cortical activity would have to be already low. Cortical activity is lowered by the hippocampus due to its increased stimulation of the PFC via the nucleus accumbens' release of dopamine (DA) performing as a neuroregulator.[43] The second lane produced by the amygdala activates the parasympathetic response, lowering heart and respiration rates, which is a characteristic of the quiescent nature of mediation.[44] From there the paragigantocellular of the medulla ceases to innervate the locus coeruleus (LC) of the pons. The LC produces and distributes norepinephrine (NE).[45] NE would normally activate the ventricular nucleus to secrete corticotrophin-releasing hormone (CRH), which then leads to pituitary gland stimulation and production of adrenocorticotropic hormone (ACTH). This process leads to the production of cortisol.[46] However, this process is counteracted with the decreased NE from the LC. Essentially, the de-innervation of the LC stops the production of cortisol in the brain, which is important for stress-relieving purposes. AVP is also released in the brain to maintain a positive mood.[47] In this process it tightens arteries in order to bring blood pressure to normal ranges. 5-HT (serotonin) is also released which works well in combination with DA for pleasantness of mood. As a practice goes on there is an increase in PFC activation. This increase is thought to lead to the stimulation of the hypothalamic arcuate nucleus (HAC). The HAC releases b-endorphin.[48] This b-endorphin is an opioid produced in the brain that is known to slow respiration, reduce fear, and reduce pain while producing sensations of joy and euphoria.[49] Although b-endorphin is believed to be a factor in the meditation process, more research needs to be done to determine its specific role in the effect of meditation. During extended sessions of meditation the brain may begin to produce too much of the excitatory transmitter glutamate. Glutamate in high doses can actually be a neurotoxin.[50] So, NDMAr (a long neuroscience term for a transmitter), which turns NAAG into glutamate, is no longer produced once glutamate reaches certain levels. NAAG has qualities much like a psychedelic drug, which could lead to either a schizophrenic or mystical state.[51]

Neural correlates of somatically dominant spirituality

Somatically dominated spiritualities are those that incorporate the body into the practice through movement. The majority of neuroscientific studies, especially imaging studies, have been conducted on somatic practices like yoga or Tai Chi. There are also studies of the neural correlates or neural impact of sport, that is fencing, weightlifting, and ballet on the brain. These studies could serve as gateways and provide implications for other somatically dominated spiritualities, especially of the Christian tradition, which have yet to be studied. It is important to note that imaging studies related to these practices were normally done before and after these practices. In the case of fMRI's, PET's, and similar neuroimaging techniques, participants are required to be still. So, the information gathered about these somatic practices also entails some lag time between the experience of the practice and the neural response—a weakness of imaging somatically dominated spiritualities.

Gao-Xia et al. conducted two studies of import to this discussion. In 2013, her team determined that practitioners of Tai Chi Chuan (TCC) had thicker cortex in the medial temporal sulcus and lingual sulcus.[52] They determined that this structural change was associated with TCC. In 2014, her team noticed that practitioners of TCC had greater functional homogeneity in the left medial occipital lobe and anterior cingulate and postcentral gyrus.[53] It was determined that postcentral gyrus (part of the parietal or self-orienting region) activation was most associated with TCC. In 2016, Tao et al. looked at the impact of yoga on the hippocampus (HPC) and memory based on resting state functional connectivity (rs-FC) in elderly practitioners.[54] They found that yoga practitioners had greater rs-FC in the HPC as well as the MPFC. This increase in rs-FC was also correlated to increases in memory retention. In another study, middle-aged fencers exhibited greater attention and single-leg balance than participants of similar age, suggesting greater activation in the PFC, parietal lobes, and cerebellum.[55] A study by Taren, Creswell, and Gianaros also showed that dispositional mindfulness practitioners had smaller right amygdalas and left caudate.[56] I am including dispositional mindfulness as a somatically dominated practice as it involves the ongoing engagement of the practitioner. Maintaining a mindful disposition requires the inclusion of mindful awareness in the various aspects of life, which include eating, walking, talking, playing, the list goes on.

Somatically dominated spiritualities seem to affect the brain differently than other types of spiritualities. TCC practitioners showed the greatest activations in the temporal lobe, parietal, cingulated cortex, and PFC. The majority of stationary spiritual practices engage the PFC, temporal lobes, and limbic systems (hippocampus, hypothalamus, amygdala, and thalamus). Although the somatic spiritualities do engage the PFC and temporal lobes it explicitly engages the parietal lobes in ways that the compassion, volitional, guided, and mystical spiritualities do not. I do think there is something to be said about the practice of glossolalia and its neural reversal of increased parietal lobe function and decreased PFC function. Carhart-Harris's 2012 study on the effects of psilocybin on consciousness gives insight into the effect of psychedelic drugs for inducing mystical or transcendent mental states. The use of psilocybin showed a decrease in positive coupling between the PFC and posterior cingulate cortex (PCC) for unconstrained thought.[57] This might be one of the main differences in looking at how "other" forms of spiritual practice differ from somatically driven spiritual practices. Aside from glossolalia, the underlying intention is a particular kind of thought that is free-flowing, yet demonstrative of the particular needs of the practitioner. Individuals engaging in somatically dominated spiritual practices may not necessarily look for a particular free-flowing state of thought but look for a free-flowing state of being, which ultimately expands the practice to an engaging awareness of the entire self. This brings me back to Newberg's study on glossolalia. Practitioners of glossolalia do self-report to have transcendent experiences. If the parietal lobe plays a large role in the transcendent experience, then this makes one ask what else may be happening neurologically if the individual can experience transcendence and the self at the same time? There might be a link to concepts of self-transcendence and unitary transcendence; however, I would suggest that more research be completed on the cognitive and psychological aspects of these two meditative states. Moving forward, I think it would be important for researchers to investigate possible active transmitters during glossolalia if brain region via BOLD signal does not prove more helpful. At the very basis of the difference between somatically dominated spiritualities and other spiritualities is the use of the parietal lobe, which helps the practitioner to maintain their sense of self throughout the practice.

Somatically dominated spiritualities and other, primarily stationary, spiritualities rely heavily on the PFC. Concentration is paramount in both types of practices. A practitioner of volitional meditation that engages the PFC and the ACC is likely focusing on the prompts of the practice while engaging in mental non-reactivity, that is, gently asking recurring thoughts to move to the side or through nonjudgmental acknowledgment of thoughts as they enter the mental window of awareness. Similarly, the TCC practitioner who is capable of maintaining their focus on the TCC practice amid both internal and external noise is probably engaging their PFC along with portions of the temporal lobe and postcentral gyrus. These spiritual exercises call upon the concentration faculties of the PFC which help practitioners successfully complete the given spiritual task. This phenomenon coincides with what E. Baron Short et al. demonstrated in their investigation concerning the ability of experienced meditators to maintain their focus and successfully emotionally attenuate in response to negative stimuli.[58]

Black spiritual practices

The complete summary of Black spiritual practices is more expansive than I would be able to legitimately catalog in the second half of one chapter. Black folks have been the initiators and adopters of numerous traditions, spiritual paths, and walks of life for quite some time. The diversity of Black spiritual practices may stem from a perspective that sees "everything [a]s natural," or a recognition of that which is spiritual in all aspects of life.[59] Barbara Holmes references how one enters this experience as one enters a "portal," between the natural and the supernatural.[60] The ideology that views everything as natural not only helps to explain the plethora of Black spiritualities and contemplative practices but also helps to explain the reason why so many of these spiritualities and practices go undocumented and academically delineated. For example, most Black contemplative practices are traditionally taught orally and through repetitious practice. Point being, through oral tradition and various forms of "on the job training," these traditions are passed down to make sure they are being done "right."[61] I am confident that as more Black scholars continue to emerge, they will further expound upon the depth and "how to" of these particular practices. An increase in the scholarship of Black spiritualities might be especially pressing as many individuals continue to turn away from the traditions of Christianity. The remainder of this section will focus on cataloguing and summarizing spiritual practices that Black folks participate in. It will also imagine the potential neural correlates of these spiritual practices as well. I will draw from the scholarship of Barbara Holmes, Stephanie Rose Bird, Darnise C. Martin, Angel Kyodo Williams, and Akasha Hull to help me catalog these practices.

In order to outline the potential neural correlates of each practice I will draw from previous research on similar activities. It is important to remember the neural correlates that I reference are positively inferred, meaning this is my hypothesis based on the neuroscientific information available. I will mention hemispheric hypotheses for some. So, it is important to remember that the right side of the brain is more closely related to visualization and abstract thinking. The left side of the brain is more analytical.

Ancestor veneration

Hull highlights many stories of Black women who participate in venerating and communicating with the ancestors.[62] This practice is meant to keep the communication open between the ancestors and practitioner. It is meant to remember the ancestors and acknowledge their presence in the world.

The neural correlates of ancestral veneration could be similar to verbally praying to God. Veneration includes remembrance and communication to a subject that is deemed real. So, it might include the anterior MPFC, which is active in the communication between the self and others. It could also include the connection of the precuneus and default network, drawing on memory of the ancestors, referencing the self in communicating with the ancestors, and social cognition with the expectation of hearing from the ancestors. There might also be brodmann's area activation when practitioners are speaking as well. Ancestral veneration feels much like prayer, because of its focus on, and awareness of, another entity. The more intense the exercise, the greater the level of awareness of the other entity or ancestor, which leads to increased levels of felt connection with that ancestral entity.

Cooking

Cooking contemplatively is done with love, focus, and a particular attention to the ingredients. It allows for focus on the activity of cooking and even creates room for the creativity of cooking. This immersive experience brings the whole person into the act of cooking. It allows for the individual or community of "chefs" to get lost in their food and turn the contemplative moment into one that is truly life giving.[63] Contemplative cooking also requires picking the right ingredients. Ingredients lead to taste, which is very important. However, health benefits are also very important. Ingredients should not be selected just for their potential contribution to the final taste, but they should be selected for their ability to contribute to the overall health of the practitioner.

The neural correlates of contemplative cooking would be more in line with the neural correlates of mindfulness. Cooking is a very decision-oriented act. Full immersion into the cooking experience should draw on the PFC. It would also draw on the parietal lobe and supplementary motor area as it requires constant movement between stations, stirring, cutting, and the selection of spices. Since practitioners need constant awareness of their surroundings, it might be a safe assertion that there should be activation in the parietal lobes. In a community of chefs there should be activation in brodmann's area 44 and 46 whenever one is speaking. There would also be activation in the Wernicke's area, because at any one time, each chef will be listening to determine what is being said in the kitchen. The brain's default network (MPFC, TPJ, temporopolar region) and the precuneus would also be active.[64] The default network would help with social cognition, while the precuneus would be active in the necessary self-referential activity of task completion of one person in relation to another. In the act of communal cooking and in personal cooking, a connectionist perspective would suggest that practitioners use a good amount of their brains. Essentially, contemplative cooking is a good exercise in utilizing the totality of a person. I think it is important to remember that complete immersion into the cooking act, just like anything else, should reduce mental chatter and increase focus. Although the MPFC is part of the default network, it is also closely aligned with mental chatter. I would hypothesize that the MPFC would be less activated in relation to the rest of the default network when immersed in the contemplative cooking exercise. Cooking allows for an interconnection between those in the kitchen, especially when done communally. It augments the sense of being with others through the method in which cooking is done. Certain actions and recipes must follow a particular level of performance, such as cutting and slicing. When you cut sweet potato slices for candied yams, they must be done in a certain way. There might not be an emphasis on exact measurement, but the key to cooking contemplatively is an intuitive movement that links the hearts of those cooking together with the foods they are preparing as they operate in the kitchen together. As such, oxytocin might be present among the practitioners of communal cooking, eliciting conceptions of in-group bonding since cooking is an act of caring for others (inclusive of those who are cooking together and those being cooked for).

Cleansing

Cleansing has many connotations in terms of contemplation: the act of bathing; cleansing via a particular fasting ritual; the cleansing of one's spirit; or even the cleansing of a space. Each entails detailed liturgical like elements based on the intention of the cleansing act. In many cases there are grounding symbolic elements in the form of oils, salts, herbs, spices; each with their own special meaning and healing capacities. There are also instances where the act of washing itself prepares the participant for another spiritual practice, which is the case of the Islamic wudū.[65]

The cleansing act, specifically bathing practices, follows a particular process. After the bath has been prepared, the practitioner enters the water infused with the symbolic elements. The initial heat of the bath can be intense depending on the temperature of the water. After entering the water, the practitioner begins the adjustment to the new environment, which goes from an intense experience to a calming one. As the body soaks, releasing impurities, there comes a point in the bathing ritual where the calm increases in relation to the release of bodily impurities. If there is a liturgy that accompanies the bath the practitioner feels a sense of self-affirmation that strengthens the connection of the bathing practice to the individual. After the practice the practitioner feels renewed, lighter, and ready to engage the world once more.

The practice of contemplative cleansing (physically and spiritually) would engage concepts of identity and personhood which are housed in the SMA, and default network. The act of cleansing would probably involve the temporal lobes, as feeling clean might invoke some form of emotionality related to the transition from being unclean or weighed down to being cleansed or released from the stress that precipitated the need for a cleansing ritual. Lastly, it may engage the limbic system. If a cleansing ritual provides a particularly potent emotional experience for the practitioner, then it has the potential to engrain the physiology of that act within the individual practitioner's intrinsic memory, as an emotionally formative practice.

Crisis contemplation

For Holmes, crisis contemplation originated on slave ships.[66] Africans who did not share the same dialect would band together through song, teaching one another. She extends the significance of this practice to today as Black folks who are suffering still come together to share song. Individually, crisis contemplations allow for individuals to withstand oppression and pain through song, humming, rocking and swaying, or repetition of scripture (much like *lectio divina*). Repetition is also mentioned here, and even though repetition is meant to reinforce ideas about the self or a specific situation, the repetition of crisis contemplation is carried out in response to a particular situation. Due to this feature of crisis contemplation it is often a reactionary contemplative practice. Contemporarily relevant forms of crisis contemplation are vigils, protests, and riots. Each is a shared reaction to an overt crisis. Many times vigils, protests, and riots are a communal response to death that results from the oppressive weight of structural violence. Furthermore, the reactionary nature of crisis contemplation calls into question the categorization of riots as a contemplative act. However, I am not sure that anyone can contest their cathartic qualities. Anyone who has released a considerable amount of "steam" usually has done so through physical activity. In this case, the cathartic exercise is done against physical property in an attempt to gain the attention of oppressive regimes. By saying this, I am not condoning riots nor agreeing with how they are normally carried out (rioters regularly end up destroying their own neighborhoods). This is an attempt to acknowledge rioting as a form of spirituality and validate its place in history and in the fight against overarching forms of everyday oppression.[67]

Attempting to outline the neural correlates of crisis contemplation is an important task. Singing activates right superior temporal gyrus (STG) more than the left.[68] Similar activation is reported for humming. This is important as singing is differentiated from humming with additional activation in the right STG, inferior central operculum, and inferior frontal gyrus.

Singing also activates the inferior central operculum and the inferior frontal gyrus more than humming does. I would like to point out that each act of crisis contemplation draws from something close to the practitioner. Since crisis contemplation is a coping mechanism limbic system activation might be a neurological component of each practice as well. There is also the possibility that the act of rocking and swaying initially starts with an internal volitional movement (SMA, PFC, parietal, and MPFC), and over time these movements become subconscious movement, mitigated by the need to soothe. If accompanied by humming or singing it would then additionally recruit the right STG, along with the inferior central operculum, and inferior frontal gyrus (singing). There are no similar activities to compare to protesting and rioting. Protests and riots are associated with anger. One is a peaceful embodiment of anger while the other is not. Cortisol and NE might be present due to their connection to anger.[69] Arginine vasopressin (AVP) may also be present during protests and riots. AVP has conditional ties to aggression, but more research is needed. These neurotransmitters are all correlative to anger. However, I think that they will be more readily available in the plasma during riots. Depending on the atmosphere of a protest, oxytocin might be present as well. Oxytocin is a transmitter recognized in bonding and trust building. It also shows up during in-group and out-group associations that increase the likelihood of aggression toward out-group individuals.[70] And regardless of the violent action accompanying rioting, the high-arousal states that carry cathartic weight may meet acquiescence through the intense expenditures of energy.

Crisis contemplation has a soothing affect. In the act of rocking and swaying, it provides an outlet to allow the shock or trauma of the situation to move away from the body through personal vibration. Humming can do the same thing and may provide added help when someone is already rocking. The same can be said regarding moving from humming alone to humming and rocking. In the case of protests and riots, crisis contemplation is a bit more cathartic in the sense of acting against the traumatizing agent. So, the protester or rioter might experience a moment of strength and even mental clarity as they act out against what they perceive as the oppressive structures that uphold marginalizing ways of life through purposeful organization or the physical destruction of property.

Dancing

The act of dancing is one that allows the practitioner to obtain a sense of freedom and spiritual connection through movement. An individual can dance alone, or a group can come together to dance. The ring shout is a traditional African form of dance brought over by enslaved Africans.[71] It was carried out in Hush or Brush Harbors as a communal act. Contemporary forms of dance, whether connected to the Black Church (i.e., liturgical dance), in connection with indigenous spiritual dance practices, or even through the variety of Black spiritual forms of dance, allow for expression of self, freedom of movement, and a contemplative space where the practice allows the dancer to be "taken" with the movement.[72] As a somatically based contemplative practice, dance takes the body to a space of mystical union through the path of high-arousal states.

Neurologically, dance has the potential to decrease activation in the PFC while increasing activation in the parietal regions. The high-arousal state, in conjunction with the increased activity in the parietal lobe, possibly takes the body into a quiescent state of calm and focus. This calm and focus still allows the dancer to know where their body is located in space, perhaps better than when not dancing. Since calm is an emotive response the temporal lobes are possibly active as well. At the height of the dancing experience one might experience what is called "unio mystica."[73] It is the complete alignment of high arousal and quiescence where the practitioner feels at one with God, the environment around them, or anything beyond the self that is deemed sacred (including the self). When practitioners engage in spiritual dancing, there is a felt unity between the self, the environment, history (inclusive of ancestry), and the divine source intended to be honored by the dance—if there is a divine force involved at all.

Eating

This practice goes hand in hand with cooking. Contemplative eating not only allows for the appreciation of the savory, sweet, or umami (most good traditional Black food is not bitter), but also allows for the group of persons to be truly present with one another. The food is the constant grounding element of the communal encounter. It does not replace other grounding entities, but in the contemplative eating moment, it becomes the conduit of the grounding entity for the family or community. It reminds everyone that they are present at the table, so that they can then be with one another in a more generative and authentic way.

Neurologically, I would surmise that contemplative eating is a combination of mindfulness and contemplative cooking. There is the possibility of reduced MPFC activation in correlation to the activity present in the default network. Individuals eating will be relating to one another with a sense of self, but immersion within the moment is an awareness of one's placement, relationality to others, and to/with the food. So, mental chatter might not be an active part.

Increased PFC activation would be an assertion as fully immersed individuals who are paying attention to the conversation and mindfully eating their meal. Each bit would be savored, while each word would be held in a generative and loving space. Everyone is held in esteem. There would be limbic activation as new memories are created, spatial reorientation is constantly occurring, and emotional bonds are created. Serotonin might be present in response to the meal and oxytocin might be present as well due to the in-group bonds being created. Eating feeds not only the body but also the soul. It brings a sense of joy that reaffirms the ability to be with others while in the same space, partaking of the same life-giving sustenance. Eating uplifts the spirit and feels like one is being recharged, where those at the table can become absorbed into the moment and escape the stressors of everyday life. Because through this practice those who are gathered at the table somehow become family—if they are not already.

Ecstatic singing

This is done either individually or communally. Ecstatic singing happens when the mind and body align. In the communal setting it occurs when everyone is on one accord and, as Holmes proclaims, a "joy unspeakable" is felt by everyone in the communally unitive moment. Like any other practice, the more practitioners partake in singing, the greater the chance the practitioner has to experience the ecstasy associated with it. Ecstatic singing is a low-arousal high-quiescence activity. It is important to note that singing by itself is not ecstatic singing, even though it does have spiritual import. Singing adds intonation to a mantra, phrase, or "word" that is relevant to the spirit of the practitioner. However, there is a specific moment when the singing act becomes ecstatic.

Singing mainly manifests as activity in the temporal lobe. Specifically, we know that singing produces activation in the right superior temporal gyrus (STG). We also know that similar activation is reported for humming, as well as intoned speaking, which is a derivative of singing with a contemplative ramification all its own. Singing is also similar to prayer because each incorporates language. So, I would suggest the ecstatic singing state has an increased parietal function and decreased PFC function, which is similar to the neurological effects of glossolalia in addition to increased right STG function.

Ecstatic singing places the practitioner in a sense of relationality with the object of song—in most cases the divine or a form of divinity. So, it would suggest that the maintenance of the self in relation to the object of song would produce a contemplative state correlative to the intent of the song itself. For instance, a song that lauds the object of song might foster an internal sense of gratitude toward the object. The lyrics of the song that often catalog stories tied to individuals or communities serve as reminders that help the practitioner embody the time of reference in the song, and thus produce a sense of connection that can be tied to joy, grace, love, gratefulness, etc. This helps to nurture the spiritual states within the practitioner and mentally tie those states to the object of song.

Listening to the sermon

Based on the repetitive and engaging nature of Black sermons, listening to it is contemplative in Black churches as the repetition is meant to accentuate a different emphasis on each point, leading to new levels of illumination for the listener. This is part of the reason people insist on relistening to a good sermon over the course of their lives, especially if they find it to be inspiring.

Contemplative listening requires many networks in the brain. Wernicke's area is essential for listening and understanding what is being said. The default network is important here. Mental chatter may very well happen while listening to a sermon, but a strong sermon (often subjectively determined) will help to attenuate mental chatter. The PFC should be active as the listener focuses on the words. Listening places the practitioner in the story. The sermon is meant to speak to the practitioner. So, one is constantly trying to find themselves in the sermon, whether it be the sermon's logic, its wisdom, narrative, or lesson. There should be some social cognition as the listener imagines themselves utilizing what is being said in their personal lives. As the preacher reiterates the point, inflecting on the different parts of a given sentence, the picture that is envisioned is amplified in the SMA, parietal regions, and visual cortex. Picturing the implications of the sermon and what it means for the listener is the point of the practice. Seeing it in the mind has the potential to spark transformation, because visualization opens up what is possible in the life of the listener. Listening to the sermon feels like an imaginative awakening of personal and communal possibility. This practice can birth hope, reflection, repentance, introspection, and more in the imagination of the listener who reconfigures life through an internal conceptualization of what it might be like to live in a world dictated by the wisdom of the sermon. Listening to the sermon feels like being immersed into the preached narrative where the listener experiences the benefits of living in that world.

Mindfulness

Angel Kyodo Williams highlights mindfulness practices that are based in Buddhism, which stress awareness of the present moment, grounding the practitioner through an acknowledgment of the body's position in the world.[74] Her work is geared toward helping those within the Black Buddhist context, as practitioners, who seek to remain aware of their body. Somatic awareness is a key component of being fully immersed in each moment, for the utilization of a nonjudgmental stance toward the inner movements of the mind.

Mindfulness is among the most studied contemplative practices because of its secular popularity. Its neural correlates are a general increase in PFC activation and a decrease in MPFC and parietal lobules.[75] The increased PFC is due to increased concentration. The decrease in MPFC, thalamus, amygdala, caudate, and parietal lobes is due to the decrease of mental chatter and the loss of the sense of self which leads to unitary mystical experiences.[76] Mindfulness also increases parasympathetic activity, aligning respiration and heart rate variability (HRV) rhythms.[77] In effect, respiration and HRV have an inverse relationship during mindfulness practice, meaning that HRV increases when practitioners lower their breath count (by breathing deeper and longer).[78] These effects also aid in cultivating the mental clarity, calm, and attention reported by practitioners. The mental clarity, calm, and attention that mindfulness is meant to create feels like every part of the body is connected and working together, beginning from the inside of the body, extending to the immediate environment in which the practitioner is engaged. It allows for an immersion within the present moment that heightens the senses while preparing the mind for sound and compassionate decision-making.

Mimicry

This is an important contemplative practice for children. Mimicry allows children to take ownership of the spiritual experience in a playful way. Through mimicking parents, spiritual leaders, and other people they watch, children recreate the spiritual moment. This also means that they are paying attention to what is around them. Using the example of the Black Church, Helen Baylor mentions through song what Holmes also reports in her book, *Joy Unspeakable*, that mothers often tell their children not to play Church or mimic Church for two reasons. First, mimicry can actually be done in a mean spirited way, which some believe vexes God's Spirit. Secondly, if the children happen to play "hard enough," there is a chance they might have an actual encounter with God.

An authentic encounter with God may be a legitimate conversion experience or emotionally corrective experience that has life-altering capabilities. However, in the moment, it might be more than any child has bargained for, which is the cost of this playful practice. So, although it is warned against, the parents actually hope for the moment that their children experience God for themselves through play.

Mimicry incorporates the simultaneous act of recalling something previously observed and then doing it. These mental and physical processes are what activate mirror neurons. Mirror neurons are located in several regions of the brain. These neurons work in a connectionist fashion employing the faculties of memory, spatial orientation, and motor function.[79] Mirror neurons are found in the premotor/supplemental motor area (SMA), hippocampus, parahippocampal gyrus, and entorhinal cortex (EC).[80] As the practitioner recalls actions from memory to impersonate an action, it draws from the memory function of the hippocampus and parahippocampal gyrus.[81] The EC works together with the hippocampal regions. It is important to episodic memory, spatial memory, and consolidation.[82] Episodic memory recalls and retrieves particular moments in life. Spatial memory helps to situate and re-situate the body's place in space. It is constantly updating itself with new bodily positions and locations. Consolidation is the process of taking memory from short-term to long-term storages in the brain. The SMA works to prime the body for movement (visualization) and then execution (movement). It is important to remember that the practice of mimicry is a priming practice. It prepares children for the actual experience of God. In essence, they mimic what they have seen until the experience of God that legitimizes the mimicked actions occurs in their own lives. So, in the instance of singing, the child might not feel anything until the spiritual encounter with God takes place. This suggests that mimicry does not produce an affect other than play, because once the spiritual experience happens the child moves from mimicry into the actual practice itself.

Prayer

Prayer is a major component of Black spiritual practices—mainly because of its contemplative nature. No matter to whom, or to what, prayers are directed, prayer is seen as an important way to communicate with the practitioner's grounding/sacred entity. Black folks subscribe to many varieties of prayer. Holmes highlights the historic role that the mourner's bench played in Black contemplative prayer. Prayers at the mourner's bench are meant to signify the outward renouncement of sin while being a conduit for the moment of conversion. People seeking conversion often kneel at "the mourner's bench" in order to demonstrate their contrite posture toward the life they planned to leave behind while awaiting an experience with God. Conversion, historically, was the reorientation of one's views toward life, as "it was hoped that while contemplating their fate in the next world [practitioners] might have a spiritual visitation or awakening, or at least a confession of sin, a disavowal of sinful behavior."[83] It was not always a quick experience. This practice often had gatekeepers, in the form of church mothers, who gave the final say as to whether a conversion was authentic or not. The mothers did not want new converts to miss or fake a real experience with God. A real encounter with God was believed to open the opportunity for communal contemplative participation.[84] The mourner's bench is not as widely practiced as it once was, but it is worth mentioning due to its multifaceted contemplative components: visualization, speaking to God, looking for meaning, and seeking visions or mystical experiences.

More contemporary versions of prayer are prayers of affirmation, prayers of repetition, and the practice of remembrance. Prayers of affirmation build up the practitioner. They can be found in several traditions across Black spiritualities. Darnise C. Martin, in "The Self Divine: Know Ye Not that Ye are Gods?," describes how prayers of affirmation work with the African American New Thought tradition to foster "interior focus, sometimes in stark opposition to that which the material world would present as real or true . . . to see beyond the physical or metaphysically into what is considered true reality—the divine as the ground of all being, and one's own unity with it."[85] These prayers remind the practitioner of where they are going, who they are becoming, and what is true for them at the moment. Prayers of affirmation help create the internal narrative that supports generative rumination and mental states of confidence. Affirmation prayers help set the tone for people, or help them reset their minds, giving them something new and generative to focus on. Prayers of repetition are similar to prayers of affirmation. However, prayers of repetition are more likely to place attention on one word or phrase, while in contrast, prayers of affirmation often have a much longer script. The repetition of one word or phrase allows the practitioner to focus on a particular part of the phrase or infer a different meaning from the word based on the inflection of his voice or context placed around the word in his mind. The practice of remembrance is special because it draws on the memory of the individual or community. It is a time of reflection on God's presence and God's goodness. The remembrance of God's presence and goodness is similar to the heartfulness practice. It creates a state of gratitude that is then cultivated by the practitioner. Very similar to the heartfulness practice, the cultivation of gratitude bathes the body's cells in generative genes, which are beneficial to health, clarity of mind, and compassion toward the self and others.

Neurologically, these prayers are similar to one another. The prayer of affirmation is reminiscent to speaking to one's self. So are prayers of repetition. Prayers of repetition could potentially be associated with changes in brain activity in the precuneus and ventromedial prefrontal cortex (VMPFC). Both areas are connected to self-referential activity.[86] Proposed changes in the precuneus would suggest decreased activation due to its connection with negative self-referencing. Changes in the VMPFC might infer increased activation since it is also connected to positive self-evaluation as well.[87] Another option might be a lessening in the resting state functional connectivity of the precuneus and anterior portions of the brain which would allow for a more positive view of the self. This is important as prayers of affirmation and repetition are intended to address personal identity and one's relationality to God and the world. Prayers of affirmation and repetition might also activate the connection of the precuneus, medial prefrontal cortex (MPFC), temporoparietal junction (TPJ), and the temporopolar region.[88] We already know that the collective activation of the precuneus, MPFC, and TPJ are associated with self-referential and social cognitive tasks.[89] This combination might play a more significant role in the prayer of remembrance when the practitioner is thinking of themselves in relation to God. Important to all three modes of contemplative prayer (affirmation, repetitive, and remembrance) is the temporopolar region. Important to the contemplative task of prayer, this region is linked to autobiographical memory and the processing of social narratives. While each practice draws from his or her prehensive autobiography and social narrative, the first two (affirmation and repetitive) apply meaning to the layers of personal biography and social narrative. However, the prayer of remembrance views past experience through a lens of gratitude. Furthermore, in comparison with glossolalia, the practices of affirmation and repetition might retain activity in the parietal lobules while increasing activation in the MPFC, because both have an active speaking component where the practitioner understands what is being said. This is in comparison to the practice of glossolalia where the practitioner is not aware of what her words mean.

On a basic level, prayer can feel like any conversation, but the contemplative component moves this conversation into an augmented sense of unitary experience for the practitioner who engages in the prayer. Even if the practitioner does not know what they are saying, as in the case of glossolalia, they feel more intensely connected to the object of prayer, even if that object is the self, which works to affirm the power of that prayer. In a relational sense, the closer one feels connected to the object of prayer, the greater potential for a sense of confidence in the actualization of the prayer's contents.

Preaching

Preaching is a contemplative practice based on the time spent in reflection, rumination, and communication with God, repeating the spoken word to the self and finally to the community. For the Black preacher the preaching moment is contemplative as it is the culmination of the studying, research, writing, and prayer that went into the sermon.

Preaching is concentration centric. So, it would probably engage the PFC because of its connection to focused attention. Whether extemporaneous or manuscript, preaching is an incredibly reflective and creative exercise. The difference can be found in their stages of application. Still, preaching might include the precuneus and/or the anterior cingulate gyrus for self-referencing while the preacher determines what she might say. It would incorporate the combination of the default network for social cognition as the preacher speaks with God and attempts to listen for a reply. I think the preaching process requires an equally active co-hemispheric activation in the temporal lobes and dorsolateral PFC (dlPFC) as one experiences God and imagines what is being said. The preaching act itself would incorporate brodmann's area 44 and 46 along with Wernicke's area, since it utilizes the ability to simultaneously listen, speak, and comprehend. While preaching, the PFC would remain active during a manuscript preaching session and has the potential to decrease activation in the PFC if the sermon is extemporaneous. Preaching feels like a multilayered conversation. On one level it is an internal conversation between the preacher and herself. On another level it is a conversation with the preacher and the congregation. And on the last level it is a conversation between God and the congregation, which includes the preacher too. So, in the preaching moment the preacher feels focused on the message, enlivened by the message itself, creative in delivering it, and excited to speak on behalf of God to God's people.

Yoga

Yoga is a broad contemplative practice in which many Black folks participate. Stephanie Rose Bird points out that there is a form of yoga which originated from Egyptian hieroglyphs.[90] Williams, who is a Buddhist, practices yoga within the Eastern tradition. Her book, *Being Black,* outlines poses like the lotus, among others, that have helped her along her path.[91]

Neurological effects of yoga participation are well documented. One's participation is correlative with decreased activation in the right amygdala, dorsal medial cortex (DMFC), and sensorimotor area. There is greater activation in the right dorsal medial frontal lobe (DMPFC), PFC, and right sensorimotor cortex. These changes in activation would result in decreased mental chatter, increased body awareness, increased parasympathetic activation, increased HRV, and decreased respiration. Overall, yoga leads to greater body control, calm, focus, and a sense of being grounded. While participating in yogic contemplative exercises, participants experience relaxation, alertness, and muscular activation. The tension of muscular engagement, relaxation, and alertness engages the entire anatomical edifice. This awakens the body's senses to its existence and strength under the intentional duress of mental concentration, balance, and eccentric movements.

Final thoughts

Someone once asked me, "What is the point of knowing what my amygdala is doing when I am meditating? How will it help someone when they are in the middle of a troubling situation? How will it help when they are in the midst of bleeding from a gunshot wound, dying in the street?" I believe this represents a real sentiment among Black folks who think that science will reduce Black spirituality to neurons and synapses. However, the neurological delineation of Black spirituality is important because its wisdom has the potential to keep us from experiencing the continued tragedy of dying senselessly. Neuroscientific wisdom is integral as it can illuminate pathways to accessing the sought after internal disposition that is required of freedom fighters. The neurospiritual approach is actually part of a proactive strategy to political action which recognizes the importance of starting at the level of the individual. It recognizes that collective efforts consist of individual entities working together, and that these individual entities need to be healthy in order to approach the very difficult task of anti-oppressive work. Since the entities in question are Black people, whose spirituality is closely tied to their identity, a strategy that cares for the spiritual nature of Black folks who are constantly moving through the dynamic complexities of a structurally oppressive environment is of dire importance. A neurospiritual approach recognizes that bodies are never still. Even while sleeping our cells are moving, replicating, replenishing, feeding. Since even the smallest levels of our body are in constant motion, the intentional actions of our entire bodies should be informed by an approach intended to deliberately cultivate a biological internality of grounded peace, clarity, and focus. Because as freedom fighters, Black folks should embody the idea that every movement is a movement toward justice, toward freedom. While the cultivation of justice is intense work, the intentional maintenance of a neurospiritually grounded disposition helps to maintain a generative internal space that does not eat away at the very bodies doing this important work. So, fostering, or cultivating, a particular spiritual disposition not only helps Black folks to cope with the unsettling nature of injustice, it helps us to establish and maintain a laser focus that precipitates the realization of a weighty goal—physically dismantling oppressive structures from the inside of ourselves to the outside world.

A greater understanding of how these spiritual practices affect Black biotechnology is key to the formulation of new Black spiritualities that are more effective, quicker to impact physiological change, and that help preserve the spiritually grounded state necessary to stop us from living as reactionaries. Accepting that physiology plays an integral role in Black spiritual practices necessitates the search to discover what might be determined as the best spiritual practices for individual Black biotechnologies. Again, I specifically mention the individual and not just Black folks as a whole, because this particular viewpoint must take into account the varying degrees of context, physiology, and psychology that situate Black folks in the multitude of spaces we find ourselves. The reality is that the current condition of the US context is not one that has successfully eliminated systemic issues that adversely affect Black folks. Honestly, there are times that many Black folks might say that the additional component of technology, on top of oppressive frameworks, exacerbates an already emotionally overwhelming environment. This is especially true when the stress of being Black is compounded by the pressures of the rat race, and the over saturation of disheartening information which has maladaptive affects which often reiterate the idea that Black folks are not safe in the United States. For these reasons we must keep in mind that the fight toward materializing freedom is simultaneously the fight against internalized modes of oppression. Oppressive structures do not sleep; they are built into the complex intersections and overlapping layers of our existence, so that those who benefit from them may sleep. A reactionary approach to freedom, one that elicits response to acts of violence and injustice will not win. Black folks have been operating in a reactionary mode for far too long. We even react to technology, allowing ourselves to be lulled to sleep by our increased access to personal entertainment, in order to take our minds off the pain we experience from viewing traumatic occurrences of racially motivated injustice on the screens of the same devices that we use to entertain us.

The point of understanding the neurophysiological underpinnings of spiritual experience, for Black folks, is to intentionally live from a grounded space while simultaneously strategizing (what may be considered a stationary act) and moving (a somatically dominated action). We cannot continue to be emotionally disrupted with every form of technologically mediated trauma, shifting our focus away from the task at hand. This is not to say that we cannot mourn; however, there is a difference in mourning and raising our voice in spurts, in hopes that it will somehow cause the technocratic operators of oppression to hear and adhere to our cries. We must remain relentless in the pursuit of freedom, guided by our spirituality. Black folks should not have to continue to pull from the crisis contemplative tradition in order to survive psychological affects of attacks on those who resemble us. Crisis contemplation pigeonholes Black folks in an attempt to reify identification with marginality and the ensuing levels of hopelessness it facilitates. This is exactly why we must construct spiritualities that are grounded in biology and a spirit of revolt. These revolt-based spiritualities can help us actively design and participate in the future we want to live for ourselves. In essence, neurophysiologically based spirituality helps prepare Black folks to be ever vigilant and ever grounded in the pursuit of materializing liberating materialities.

4

Black Transhuman Liberation Theology

Black transhuman liberation theology asserts that transhumanist modes of enhancement have the potential to further infuse spiritual dispositions into Black biotechnology. It recognizes the reality and pressing concern of anti-Black racism and its potential for the complete social death of Black folks. However, being a theistic transhumanism, the theological turn imagines/reimagines the Black body as a technology infused with vitalism. Here, Black folks embody the transhumanist capacities of malleability, flexibility, and evolutionary adaptation. So, while anti-Blackness places Black folks at odds with the notion of "humanity," whether it be through an attempt to achieve humanity or defend it, Black transhuman liberation theology presents an opportunity for reconstruction and recapitulation through a distinct merger of Black spirituality, Black biotechnology, and technological advancement. The fusion of these three components may prove to be the perfect tool in the fight for liberation, now and well into the future. Still, the linchpin of Black transhuman liberation theology is Blackness—what Blackness might do with technology, and how Blackness handles its own biotechnology.

Although Blackness currently has an amicable perception of technology, one can argue that the relationship between Blackness and technology remains tentative at best. A growing demographic of Black folks is embracing the use of technology in their lives. There is a growing contingent who are beginning to become skillful in it. However, underneath frequently used technology there still flows an intimation of science, which is the foundation of technology. These technologies are often systems constructed by mathematically derived languages. So, while these Black folks have readily accepted the implementation of technology in their lives, it can be said that a strong cohort of Black folks have not completely accepted the science behind it, or their ability to participate in that science.

I would submit that the tentative nature of the relationship between Black folks and science arises from the combination of the malicious medical treatment that Black bodies have received in the United States (stemming from antebellum slavery), and the manner in which scientific racism has used its platform to promote anti-Blackness. Black scholars, such as Harriet Washington and Dorothy Roberts, have done extensive work to outline the lasting effects of scientific racism. Yvone Harris has added to the discussion by exploring why Black folks still do not want to participate in scientific inquiry.[1] Their work points to the manner in which scientific racism was, and continues to be used to shape social perception, situating Black folks as necessarily expendable. They also highlight the way in which historical perceptions persist in present day. Prime examples of this necessary expendability are the denial of Black humanity through the Black only ailments of antebellum slavery, coerced participation in medical experiments (think J. Marion Sims), subjection to grave robbing and dissection, or the federally funded eugenics movement meant to handle the negro problem.[2] The collective narratives shared within Black communities were inspired by these historical events and grew into legends warning against body snatchers, doctors, and science overall. These effects were compounded when coupled with the inability of Black churches to adequately navigate and to engage scientific inquiry in their teachings.

Around the early twentieth-century Black churches began to struggle in their work of attending to the increasingly complex needs of their congregations. The great migration played an intricate role in shifting the internal layout of Black churches. Gayraud Wilmore describes three distinct categories within Black churches of that time period: (1) those who remained committed to the self-conscious Christian movement of Bishop Henry McNeal Turner's radical tradition. This faction did not garner much backing as the Black community began to eschew radical social upheaval; (2) the secularized Black hatred of White people, most commonly found in the poorest of neighborhoods. Members of this group in many cases eventually became part of the Nation of Islam, Black Nationalist, or Black Power movements because of their affinity toward nonconformity and their opposition to whiteness; and (3) those who sought the democratic social integrationalism espoused by the NAACP and Du Bois, which was championed by the Black middle class.[3] Churches were ill equipped to simultaneously placate to the radical tradition, handle the struggles of poor Black folks, and appease the secularized respectability associated with the emerging Black middle class. In addition, Black preachers had no real response to scientific racism. Historically, Black churches emphasized freedom and liberation. But, amid the internal movements of the time Black churches were beginning to prioritize upward mobility. Preachers often relegated references of Black worth to messages of God's love for the oppressed and the intrinsic worth of their humanity.[4] Theologically, Black churches were affirming Black worth through rebuttals to scientific racism's attempt to uphold proto-normative white supremacist notions of existence. So, while Black churches were home to after school programs which helped produce prominent Black scientists and intellectuals, the teachings of Black churches was becoming overwhelmingly unintelligible/irrelevant to the same crop of educated Black folks it helped raise. Gayraud Wilmore has already argued that Black churches of the early twentieth century were focused on maintaining their relevance amid the demographic shifts of that time, which may suggest that Black churches did not find dialogue that explored the intersections of theological suppositions and sound scientific inquiry significant to their cause. I highlight the early twentieth century, in terms of Black churches and scientific discourse, because it marks an important moment in history that highlights what, in hindsight, appears to be a missed opportunity. A missed opportunity that may have had the potential to speak to all three groups who were experiencing differing levels of distance from Black churches. Hence, it can be argued that since Black churches did not intentionally engage the intersections of science and theology during the important demographical shifts of the early twentieth century, the arc of Black churches since that time period have maintained a contentious stance toward science simply by neglecting the wisdom science may offer to theological discourse. By focusing on freedom and liberation or upward mobility without attending to science, Black churches have allowed technological revolutions to occur without their involvement.

Recent technological revolutions have captured the attention of Black Church adherents, but Black churches have placed little value on the ways that the science undergirding technology can be used to enhance Black spiritual experiences or Black theology. Black churches have utilized technologies to update outreach or modernize their services. And even though discussions of science are more accepted in Black communities than in the past, not much work has been done to connect Black religion, inclusive of spirituality or theology, with science. So, while some Black churches have recently begun opening themselves up to the possibility of exploring the connection between science and religiosity, a disconnect still remains prevalent among Black folks, who attend church or not.[5] So, it is for these reasons that it might be realistic to imagine how some might still perceive science as antithetical to Black religious expression.

Black transhuman liberation theology proposes that technology is key to Black revolution and liberation. Within this theistic transhumanist framework technology is viewed as an unavoidable and pertinent component of futuristic iterations of society. There are very few places in twenty-first-century everyday life that have not already been turned over to computer automation. It is estimated that over the next twenty-five years millions of jobs, leading up to 47 percent of the entire workforce, will be replaced by the further implementation of computers, artificial intelligence (AI), emotional intelligence, and or robots.[6] Economists and theorists have projected that this will lead to an incredible time of leisure, where people can pursue art, personal enjoyment, creativity, and purpose. Yet, experts have also warned of the legitimate potential for social collapse. If the right measures are not taken to ensure a proper transition from an economy dependent upon low-wage jobs, the majority of society will no longer have a means to provide for themselves.[7] Disregard for technology's potential to increase societal volatility may prove detrimental. Increased automation serves as a risk for the rich. If theorists are correct, people will not take kindly to having the workforce being substituted en masse. As George Dean puts it, work serves as a form of identity for people, while simultaneously allowing them to participate in the larger economy.[8] If people can no longer participate economically through pride in identity, then the probability for social peril rises significantly. Conversely, if considerations/personal changes are not made by those who are employed in fields susceptible to automation, then they are placing themselves in harm's way of experiencing the widening wealth divide. The tough part is determining exactly which jobs are susceptible to automation. Significant to this debate, Pew Research conducted a survey which showed that the majority of job holders in the United States (~80 percent) recognize technological automation as a threat to replace jobs. However, less than one-third of American workers actually believe their jobs are in jeopardy.[9] It seems that people recognize the potential of technological automation, but do not have the foresight to rightly anticipate its impact on the job market. This is especially alarming as history has shown that people are not good at predicting the potential of technological advancement. For instance, very few people could predict the Wright brothers' flying machine. Few people could have predicted the rate of data storage advancement. We are now able to write millions of terabytes of data on DNA strands![10] The human inability to foresee the declining utility of human capital is closely tied to the identities derived from work. For centuries familial lineages bore the names of their craft—Blacksmith, Butler, Baker, Brewer, Knight, Judge, Fisher, etc. Although many people are no longer nominally connected to their trades, it is understandable to see how humans struggle to envision a future where their contributions are deemed expendable.

The reality is that human capital is being phased out by the same force that was created to improve human quality of life. In fact, automation is an attempt to make life easier. However, one can determine on their own whose lives are improved through workforce automation—businesses (governments, executives, and infrastructure) or individuals. Nevertheless, as technology advances, a chasm appears that will have already taken the form of a classist discussion. I would like to submit that this is more than a discussion on class. This is undeniably a discussion of race as well. The old saying "When white folks catch a cold, Black folks catch pneumonia" is often used to demonstrate the wide disparities that effect people of different races and ethnicities that have institutional and socioeconomic meaning. During slavery, Black folks were the robots that made labor cheap. Free is a more accurate assessment—slave labor was free. When the slaves were freed, sharecropping began around the 1870s, and kept the lines of free labor open through debt until it ended around 1950. As Black folks gained ground in the civil rights movement, education, or through what was perceived to be greater opportunities in the North, albeit not by much, labor costs began to rise. Labor was then incrementally moved overseas and into prisons. Overseas labor began in the 1960s with manufacturing jobs. Prison labor has undergone a several evolutions. Initially there was the convict lease that existed in the South before penitentiaries. It leased convicts for work at private firms. In 1934, federal prison officials lobbied to institute a prison-based work program, but it was not until 1979 that the possibility of prison labor, in connection with private firms, was reintroduced.[11] Current overseas labor is largely a combination of African workers who exist in conditions akin to slavery and sweatshops spread throughout the Third World and the Global South. Prison labor remains another example of how the United States began to, and continues to, place free labor on the backs of a disproportionately Black population to uphold its racist capitalist order.[12] Any population labeled "prisoner" while being forced to work for little to no pay is an enslaved population. Prison labor is slave labor reincarnate. As a result of these economic moves labor costs were lowered once more. Now, with the rise of automation, jobs that were once thought to be staples in the American workforce/economy may now be on the brink of total extinction. So, while automation may present leisure to some (the wealthy), it may also prove to be the playground of revolution to others.

Conversations concerning the concept of basic income have grown in an attempt to conceptualize abating the potential cataclysmic nature of the shifting economy. In 2016, Y-Combinator, most reputable as a start-up incubator, began the piloting of a study in Oakland, California, testing the concept of basic income. People received $2,000 a month, for a year, with no strings attached. The goal was to see if people will really be productive without having to worry about life's basic needs such as housing.[13] The concept of basic income raises the question of equity. When implemented, who gets to decide the qualifications that make one eligible for basic income? Do felonies terminate eligibility? Are the most poor or the most rich going to be the first benefactors of a governmentally run basic income program—if it ever materializes? And who determines what is basic? Essentially, several questions arise, including (1) What disqualifies someone from receiving basic income if it is ever rolled out? (2) What other options will be provided to someone whose basic income disbursement has been revoked? (3) Will basic income be another way to exclude/ostracize Black folks from participation in the larger economy?

Without basic income the imminent wealth divide could prove cataclysmic for Black folks. In 2018, Black folks only made up 10.5 percent of the technology industry. That number drops to 9.3 for computer programmers, and 3.9 percent for software developers (this is down from 5 percent in 2016). However, Black folks do make up 12.3 percent for information security analysts, which does coincide with our roughly 13 percent of the overall US population. We also make up 15.3 percent of statisticians, which is above our overall percentage of the US population.[14] But that is not nearly enough, especially in reference to power structures and influence. In the engineering industry the numbers are worse. In 2018, Black folks only made up 6.5 percent of the engineering workforce. With the current inundation of technology that has occurred in the last twenty years, it is hard to imagine how much more integrated technology will be in our everyday lives within that same time period going forward. If Black folks do not become creators within the technological space, placing themselves in positions formative to its future, then the future does not look good for Black folks. Recent progress in intelligence and facial recognition might grow to replace psychologists, social workers, security guards, and military/law enforcement—jobs that are thought to require the human element. These are also fields that employ higher rates of Black professionals. It is important to consider that these statistics probably include Caribbean and African immigrants, along with recent descendants of the Caribbean and African continent. The inclusion of Black bodies who are not descendants of US chattel slavery might inflate these numbers. But if the focus solely becomes those whose heritage includes enslaved Africans, the actual percentage of workers in the technology industry might reflect even greater disproportionality regarding participation and influence.

Given the societal push toward increased technological dependence the question becomes, "How do Black folks merge one of our strongest collective strengths—spirituality—with emergent technology?" First, Black folks must begin to recognize the ways in which we are already transhuman, malleable, flexible, and adaptable/augmentable. A reflection of ways Black folks already augment their physical, intellectual, and psychological capabilities through technological interaction will help to demonstrate how it is only reasonable to move further into transhumanism. This chapter will begin with an outline of what already makes Black folks transhuman. Then, it will demonstrate how current and emergent technologies can be harnessed to understand spirituality, and subsequently be paired with spirituality. Harnessing current and emergent technologies and paring them with Black spirituality will illustrate technology's spiritually augmenting capabilities as it interacts with Black biotechnology. I will end by looking at the potential for Black transhumanism to ignite a spirituality of revolt within Black bodies, and a practical sketch of Black transhuman liberation theology in efforts to attain full immersion in the technological.

Already transhuman?

Basic biotechnology

Lee Silver in "Biotechnology in a World of Spiritual Beliefs" outlines the history of biotechnology and how its prevalence leaves its presence virtually undetectable.[15] He begins at the edge of the Ice Age when the human population grew. Hundreds of large game animal species were hunted into extinction, and vegetation was over foraged. Prior to this point, humans depended on their nomadic qualities, but they pushed the biosphere past its human carrying capacity. This string of events pushed humans to intentionally embark on what has been coined as the agricultural revolution. In that same chapter he asserts that the agricultural revolution was fundamentally a revolution of biotechnology.

> The Agricultural Revolution emerged out of the human discovery of genes—the invisible abstractions that carry specific characteristics of plants and animals from one generation to the next. Genetic conceptualization allowed people to create novel organisms expressing domesticated characteristics built to satisfy human needs.[16]

In Central America, teosinte, a slender weed, was engineered into corn.[17] In South America poisonous shrubs became red tomatoes, sweet potatoes, potatoes, and peppers. In South Asia, inedible weeds from Malaysia and India were merged to create bananas. Animals were bioengineered through domestication. Threatening bloodlines were killed off. Loyal and obedient bloodlines were allowed to breed.[18] The dogs, descendants of gray wolves, are prime examples of this breeding technique. In the Middle East, oxen were engineered into cows that produced milk. The amino profile of their milk was expanded and altered to fit human consumption. The weaning age of calves was reduced, and humans began drinking milk regularly.[19] Eventually, the discovery of microbes opened the door for the creation of fermentation: cheese, alcoholic beverages, vinegar, etc. Today, Black folks benefit from these biotechnological advances regularly. These advances have become so engrained in the mundane that a realization of their status as technological progeny is lost.

Black folks use pharmaceutical drugs and dietary supplements that augment their psychological and physical capabilities. In the United States, an FDA-approved drug is a medication that is used to diagnose, treat, cure, or prevent a disease. These drugs simply speed up the body's recovery process by decreasing symptoms. For example, pain-relieving drugs can be taken for several symptoms: arthritis, menstrual pain, muscle soreness, headaches, etc. Pain killers are intended to reduce discomfort so that users may resume normal activities with little to no pain. This biochemical response to laboratory made substances helps soothe bodily ailments and aches. Psychologically, the reduction of pain increases the likelihood of users sustaining normal activities. Substances like Adderall make people more alert and increase productivity. Cough syrup represses the cough reflex. Lactose free protein supplements are made through microfiltration processes that remove lactose while making protein more easily digestible. Amino acid compilations aid muscle recovery, boost mental concentration, and increase neuromuscular capacity which primes the body for increased strength and active recovery.

Technological apparatus

Prosthetics serve as the perfect example of combining technology and personal biotechnology. Hearing aids work as either a cochlear implant or attachments. Hearing aids augment the physical ability to hear. Hearing is considered a neurological system. In unaided ears, the cochlea, a spiral and hollow bone, allows humans to hear with a combination of pressure, inner ear fluid, and tiny hairs called "cilia." Sounds are determined by the high or low vibrations they cause within the cochlea and how much force they apply to the cilia. Cilia then send afferent signals to the brain in accordance to the sounds that were heard.

This process happens in millionths of a second, so that we can decode and understand what is happening around us.

Artificial limbs help in similar ways. Prosthetic hands that are mechanized allow for people to grab and grip. Prosthetic legs help people walk and run. Recent developments in neuroprosthetics can decipher how much pressure to apply when gripping objects and even offer users the ability to feel.

I went to college with Jerome Singleton. He is a single-leg amputee and two-time Paralympian. In 2008, he came in second to Oscar Pistorius in the 100-meter sprint during the Beijing Paralympics. In 2011, he beat Pistorius in the 100-meter sprint at the Paralympic World Championships in Christchurch, New Zealand. As a single-leg amputee, his personal best in the 100-meter sprint is 11.1 seconds. His story is an example of how prosthetics help people do things that they would otherwise be incapable of doing. Every day he wears his prosthesis, Jerome Singleton embodies transhumanism.

Andrew Jones is one of the strongest examples of Black transhumanism. He is a Black man who lived with an artificial heart. He had no pulse and no heartbeat, but his artificial heart kept blood coursing through his veins. He is a bodybuilder who called himself "the best looking zombie [anyone] would ever see."[20] In 2012, he was diagnosed with cardiomyopathy and needed a heart transplant. While waiting, he was given a device to continue pumping blood through his body. The device is called a left ventricle assist device (LVAD). It is battery powered and requires him to keep it attached to his body 24/7.[21] Unlike a SynCardia device, which works without a heart in the body at all, Jones still had his heart while awaiting transplant.[22] He received his heart transplant at the end of 2016.

Pen, printing press, typewriter, etc.

The pen, printing press, and their technological offspring have benefited Black folks intellectually. Handwritten books provided written access to the wisdom and information of authors from nearly every subject. But, writing by hand was incredibly time consuming. So, the invention of the printing press made the mass production of written information much easier. The increased production of books, newspapers, and magazines allowed the information contained to on their pages to become wide spread. Literacy is a new privilege for Black folks in America. It is an opportunity whose legality is less than 200 years old. But even before it was legal for Black folks to read, Black folks risked their lives to reap the benefits of increased intellectual acuity. When access to public libraries became a reality for Black folks it opened books up to our ancestors in a greater way.

While the geographic location of libraries has not always been close to Black neighborhoods, their existence matters. As the production price of books and pamphlets continued to drop, the increase of educated Black folks lead to the proliferation of personal libraries. Simultaneously, the use of the typewriter by Black folks widened the scope of Black thought. Black readers were eager to get their hands on the writings of people who were Black and shared similar contextual experiences. Thus, Black literature gained popularity as exhibited by the writers of the Harlem Renaissance who were influential to Black readers. The advent of the computer, along with its personalization, brought information right into people's homes. The information age, which brought the internet, search engines, social and real-time data along with it, digitally augmented Black intellectualism. For instance, Black children today are more likely to learn about Black history from the internet and social media than they would at school. Mobile devices are the current manifestation of writing, reading, and technology. They bring information directly to the palm of the user's hands. The use of mobile devices is so prevalent that many people are now nomophobic. The connection these devices provide to information is unlike anything in history. Beyond the basic concept of intellectualism, people who use these devices regularly are learning how to interact with and become more technologically sound. I want to be clear—intellectual augmentation does not happen through osmosis or digital transfer; however, access to information, especially conflicting views, provides the atmosphere for it.

Black folks are already transhumanist in practice. There is no way around it. Black folks routinely and intentionally seek out technological advancement to increase their quality of life. Considerable portions of Black scholarship are still trying to prove the worth of Black humanity.[23] However, if we accept our transhumanist existence, Black folks, and every iteration of folk, must question whether we have ever been just human. With the first human to use a rock as a tool all "humans" became transhuman. When we add concepts of incarnation and deities, we begin speaking of the capacity for human bodies to hold elements of the divine. Some scholars, like Bill McKibben, author of *Enough: Staying Human in an Engineered Age*, suggest that technology is only useful when its power is harnessed for human enjoyment, or to make life easier.[24] He asserts that technology should be limited in the power it has over humans. He also thinks that humans have enough power and should exercise restraint in the pursuit of technological advancement. But if the question is of nature, or the prescribed order of humanity, then is it not too late for these questions? Is it not a denial of what we have already done, not to mention our potential in the world?

People have a history of adaptation. That is how people have survived. That is how Black folks have survived. For those who use God as a reason for not fully exploring scientific possibilities I ask, "If no one can remove God from God's place of sovereignty, and God gave people these creative abilities—including natural curiosity—then how can the exploration of God's natural world result in any legitimate replacement of God?" Is it not God who ignites human ingenuity and innovation?

I grew up in a Word of Faith church, and a common ideology in that tradition is that the end is better than the beginning. In tandem with transhumanism, one could suggest that, historically, humanity has been in search of better ways to exist and experience life. It also acknowledges the nonlinearity of what might be considered as "better" in relationship with what is worse: heinous, brutal, or terrifying. Applied scientific innovation, resulting in technology, can be presented as an example of that search for improvement. This is not to dismiss the harmful means through which social technologies, or technical innovations, have been used to abstract life and justify monstrous acts against select groups. This is especially troubling since many people are still trying to figure out what it means to be human—or if human is the best designation at all. But this might also ease the transition to a full immersion within Black transhumanism and an acceptance of the posthuman phase. Nevertheless, an acceptance of Black bodies as biotechnology would implicate them within the larger milieu of interdependent biotechnology. Black bodies participate in the natural world, which supports our biotechnologically meditated existence. Through this lens Black bodies are proliferating and coevolving along with other biotechnologies. So, the question becomes, "Why not become intentional about the direction of the biotechnological evolution already taking place?"

Harnessing the technological

The neurophysiology of Black spiritual experience serves as a bridge between Black biotechnology and science in a generative way. Understanding the neural underpinnings of Black spiritual experience can be life giving as Black folks may finally see/record the physical manifestation of their beliefs on their bodies and the world around them. Many Black folks have died without seeing the physicality of their beliefs—Nat Turner, Fannie Lou Hamer, Martin Luther King, Malcolm X, etc. In the neurospiritual case for freedom, materiality matters most. Beliefs may precipitate material reality, but in terms of freedom, immateriality is almost a nonfactor. Now technology, as a form of materiality, can illustrate the correlative connection between particular spiritual practices and neurophysiological body states. A comprehension of these bodily states will open the door for determining the quantitative utility of Black spiritualities, putting them on the table of critique and empirical analysis. Black folks should not be afraid of this. For centuries Black folks have been unwilling to question their faith, because faith has been the one thing that has kept Black folks through the years. It has functioned as the tapestry that "kept" their reality together. It is important to know that the term kept is used in Black religious settings as a means to explain either how one is kept from danger or how one remains physically, psychologically, or spiritually well in the midst of tumultuous surroundings. To question Black faith is essentially questioning the backbone of Black resiliency. What I am proposing is not a questioning of Black faith for the sake of belittling and dismissing it. I am proposing a questioning of where Black folks place their faith, as a spiritual practice, to determine what it means to have a potent and satisfying spiritual experience that is readily accessible in any environment. I am not advocating the parsing out of Black spiritual experience for the sake of deconstruction. I seek to parse out the Black spiritual experience in order to determine what makes the most effective spiritual practice that produces the most sustainable spiritual affect. This is a constructive exercise. In this section I am going to demonstrate how current and emergent technologies can provide insight into the affect of the spiritualities we practice. Specifically, I will look at neuroscientific methodologies and consumer-based methodologies. While I have mentioned genetics research throughout this project I think its use in Black transhumanist approaches to liberation would require greater attention.

Using neuroscientific measures gives insight into the effects of a practice. Consumer-based methods allow for practical application of the wisdom neuroscience provides. The specific neuroscientific measures I will focus on include functional magnetic resonance imagery (fMRI), single-photon emission computed tomography (SPECT), positron emission tomography (PET), electroencephalogram (EEG), electrocardiogram (ECG), electromyography (EMG), galvanic skin response (GSR), phlebotomy (BD), and emergent methods as well. I will highlight what each methodology does, its potential, and its limitations. I think it is important to note that EEG is currently the only imaging methodology not bound by the confines of the laboratory. All other current imaging technologies are limited to analysis in the laboratory setting. So, while many examples of spiritual practices may be explored through laboratory-based instruments, spiritual practices that involve movement cannot be conducted in those spaces. They can only show the effect of a practice based on residual brain activity. Immediate limitations to methods that focus more on the physiological side, such as ECG and EMG, depend on their connective apparatus; they may be seen as obtrusive and uncomfortable to the participant who wears them. The specific consumer measures I will examine are heart rate monitors (HR) (i.e., Fitbit variations, Spire), a breath monitoring device, and mobile applications. These applications either already draw on knowledge of neuroscience or have the ability to do so.

fMRI

fMRI gives researchers the opportunity to see inside of the brain with real-time capabilities, and it is currently the gold standard of brain imaging technologies. By tracing the brain's dynamic blood oxygen levels (BOLD) it illustrates which parts of the brain are more active during certain tasks, such as thinking about driving, prayer, remembering, speaking, etc.[25] Interpreting the BOLD signal requires understanding of brain anatomy and inference (forward or reverse) to determine correlative speculation as to what may have caused any particular part of the brain to respond to a given task. The strengths of this method are its visual capacities. It can easily show active brain regions associated with specific tasks, along with their artifacts. Artifacts are leftover brain activity related to a particular task that do not show real-time reactivity. fMRI can also show the speed of reaction in the brain and a depiction of individually highlighted brain structures. These strengths provide strong implications for understanding the impact of Black spiritual practices on individuals and small populations. For instance, fMRI can show which brain regions are most associated with a particular spiritual practice. It can show structural change associated with longitudinal use of a particular practice. It may even show structural changes that take place as a result of being in community. However, fMRI is not a perfect tool. Its problems start with the fact that it cannot determine causality without brain lesions (brain injuries). Due to the vast differences of individual brain structures, the pictures it produces when testing larger populations are really only an average of activation, meaning that all the brains used in a particular study have been stretched or shrunk to fit a predetermined average brain so that region activation might match.[26] The reality is that all brains do not look exactly alike, so what may be the dorsolateral prefrontal cortex for one person might actually be the motor region for another. fMRIs are also expensive. The cost of using this device normally leads to an acceptably smaller participant pool, making it harder to make more concretized determinations from gathered data. Due to the technical nature of the fMRI, a specialist is required to read the images it produces.

PET

PET scanners create images using positron-emitting radioisotopes (an intentionally unstable chemical which emits radiation as it decays).[27] PET imaging is based on the tracer principle, which utilizes radioactive compounds to help trace the functional components of nonradioactive compounds in order to better understand the flow and distribution of bodily substances.[28] This differentiation in process allows for stronger images to be made due to the relationship of multiple decaying isotopes in contrast to a single radioisotope. It is also important to note that PET radioactive isotopes have a much shorter half-life than SPECT radioisotopes. As PET isotopes decay in the body they are believed to split in pairs and go in opposite directions. The PET scanner detects where pairs of isotopes decay together to create the image that will later be reconstructed in 3-D. PET images are produced once every forty seconds, so there is not a steady functional image product in comparison to the fMRI; however, the PET image is still more detailed than SPECT and is easily read since the isotopes injected into the participant create color-coded images highlighting the areas of the brain receiving the most oxygen. PET imaging capabilities are similar to fMRI. As an imaging technique, PET is a useful tool with the capacity to see biological responses to Black spiritual practices, spiritual thoughts, or stimuli. It has the ability to show which areas of the brain are more responsive to particular rituals in comparison to others, and it helps to bring clarity to the neurological responses when comparing particular traditions. The main weakness of the PET method is that, even though its images are clearer than SPECT images, they are still not as strong as fMRI images. Since image production is parsed over 40-second intervals, real-time assessments are not possible with current PET technology. Similar to SPECT, PET is best when compared against an MRI or Computer Tomography (CT) to increase the strength of results shown. Due to the technical nature of PET, a specialist is required to read its images.

SPECT

SPECT creates 3-D images of organs to determine their functionality. Its imaging process follows a single photon to show bodily processes instead of isotope pairs in the PET model.[29] It is a nuclear medicinal technique that utilizes gamma rays in combination with a radioisotope, either injected into the bloodstream or inhaled to help create the picture. The radioisotope emits a single gamma photon that can be traced throughout the body as the image is being captured. The radioisotope, in conjunction with the gamma camera, takes pictures in slices and through reconstruction builds the desired 3-D image.[30] Much like the fMRI, SPECT works with oxygenated blood. Through the radioisotope attached to the oxygenated blood, a computer is used to identity high levels of oxygenated blood in various areas of the brain to determine their association with a given task. So, as with all functional imagery, SPECT captures brain activity in a working capacity. This is helpful in assessing Black spirituality, as structural functionality and neuroplasticity are important factors for understanding the impact of a practice or ritual on the individual in real time and through longitudinal methods. These methods allow for measuring lasting effects of continual practice or residual effects of a prescribed set of practices after an elapsed amount of time. SPECT does come with its limitations. Due to its use of only one photon, it is not incredibly clear, so it is normally combined with a CT scan. It is a cheaper version of PET, which results in a lower resolution image. However, each SPECT session can last longer than PET sessions since the radioisotope is not metabolized by the brain tissue as quickly. The gamma in the radioisotope is radioactive, which limits the number of times any one individual can undergo a SPECT scan. Due to the technical nature of SPECT, a specialist is needed to decipher its images as well.

EEG

The EEG measures electric activity in the brain. Electrodes connect to the various parts of the scalp and forehead to determine the level of electric activity in the brain. Electrode numbers on an EEG range from 8 to 256 electrodes.[31] The greater the amount of electrodes on an EEG, the more intricate an image it can produce. An EEG is a strong instrument for reading brain wave activity.[32] It is not an imaging device that peers into the brain, giving insight into its structure and functionality. It shows electricity in brain activity in particular regions by providing a surface view. The EEG process usually takes about an hour. EEGs can be useful to practical theology as it provides a synopsis of brain wave activity in response to Black spiritual practices, rituals, and forms of worship. For instance, alpha waves are correlative to calm and relaxation associated with mindfulness meditation. Theta waves are correlated to deep meditation,[33] whereas beta waves are connected to active thinking which could imply stress. EEG can be helpful in deciphering brain wave type and inter-hemispheric coherence resulting from practices done in a laboratory setting or beyond. EEG cannot take anatomical pictures and thus falls short in understanding the complete picture of brain wave activity that it records. It does not create slices like fMRI or PET devices. There is no limit to the amount of sessions one can undergo an EEG, because it is not a radioactive medicine like SPECT or EEG; however, it does have real-time functionality in recording brain wave activity. Also, EEG is not limited to the laboratory setting like the other imaging methodologies, but EEGs taken outside the lab have traditionally been weaker in their ability to produce high-level imagery/readings. Emerging EEG capacities are being explored to alleviate this issue.

ECG

ECG readings demonstrate the beat-to-beat changes in the heart. It is a neurophysiological measure that reads the P and QRS waves of the heartbeat, and breaks down the electrical mechanism of the heart.[34] This is not the same as the mechanical mechanism that HR measure, making the ECG a much stronger method than HR, specifically because mechanical phenomenon can be perceived as an artifact of the electrical beat.[35] The P wave is the depolarization of the atria, known as the "atrial complex." The QRS wave is the action potential (depolarization and repolarization) of the ventricles or ventricular complex that occurs during each heartbeat. The importance of the heartbeat lies in its heart rate variability (HRV). HRV measures the difference in beat-to-beat changes to determine coherency within the heart. Coherence is a strong indicator of emotional states.[36] The heart has the capacity to override intentional thinking by its influence on the brain through the vagus nerve.[37] Heart rhythms, indicative of chaos, administer a sense of internal chaos, instability, and stress. In contrast, rhythms, indicative of calm and coherence, relay those messages to the brain, and in turn influence the body to emotionally and mentally relate in a calm and coherent manner as well. This is critical for Black spirituality because HRV can be utilized as a method to actively monitor bodily states correlative to Black spirituality and the impact of Black spiritual practices, worship, community, ritual, etc., on the individual and larger community as well. The strengths of this method are that it provides real-time feedback to neurological states, it is not limited to the laboratory setting, it is a noninvasive or non-obtrusive method, and it has multiple means of application such as a chest strap or finger monitor.

This method's weakness lies in the fact that it requires self-reporting to determine efficacy, it is not an imaging method directly related to the brain (this may not be a true weakness because ECG is more related to the physiology that influences the brain), and although the science supporting the neurological impact of HRV on the body is strong, ECG only reports on the heart, which affects the brain through the connection it has via the vagus nerve.

EMG

EMG is a method that records muscular activity. It requires participants to be connected to electrodes to help determine the types of isolated or compound muscular movements on either the face, shoulders, or other parts of the body that are in relationship to a given stimulus.[38] For instance, participants could be asked to watch the sky while having electrodes connected to their face to see if there is a facial response to looking at the sky, especially when a cloud is spotted or a bird is pointed out. EMG should be carried out in conjunction with another method such as self-reporting, ECG, or EEG, depending on the variables being tested.

EMG has the potential to dramatically alter practical and theoretical theological work. For instance, it can potentially measure the result of meditation on physical strength (something relevant to athletes or the elderly). It can also potentially examine whether physical acts can impact the Black internal spiritual state. For example, EMG can determine whether the act of smiling or the opening of one's hand as opposed to clenching it does something physiologically to the individual that makes one action more desirable for spiritual outcomes. EMG inclusion in relation to religion as a whole is fairly new and mainly relegated to understanding what happens to the face during meditation,[39] although some studies have begun to include somatic-based practices.[40] However, EMG's possibilities for impacting Black spirituality are vast. Its strengths lie in the ability to assess the muscular activity in relation to experience, and the impact Black spirituality, rituals, and worship may have on muscular output. It has real-world and real-time capabilities, which makes it a helpful tool when looking at spiritual practices in their natural setting. Its weaknesses include the fact that it does not provide direct insight into the brain or anatomical structures through imaging, and depending on the type of EMG apparatus employed, only a limited number of actions can be tested at a given time. EMG is not a method that can stand on its own. It works best in cooperation with methods that have some form of measurement to aid in deciphering the information it provides, like, ECG, EEG, etc.

GSR

GSR is a method that uses electrodes to measure electrical changes in the skin through exocrine secretion. The signal can be used for capturing the autonomic nerve responses seen in the activity of sweat glands.[41] GSR is mainly a stress response measurement and has implications for investigating self-regulation through Black spiritual practices, traditions, and rituals; however, to acquire the strongest reading, GSR requires participants to remain still, so implementation outside the laboratory setting is limited as it is not well calibrated to withstand the constant movement of bodies outside laboratory settings. Participants would have to stop and remain still while engaging in a spiritual practice before going about the rest of their day. It is also important to note that GSR sensors may slip, which add to the noise of its recorded measurement.[42] GSR's strength is in its ability to assess stress responses to outside stimuli and even track self-regulatory responses as a peripheral neurophysiological measure. Yet, its weakness is found in its inability to be utilized in real-world situations, provide constant and continual assessment, or perform outside of the perfect and sterile laboratory.

Blood draws (BD)

Phlebotomy assesses the neurotransmitters and hormones present in blood plasma. Neurotransmitters such as arginine vasopressin (AVP), which is associated with anger and aggression, oxytocin (OT), which is associated with love, trust, and inclusion, or dopamine (Dopa) or Serotonin (HT5), which are associated with happiness and calm, can be traced through blood flow.[43] Transmitter assessment in blood plasma is important to understanding mental and bodily states as neurotransmitters encounter the 10,000+ receptor sites in each cell which ultimately impact mental and body states.[44] They can be a peripheral indicator of the autonomic nervous system's response to outside and internal stimuli including spiritual practices such as worship, ritual, and communal engagement. Through blood draws, investigators can assess which transmitter is present in response to listening to a sermon or participating in a meditation practice, and compare the pervasiveness of particular transmitters in comparison to when participants engage in the same practices either alone or with others. This is another considerably important methodology for theology. With the importance placed on communal and individual spiritual implementation, theologians who engage in this kind of work can measurably see the physical effects on both the individual and communal event in relation to particular spiritual practices and traditions. When blood draws are used in tandem with other mentioned methodologies such as ECG or fMRI, the results become even stronger. This is where correlations can then be made to infer the impact of Black spirituality and hopefully spark the construction of new spiritualities, whose intent is stronger and has a more lasting physical effect. This may also lead to further exploration and new discoveries in spirituality and practical theology. BD is an expensive method which would require adequate funding or the acceptance of a smaller participant pool. It does not provide an anatomical image of the body, and any correlation to brain regionality would have to be determined based on either a hybrid methodology which includes imaging mechanisms or other studies with paralleling factors, such as, behavior, chemistry, emotionality, etc. BD requires quick and precise action to ensure the samples remain viable for assessment. Skilled phlebotomists are necessary for this procedure, which presents an additional cost as well. Investigators must also find a willing population as strong BD designed studies require a baseline draw before the actual draw in response to the independent variable.

Emergent Neuroscience Technologies

Diffusion Tensor Imaging (DTI) is an emergent technique that allows the axons in the brain and their subsequent connections to be tracked as their connections actively move across the brain. This is based on water diffusion in the brain as opposed to BOLD signals in MRI-based imaging.[45] DTI is color coded to demonstrate different areas of brain activity. Within DTI imaging is white matter fiber tactography, which tracks white matter (glial cells or myelin) connectivity. This tracking may prove to be a remarkable resource in understanding how the brain is connected/wired for spirituality in comparison to other bodily states. Seeing how white matter tracts act within the brain during Black spiritualities might give a more holistic understanding of how the brain collectively works and also how those connections are impacted during Black spiritualities. However, DTI is limited in its ability to differentiate between tracts that cross one another on its color-coded scheme.

Matrix-assisted laser desorption/ionization mass spectrometry (MALDI-MS or MS) imaging analyzes ion distribution among tissue sections.[46] Its precision allows for the discovery of molecules that would not normally show up on larger tests. Neurologically, it is used to decipher brain chemistry by determining which molecules are most profuse in a given section. It can be used by practical theologians to determine individual brain chemistry in response to religious practice on the brain. One limitation of this method is that it requires tissue sections that have been removed from the body.[47] So, while it may determine levels of molecular profusion within a particular region, with high levels of precision, it will most likely require participants to be in a post-mortem state, or a brain surgery patient, due to the nature of brain section acquisition.

Implantable technologies

Implantable technologies are in a hybrid space. Due to their placement inside the body, the exploration of their use normally requires clinical research and extensive animal testing prior to advancing to human trials. Implantable technologies are incorporated in the neuroscientific technology section, because the implantable techniques mentioned specifically deal with neuroscientific inquiry.

Implantable technology demonstrates significant potential for biological advancement. Implants are available in various forms such as microchips, pacemakers, carbon-fibers, and nanobots. Implantable chips can regulate brain function via electrical signal. Recently, microchips have been used as a wireless drug delivery system for women with osteoporosis.[48] Brain pacemakers have been used to moderate certain uncontrollable tremors by sending electric currents via deep brain stimulation (DBS) into brain regions to mitigate involuntary movement.[49] Similarly, a company named NeuroPace uses DBS and artificial intelligence, in a closed-loop brain computer interface (BCI) system, to detect the onset of seizures, and help reduce their occurrence.[50]

Carbon-fibers have many applications. Currently, scientists are looking into how carbon-fiber wires work to record neuron activation in tightly bundled clusters.[51] Elon Musk's Neuralink is an excellent example of this. Neuralink uses electrodes attached to thin film polymers (similar to, composed of, or symbiotic with carbon-nanofibers). Neuralink was created to connect people to machines through personalized brain machine interfaces (BMIs). Their ultimate goal is to provide access to superintelligence through their implantable devices. Neuralink's initial device, the N1, is purported have five unique capabilities: (1) spike detection (detection of action potentials, or the brain's release of strong electrical impulses), (2) the ability to determine individually activated neurons, (3) computation of neural activity at speeds faster than that of perception, (4) the smallest bioactivity converter from brain activity to digital information, and (5) the capacity to stimulate up to 64 individual neurons at a time.

Carbon nanotubes (CNTs) are being used in the tissue engineering field as possible regenerative tissue stimulators because of their ability to conduct and act as a semiconductor in the body.[52] Nanobots have been used to examine disease and diagnose cancer. Nanobots have also been used to conduct surgery, deliver medicine, and they have served to fight viruses.[53] Wireless microchips can be helpful to augment Black spiritual experience through time releasing amino acids and hormones that increase the likelihood of spiritual experiences. Neural pacemakers could prove helpful as behavioral aids by wirelessly engaging brain regions that would promote concentration, increasing motor functions, or altering moods. Carbon nanotubes could work to rebuild or grow brain tissue more associated with spiritual experience (PFC, TL, TPJ, PSPL, etc). In the future, Nanobots could prove helpful in healing wounds, stimulating cells, neurogenesis, or synaptogenesis to accelerate structural brain changes associated with intentional spiritual development.

Biomechanical (Biomech or Bionic) limbs

Biomech limbs are either roboticized (bionic) or thought controlled. Bionic limbs use mechanized joints that realistically mimic movement. Mechanized joints have helped to normalize walking gait for leg amputees.[54] Bionic exoskeletons use various joints, spinal support, leg support, and arm support to enable individuals of various physical ability to walk. Neuroprosthetics use either BCI or brain machine interfaces (BMIs) to control modular prosthetic limbs (MPLs).

> There are many signals from the brain that can be leveraged, including the spiking rates of neurons in the cortex, electrocorticographic (ECoG) signals from the surface of the cortex, and electroencephalographic (EEG) signals from the scalp. Unlike micro-electrodes, which record spikes [which are internally planted], ECoG does not penetrate the cortex and also has higher spatial specificity, signal-to-noise ratio, and bandwidth than EEG signals.[55]

Neuroprosthetics are used to help differently abled individuals control MPLs.

Biomech is steadily progressing. For instance, SuitX is an exoskeleton created by the Robotics and Human Engineering Laboratory at University of California, Berkeley. It is the lightest exoskeleton at 27lbs. Electrode and ECoG neuroprosthesis are making small strides in the ability for thought controlled prosthetics. These technological advances can aid in augmenting Black spirituality by freeing individuals to move on their spiritual aspirations through action. The intentional action of Black biotechnology is presented as the fundamental ingredient of Black transhuman liberation. Biomech has the potential to allow folks to move, whether through regaining certain faculties, or for the very first time.

Consumer technologies

Consumer-based technologies are not clinically strong. However, their utility is helpful in terms of how they can be used to apply the wisdom neuroscience provides to augment spiritual abilities.

HR devices

Heart rate (HR) monitors like the Fitbit, Apple Watch, or Galaxy Watch work to track heart beats and movement (steps). These devices measure heart rate through photoplethysmogram (PPG).[56] PPG uses LED light sensors to track the pulse as it travels through the vein. It uses gyroscope and accelerometer technology to determine movement and location. PPG technology does not carry the same accuracy as ECG technology. It does not measure heart rate variability (HRV), nor does it maintain strong heart rate precision—even though marketing literature says it does. An understanding of HRV principles and their importance to spiritual coherence can make HR monitors useful in assessing stressful states. Fitness monitors track HR throughout the day. These devices have additional/complementary applications to go along with them which demonstrate the variations of HR throughout the day. Someone who is intentional about cultivating their spiritual disposition may use HR monitors like these to see what times of the day they experienced heart rate increases outside of exercise. A person can take inventory of their day and recognize what elevated their HR. They can either be mindful of things that correlate with their triggers, and work to cultivate a spiritual disposition that is geared for engaging events that were once triggering events, or prepare "in the moment" practices that will help them the next time they encounter something that could potentially be an unhealthy stressor. People who complete spiritual practices while wearing these devices might be able to see their HR decrease as a result of the practice. Decreases in HR can add some validity to their experience of the practice.

Spire

Spire is a wearable device that attaches to belt clips. It measures the depth of one's breathing. Stress normally induces shallow breathing. Spire takes notice of when breathes becomes shorter and sends out a vibration that reminds the wearer to breathe more deeply. Lehrer, 1999, established the benefits of longer breaths.[57] HRV can increase simply by breathing more deeply. Spire's promptings help with intentional breathing. Studies have been conducted on the differences between intentional breathing and spiritual practices associated with breathing. Spiritual practices completed in tandem with the Spire device could prove beneficial as they should work to keep the breath steady while performing the practice. The constant feedback of the device might help in building habits that align with generative breathing and a perpetual spiritual state.

Mobile apps

There is a steadily growing reserve of mobile applications with spiritual value. Headspace and Calm are apps that teach users how to meditate through progressive stages. Headspace has meditations for just about any occasion. Calm promotes a daily regimen. Each application has a subscription service that grants users more access to content. Liberate Meditation is a meditation app that is specifically for Black, Brown and Indigenous folks. It's goal is to connect the benefits of meditation practices to the needs of Black, Brown, and Indigenous peoples. There are applications that help with yoga and fitness. There are also an array of free meditation and spirituality apps that time breathing, and provide affirmations from various traditions or inspirational quotes.

The benefits of meditation and breathing have been presented along with their neurological benefits which I have already explored. Intentionality and awareness are key components to spirituality that could be augmented through technology. A spirituality app that takes the wisdom of meditation or other spiritual practices such as breathing or compassion, and combines them with modalities that help individuals cultivate their intentionality and spiritual awareness through notifications or games, would further regiment the augmentation of spirituality in a palatable and almost subliminal manner. A technologically inspired intention that breeds greater awareness of spiritual practices and sacred entities has the potential to create and maintain perpetual states of grounded spiritual dispositions, and these spiritual dispositions may be primed to fight for freedom.

Electrical stimulation

There is a new category of wearables that make transcranial electrostimulation (TES) suitable for mass consumption. TES has been used previously to effect behavior stages by the stimulation of the brain through the skull—originating from methods such as electrosleep (ES), electroshock therapy (ECT), and transcerebral electrotherapy (TCET).[58] These wearables use electrical stimulation via alternating current (AC) to help wearers achieve calm, greater energy, focus, or muscle activation. Thync is a set of strips that users place on their head and neck. It releases low-level electricity to help wearers attenuate stress. Halo, another form of TES, is a wearable device built like a set of headphones. It sends electrical currents through the skull before workouts to serve as a neuromuscular primer, intended to increase muscle activation during physical training.[59] The perception of mood and its impact on bodily states is important. Technologies that help attenuate mood can be useful in the moment-to-moment changes in the environment, and the need to navigate through them quickly. Muscle activation can prove helpful in physical training as recruiting more muscle fibers triggers muscle growth, strength gains, hypertrophy, and increased power output.[60] The physical benefits associated with strength training also accompany mood enhancement. A spirituality of looking to dismantle oppressive power structures in the physical world asks its practitioners to be physically fit, so that technology could assist in that work. Although these methodologies are based off of previous research, further examinations of their benefits and outcomes are needed for a more definitive stance on their usefulness.

Pharmaceuticals + Supplements

Drugs are an easy and effective way to change neurochemistry. Neurochemistry is responsible for mood. It also influences perception. Persons with elevated levels of dopamine are at risk to experience manic states. In contrast, persons with decreased levels of dopamine over time are at risk for depression.[61] Nootropics are drugs that claim to pass the blood brain barrier (BBB) and affect the brain, but little work has been conducted to prove that. However, drugs such as +3, 4-methylenedioxymethamphetamine (MDMA), or ecstasy, disrupts BBB integrity.[62] For instance, ecstasy's neurological effects strongly influence perceptions of close relationality, empathy, and bliss. Psilocybin is another psychedelic drug that mimics mystical states. Selective Serotonin Reuptake Inhibitors (SSRIs) and noradrenaline reuptake inhibitors (NRIs) both work on different brain regions to attenuate emotional responses and perceptions of self among users. SSRIs work to decrease amygdala-hippocampal, frontal, and medial activity. NRIs decrease frontal and medial activity. SSRIs suggest decreased emotional reactivity (negative/maladaptive reactivity) while NRIs suggest intentional emotional regulation.[63]

Creatine is a prominent amino acid in the bioenergetic cycle.[64] It is most prominent in skeletal muscle fibers and in the brain. Creatine not only works to increase the intensity of muscle contractions, but it also works in the brain to increase concentration and protect neurons. Testosterone works for muscular development. It can also play a role in assertiveness and outgoing personality types. As described earlier oxytocin is correlative to in-group bonding and protection from out-group association. These pharmaceutically derived proteins, transmitters, and hormone influencing agents can be used to augment spiritual dispositions psychologically, somatically, or neurophysiologically based on their intended use. For instance, someone could use psilocybin in conjunction with testosterone or creatine for added concentration while operating from a perceived spiritual state. The employment of pharmaceuticals to achieve a spiritually induced state might border on the line of spiritual fabrication; however, if spiritual states present themselves as neurophysiological states, how can we limit/control the way that these states are attained? Abuse of chemical compounds is a legitimate concern, but if pharmaceuticals are tied to a bioengineered implant or prosthesis (i.e., a constant morphine drip connected to a mechanized arm to mitigate the pain of its attachment post surgery), then it may be a more readily accepted form of disbursement. Realistically, Black folks would first have to begin accepting transhumanist ideas of existence (personal embodiment as biotechnology), along with the possibility of mechanized and surgically connected limbs.[65]

The internet of things (IoT)

IoT brings all the aforementioned methods together—clinical and consumer. The IoT allows communication and synchronization between objects. Communication through near field communication (NFC) between objects allows for pertinent information from one device, such as the fMRI or ECG, to be sent to another device, like a wearable HR monitor for instance.[66] The connection between these devices could potentially infer what regional activation occurs during particular HR cycles closely correlated to similar HRV intervals. This may seem far-fetched with the current state of technology, but the IoT will eventually be able to perform with greater synchrony than the described example. Within this line of logic, the IoT should be able to connect all pertinent spiritual information logged on other devices that aid in physiological regulation or intentionality and awareness, and lead to a seamlessly integrated way of being. The IoT will likely be connected to the body through implants or nanotechnology. It may potentially be the portal that leads transhumanist existence to a technorganic way of life, where the line between biology and technology completely blur. The IoT could prove helpful in augmenting spirituality as it monitors, logs, correlates, and helps to reproduce spiritual states through a greater understanding of correlative physiology. An example could be of an implant which releases dopamine whenever there is a prolonged decrease of dopamine in its presence. Every release is accounted for on an individual's mobile device via blockchain technology. Simultaneous with the individual's dopamine release is a prompt from their phone or wrist-based monitor to begin a short breathing practice where they intentionally focus on an aspect of their sacred entity. When the person engages in the practice, and the monitor notices a change in physiology, the blockchain ledger could monitor the correlative action to its preceding prompt. Even if there is no physiological change the user could tap their device signaling the completion of the practice, which is also logged in their mobile device. The HR, over the course of the time between the reactionary release of dopamine and the completion of the practice, can be calculated, and an algorithm would be used to determine meaning of the data along with the effectiveness of the events that took place. The data would be stored for later viewing of the person who would like to further their intentional spiritual disposition over time. Security of information would be an essential component of the IoT, which is why blockchain might be a useful technology for monitoring and securing sensitive spiritual data.[67] Still, much discussion has gone into the topic of personal data security given the level of access to personal information that the IoT needs to function successfully. Security options and greater security overall might be necessary for people to feel comfortable with information of this nature being logged continuously.

Conclusion

The manner in which emergent technology arrives presents vast opportunities. But for this Black transhumanist theology, two opportunities seem to be of the utmost importance. Both opportunities come in the form of questions. The first is how might we imagine the utilization of these emergent technologies, some of which are in their conceptual stages, in a way that augments Black spirituality? The second, how might these technologies be used to augment Black biotechnology? I think the answer to these questions has more to do with acceptance of Alexander Weheliye's description of Blackness as possibility.[68] It functions as potent matter with infinite possibility. This infinite potential is seen through the manner in which individuals and communities of Blackness are willing to engage in technology as a spiritual exercise. This spiritual exercise would include the movement into a transhumanist nominal designation. It would require an acceptance of the responsibility to become stakeholders in the inevitable technologically mediated future. Finally, it would necessitate a willingness to wrestle with the historically positive and negative potentialities associated with technological advancement. In returning to the logic that was introduced in Chapter 2, if the only way out is through we must be willing to explore all options of what "through" means. Even if that suggests we operate within a spirituality of revolt.

5

Black Transhumanism as Revolt Spirituality

This entire project has led to this point. So far, we have engaged in four distinct explorations: (1) a trek into Black transhumanism; (2) a theoretical outline of panpsychic vitalism which is intended to ground Black bodies as biotechnology; (3) a reflection upon the potential effects of Black spiritual practices on Black biotechnology as a preemptive means to combat a racist white supremacist world; and (4) an exploration of the ways that Black folks are already transhuman, which imagines the potential for emergent technology to interact with Black biotechnology. This chapter will attempt to bring all of these together through the underlying idea that in order for Black folks to materialize liberating realities it is imperative that Black folks operate from a disposition that I call the spirituality of revolt. This chapter will begin with an exploration of the spirituality of revolt. Then it will imagine two futures: a Black transhuman dystopia and an illustration of Black transhuman liberation.

Revolt spirituality

The spirituality of revolt is embodied by nonconformity, rebellion to indoctrination of docility in all forms, and the insistence of absolute justice. It is dependent upon the action of transhumans for the liberation of transhumans. In the case of Blackness, it is dependent on the actions of Black biotech for the liberation of Black biotech. It does not look to God, or the hills, for help. The spirituality of revolt becomes a spiritual disposition originating from individual and communal remembrance. Biotechnology remembers. It combines a recollection of historical pain and ancestral histories. It assesses the limitations of historical actions as it imagines liberative possibilities. It knows that liberation will not come from a God who is somewhere else. God is us. We are . . . incarnate with life itself. Revolt spirituality results in a posthuman spawn that acknowledges the convergence of spiritualities, actions, and complexities toward the goal of freedom. It recognizes the potential for teaming up with others in the fight for freedom and acknowledges historical alliances demonstrated by Bacon's Rebellion, the Populist Party, and the Poor People's Campaign. However, based on the fragility of those alliances, it takes seriously the belief that the action of Black biotechnology is key to Black freedom. Realistically, it realizes the fragility of organizing actions that are intended to topple power structures (think COINTELPRO or the betrayal of Denmark Vesey). And so, it employs a mixture of skepticism, foresight, and strategy. It considers technological trends and imagines synchronistic and projective measures to work with while imagining unforeseen tech to fit its own needs. Imagine it as the merger of Black biotech, spirituality, and technology as a means to embody (through the totality of action and thought) the directed evolution of Black biotech, Black spirituality, and Black life, for the freedom of Black folks from organisms of oppression.

Organisms of oppression

An organism of oppression can be seen as an extension of the Joe Feagin's system of oppression. Oppression is multivariate. On top of that it contains its own set of subsystems which appear in a "material, social, and ideological reality that is well-imbedded in . . . institutions."[1] Much like the biotechnology of people, organisms of oppression have many parts, which, together, allow for oppression to emerge. Viewing oppression as an organism accepts oppression as dynamic and fluid, structured and alive.[2] While oppression functions in many realms, it originates from an epistemic of domination. Domination is not something novel to recent colonial expeditions. Oppression is cybernetic (in its capacity to operate metaphysically) and biological (in its capacity to be embodied). In this case it is a metabiological organism. Even more so, it would function as a meta-biotechnology. It precedes biology (biotech), yet informs biology's movement. In doing so, it simultaneously ensures the preservation and quality of life; of itself and the biotechnology it embodies. Thus, as an organism, it would follow that oppression is a technology unto itself, committed to defending its existence.

Sylvia Wynter warns of the sinister qualities of metaphors involving simpler organisms in "The Autopoietic Turn."[3] Here, she highlights Thomas Nagel's 1974 essay "What it is like to be a bat" to analyze notions of sentience and barriers of entry into that category, which have been constructed by Western thinkers.

For Nagel, the only way something might have sentience is for there to be an account of what it is like to be that thing. Wynter goes onto say that questions of sentience have been constructed to maintain notions of stratification in societies (human, subhuman, nonhuman, savage, animal, nonhuman animal, etc.). In this regard sentience has been determined through a human-centered lens. While Wynter suggests that no one may be able to construct an objective phenomenology of experience itself, her stance still stems from someone who identifies as human, although, more in line with Fanon's notion of "the new human." Regardless of Fanon's potentially transhuman assertion this might still be considered an anthropomorphizing of oppression. Doing so would place qualities congruent with the perspectives of people onto oppression. While we may not be able to assert what it is like to be "oppression" there is something like what it means to be oppressed or to oppress others. In this way, as a meta-biotechnology oppression becomes experienced as a lens that colors one's experience. But it raises questions regarding the "goodness" of those who take up the meta-biotech of oppression. This highlights the potential separation of oppression as an apparatus that biotech "puts on" to express that which is "put on." But what about the dynamic and lively qualities that oppression possesses apart from the biotechnology needed to carry out its goals? This speaks to the vital components of cybernetic epistemologies. Ideas themselves come equipped with their own lives/vitality—the logical ends of their existence. So, when someone puts on the technology of a particular meta-biotechnology, such as oppression, they might not consider themselves as separate from the logic that results from embodying it (think about the inability of certain privileged folks to recognize their participation in certain organisms of oppression). Technologically speaking, this lack of separation might be understood as a halting problem. In this case the lack of separation might lead to an infinite loop where oppression becomes the overarching viewpoint of the biotechnology it is attached to. But, if oppression is equipped with its own vitalistic components, and, vitality is the closest conceptual configuration to God, that which is beyond the self (the sacred) then what does it mean that oppression has vitality (sacred worth)? Does the sacred nature of vitality justify the existence of oppression? Historically, the assumption has been that oppression, in and of itself, is bad or something to be opposed. But, in the question regarding the value of oppression I would like to echo Calvin Warren.[4] Inquiring about the existential worth of oppression might stand as an example of Fred Moten's "unasked question" meeting Hortense Spillers's notion of the "abandoned site of inquiry," in liberative discourse.[5] So, I ask, is oppression good?

I raise the question of oppression's "goodness"/"worth" in an attempt to parallel it's "worth" with the idea that anything that exists has vitalistic worth (having originated from the sacred), and things that possess this worth are good. Now, this can be taken in two directions. The first would be an account of some thing's moral goodness, that is, whether it can be held accountable for its ability to act in the environment. The second would be an account of some thing's existential worth. The first raises questions of whether oppression, as a meta-biotech, can ever be held responsible for the mobilization of its ideological principles since it is a technology which requires a body to enact its infrastructure. Now, the answer is yes and no. On the one hand a meta-biotechnology can be held accountable for its ability to act if it is placed in a body which a meta-biotech commands on its own. An example of this would be an artificial intelligence capable of overwriting its initial code to fit its current temporality. Both Facebook and Google have had instances where their AI did not perform according to its initial programming. In 2017, Facebook worked on an artificial intelligence that began to change the language it used to communicate with itself. The new language it created was determined to be more efficient for the AI than for people. This suggested a level of agency that was not initially programmed into it.[6] It was subsequently shut down. An AI built from Google's DeepMind project learned that cooperation provided the best chances of survival in a game scenario. As a result, its AI began to demonstrate violent and strategic behavior.[7] In these instances, oppression as a meta-biotech might be held accountable for its ability to move and manipulate the environment. Some might argue that digital embodiment in this way is still not a body, and meta-biotech maintains its immateriality. But if digital embodiment is accepted as biotech possessed by a meta-biotech (when its intention is solely created to carry out the framework which extends from a particular meta-biotech), its materiality would only count for a narrow AI.[8] More general AI would have to encompass more meta-biotechnology (in the case of cognitive faculties/lenses), so in that instance the more lenses/wider the cognitive capacity of an entity the less a meta-biotech can function on its own. But in the case where oppression functions only as a lens through which one views the world, the weight of decision-making falls to the biotechnological actor. So, we move to option two. What if the existence of oppression is a good thing?

Since oppression exists, then, we must consider why it exists. This does not necessitate an inquiry into its utility. But there may be something to be gleaned from reflecting on the purpose of its existence. Are the harsh conditions that arise from oppressive situations meant to provide one with a reason to search for the sacred? If oppression's existence supposes vitalistic worth, then, does that mean it is supposed to *be*? Additionally, if it is not just some perversion of the beloved community then would that help to make sense of the material world's "supposed" natural inclination toward expressions of dominance in sociality?[9] I recognize that decolonial scholarship looks unfavorably on conjectures steeped in empirical mythos that reinforce dominance as opposed to equity. But if Black scholars (in particular) continue to pretend that oppression is inherently bad (after being historically situated as the recipients of its manifestation in the West) then we may not gain a greater understanding of it as a meta-biotechnology. Oppression is often classified as something dark and to be avoided.[10] The proposed relationship between darkness and Blackness has come to evoke a sense of innate sub-humanity/monstrosity as an implicit reaction to the latter. The cultivated implications of the connection between darkness, Blackness, and oppression might explicate any unwillingness to traverse into the dimly lit tunnels that house the capacity to reveal whether oppression possesses liberative potential. Still, if vitality justifies oppression through existence, then, again, what is its purpose? Can we say that the prevalence of oppression we have witnessed throughout history might qualify oppression as a natural element of physical existence? Or, might that undue thinking that places oppression as some exilable entity whose presence is a nuisance to our existence? This nuisance might be what stands as the barrier between our imagined existence and the one we have now.

Viewing oppression as the barrier to a peaceable world is an illogical stance that does not take into consideration the role that oppression plays in notions of what is peaceable. It may seem like a conjecture that posits dominance as the norm of the social realm, a descendent of Darwinian intellectual lineage. But this critique is a distinct privilege of people who are oppressed, who have fallen to the lower rungs of that environment. Even more so, it is a privilege of theological thinking. It posits that another world is possible, and, as that may be the case, it does so behind the assumption that the variables which situate one's placement in the social ladder do not allow for options outside of theorizing or democratic participation. The arc of history has shown that these efforts are fruitless in providing the terms for liberation *qua* Black liberation. Calvin Warren agrees,

> Black ~~being~~ begins to get over the human and its humanism fantasies. We've tried everything: from marches, to masochistic citizenship (giving our bodies to the state to brutalize in hopes of evoking sympathy and empathy from humans), to exceptional citizenship and respectability, to protest and armed conflict;

> in the end, either we will continue this degrading quest for human rights and incorporation or we will take a leap of faith, as Kierkegaard might say, and reject the terms through which we organize our existence.[11]

But it remains, the ease through which individuals who openly function from a place of social dominance allow for oppression, as a meta-biotech, to evolve. Oppression's evolution is closely tied to the cognitive structures it aligns itself with. This has nothing to do with stratifying people by their choice to participate in dominance. It is the opposite. People enter into stratification based on their willingness to peer through oppression-based meta-biotechnology. So, as oppression is attached to individuals, communities, and societies, it evolves based on the factors in said contexts and the bodies it is attached to. So that it might stay alive. It's kind of like Marvel's *Venom*.[12] Oppression can be thought of as a symbiote, a meta-biotech that primarily functions through the biotechnology it inhabits. The determining factor indicating whether one is inhabited by oppression stems from one's behavior. If one is inhabited by oppression then they would have oppressive thoughts which lead to oppressive actions. This might implicate everyone. Oppressive acts are oppression's most problematic quality, because of their reverberating impact in materiality. Mostly plainly, oppressive acts are violent acts.

Again, on violence

Again, on violence is a nod to Frantz Fanon's chapter, "Concerning Violence" in *Wretched of the Earth*. In that chapter he refers to violence as a natural force.[13] However, in doing so, he reaches beyond the merely empirical formulation; force equals mass times acceleration ($F = m \times a$). He is describing a particular mode of existence that is capable of imposing itself upon the natural environment through various derivations. Yet more specifically, he is talking about the language of force. Its message is conveyed through observation and sound. It is observable through socially imposed boundaries of existence. It is communicated through sound: inflections, verbalizations, vibrations, etc. The combined communicative capacity of these properties results in a shared consciousness that establishes force as the most appropriate problem-solving tool. For Fanon, those who occupy spaces that are nearest to colonial power speak the language of force in its purest form—power stemming from (perceived) places of power. He also very clearly states that the way to challenge, disrupt, or topple the said relationship of domination is through an acceptance of "absolute violence." While governing authorities speak the pure language of violence, this same language for the "native . . . is not simply informatory, but also operative." This suggests that the recipients of violent oppression may successfully appropriate the wisdom of violence in order to shift the state of the political domain.[14] He engages the logic of the colonized as it calculates the viability of the violent option (given a lack of nutrition, resources, technology, etc.) and infers that violence is the natural response regardless of disproportionate disadvantages, because it somehow manages to emanate from the internality of the dispossessed. Conditions do not remove the inclination toward violence. Conditions only work to direct it, even if that direction is to squelch it. Fanon goes on to outline various scenarios of colonial and anti-colonial violence. Within this dialectic he asks, "What is the nature of this violence?"[15] And so, I ask the same question.

If we accept what Fanon provides as a definition, then, violence is the language of force—at its core. But with that logic what is not violent? There is extensive work that covers the primary realms of violence, which are psychological violence and physical violence.[16] From these two realms stem explorations of contextual violence: ontological, epistemic, domestic, sexual, structural, biochemical, gender, religious, technological, colonial, etc. This would support claims that violence extends into many, if not all realms. While some have argued that the abuse of these "realms" would be classified as violence, I would submit that the natural inclination of these realms is violence. I would go onto say that within each realm lies a social hierarchy, of sorts. And even in the most congenial, or loving, spaces/realms hierarchies are present. I agree with those who precede me in submitting that hierarchies are violence.[17] Any shift in hierarchical movement might be classified as violent, and even the balance it takes to make said shifts can be thought of as violent. Let's try another example. Movement of one's physical body can be considered violent. The use of muscles, tendons, fibers, joints, and organs places wear on them that requires repair. The fact that something needs repairing or replenishing suggests that it needs to be cared for. Needing care suggests trauma. Trauma is violence. Maintaining one's existence, aside from interacting with anyone else is violent. I'll say it more plainly. Existence is violent. We cannot escape violence, nor can we escape the imposition of dominance that it stems from. Theologically, one might wonder about the relationship God has with God's people. Can the stipulations God places upon people be oppressive? Furthermore, does a relationship with God create an infinitely disproportionate power structure/dynamic? If so, how is that not violent? What about God's unwillingness to reveal God's self to God's creation (i.e., the creation stories of Abrahamic faiths)? If one were to argue that God's love is what prevents this relationship from falling into oppressive violence, then why is God placing boundaries for engagement with God? Is God afraid of people? And, in theologically grounded situations where God blesses and curses, does that not function as a form of divine manipulation and will bending? Is the threat of punishment from a divine figure a means of violence? I think quite simply the answer to these last few questions is yes. If one's relationship with God is grounded similarly, then it can be considered an oppressive relationship. Even if one does not situate themselves as being in relationship with God, any act of self-discovery implicates the lifelong journey to know thyself. The psychological barriers we create that manifest with or without our awareness prohibit us from fully knowing who we are.[18] Similar to God our internal selves present a gulf, dividing our current selves from the one we seek to know. The barriers we erect to keep ourselves from ourselves might be considered as acts of violence against ourselves (if we count knowledge of self as something integral to one's path on earth). It appears to me that we cannot physically move, think, or be in any social environment (not even with God) and avoid violence.

An acceptance of violence as the offspring of the meta-biotechnology of oppression reinserts it into the liberative conversation as a viable and natural option. Here, I return to the vitality/logic of a meta-biotechnology. This becomes important when deciding which meta-biotechnology to embody. As alluded to previously, the vitality of a particular meta-biotech can be found in the logical arc of its use. At this point I move to question ethics that emphasize love or peace (as meta-biotech) over against the violence of oppression-based meta-biotech. When a liberative actor employs a meta-biotechnology of love or peace with the goal of liberation or absolute freedom the logical end does not seem to lead to liberation. Ideally, and this is based on a best case scenario, when employing an ethic of "love over all" the entire world is thought to eventually choose to embody the ethic of love that will usher in a new era of existence. But major historical movements have demonstrated that this ethic does not lead to its proposed ends. Furthermore, it might be argued that the progress these movements have provided had much credit to give to those who posed a threat of violence: The Nation of Islam, The Deacons of Defense, and The Black Panthers—as prominent examples. Similarly, the logic of violence as an option could be argued against as well. A considerable amount of violent insurrections have been squelched throughout history. It is no secret that they often end in far-reaching blowback. I do wonder if there might be any difference between active violence (offensive/pre-emotive) versus defensive violence (retaliatory) At this point one may ask whether there is any merit in any option, so far. In that case the option of assimilation may be explored as well. However, assimilation in the current world climate ultimately reiterates white supremacist proto-normativity. So, that immediately looks like a dead end. Some might say that assimilation practices are important/effective when they assert that change happens over many generations. An example of this thinking is that the United States congress is now more racially and ethnically diverse than it has ever been.[19] White populations are decreasing, and the country is leaning more to the left. But, the problem still remains. If assimilation tactics were to persist, how would you remove white supremacy from the air we breathe when it is just as prevalent as the hydrogen molecule? You might even argue that this book project is an exercise in white supremacy given the logic I employed and the methods I privilege.[20] At this juncture an Afro-pessimist might suggest that no option is beneficial. An Afro-pessimist might have said that from the beginning. They might even say that the anti-Blackness which grounds this country, let alone this world, is not leaving—no matter what happens. Essentially, it does not matter which route we take.[21] I would admit that I follow Afro-pessimism to this end. Theologically, I think that hope is the response to the Afro-pessimist. Here hope emerges once violence is reinserted into the equation. One could suggest that the love/peace ethic inserts hope where violence might fit. Or, that the assimilation ethic inserts hope in the belief that everything will change *in time*. Fanon mentions absolute violence. But I am inclined to think that this absolute violence stems from what he projects as the willingness/commitment to do whatever it takes overcome all obstacles.[22] Malcolm X is heavily quoted as suggesting that one might undergo this endeavor by any means necessary. But according to the logic/vitality of violence everything is violence. If I were to name the qualifiers for choosing a mode of action there would be two: logic and results. However, no one can determine, with certainty, which route might produce the desired results. So, the meta-biotech with the most logic *is* the one that actually topples the system. The question now becomes which route/meta-biotech do you choose?

Let's circle back to revolt spirituality. Given the variable nature of life one cannot determine for others which route to take. The apparatuses of nonviolent love/peace, potentially anti-white supremacist assimilation, or active violence each become wildly acceptable means of engagement. So, I'll reaffirm what was said in Chapter 2. Vitality justifies biotechnology, even meta-biotechnology and its use. Revolt spirituality is an opportunity to live from radical modes of being one's self. Revolt spirituality is a switch in biotechnology, preoutfitted with existing overlays (programming) that make being one's self the most generative option, regardless of the outcome. This is not being yourself as in just randomly doing what you want. This is a call to demand the most of what makes you you while engaging in the absolute violence that dismantles the system. Since being one's self is a mode of violence it becomes an epistemological affront to proto-normative modes of existence. Colonial frameworks work in the binary. Revolt spirituality works in the multivariate. It is an everyday way of pushing against the grain as a way to combat harmful modes of existence that maintain white supremacy. It is a commitment to the expansion of one's self into the very essence of their Blackness (potentiality). It affirms oppression as a viable means to establish and reassert dominance in the social sphere. So, *be* you in the most indignant way. Engage in the violence of being yourself. I think the late Neighborhood Nipsey Hustle (Nip tha Great) might have described Revolt Spirituality the best. Revolt Spirituality is being "disrespectful and arrogant, but who gon' stop us."[23] It signifies a violently antagonistic approach to organisms which seek to subjugate. It's engages in the violent tactics of oppression for the sake of liberation. And its paradox is a statement to its complexity. But that should not discourage from its embodiment.

Historically embodied revolt spirituality

Revolt spirituality requires a consideration of what may be thought as its former embodiments. Nat Turner can be seen as an example of historical revolt spirituality. His vision of fighting spirits that represented what he perceived as an impending apocalypse ignited his plan which culminated in his all-out attempt to overthrow slavery on August 21, 1831. Harriet Tubman's clandestine network was an example of revolt spirituality, as a communal practice. The boldness of Ida B. Wells to risk life and limb through her journalism and through her systematic documentation of the lynchings of Black folks across the United States was another example, too. W. E. B. DuBois's scholarship provided a strategic vision of self-determination which became part of the foundation of decolonial discourse.[24] Bishop Henry McNeal Turner embodied revolt spirituality through his insistence on self-consciousness, which he urged was key to revolution. The legendary punch thrown by Stormé DeLarverie that sparked the Stonewall Riots was another example. So are Octavia Butler's speculative visions, and Assata Shakur's willingness to participate in self-defense. It is important to note that these are not the only examples of revolt spirituality in history. It is also important to note that the Black spirit of revolt requires a "hundred year plan," that simultaneously carries the weight of more than 250 slave revolts (conspired or materialized) during the antebellum period, the cunning wisdom of the Marooners, the defiant fortitude of the Deacons for Defense and Justice, the economic strategy of Robert F. Smith, along with the strategic fire of the Black Panther Party.[25] The necessary coupling of patience and intensity that an intergeneration plan like revolt spirituality requires can be considered an upward apocalypse; accumulating positions of power and physically dismantling systems of inequity. Because before Black revolt spirituality can make itself known, the moving variables need to be accounted for. The wisdom provided by a hindsight view of the civil rights movement informs Black revolt spirituality. Its manifestation cannot afford the loss of its leaders. It also cannot afford to have just any leaders. Most importantly, it cannot wait and act in reply to acts of injustice. Black revolt spirituality must materialize as an intentionally relentless holistically calculated strategic plan that culminates in a spiritual disposition that will accept nothing less than freedom—nothing less than justice.

I think complete and utter freedom has not been attained because the line of freedom is elusive and continues to move. So, while tremendous organizers like Angela Y. Davis, Fannie Lou Hamer, Shaun King, W. E. B. DuBois, Malcolm X, Martin Luther King, Alicia Garza, Patrisse Cullors, Opal Tometi, and Marcus Garvey have been able to rile the people, garnering strong support not only from the Black community but also from people all around the globe, Dick Gregory so rightfully stated, "Civil rights [are] what black folks are given in the U.S. on the installment plan, [of] civil-rights bills. [They are] not to be confused with human rights, which are the dignity, stature, [personhood], respect, and freedom belonging to all people by right of their birth."[26] The stark reality is that dialogue has not brought freedom. Marching has not brought freedom. Speeches have not brought freedom. Legislation has not brought freedom. Riots have not brought freedom. Slave revolts have not brought freedom. Advocating for the humanity of Black folks has not brought freedom.[27] Black folks have historically found themselves contentiously staring at a gaping ravine. Freedom is on the other side, but there is a constant struggle to define what we see and decide on the right action that will get us there.

Black transhuman dystopia

Black transhuman liberation theology recognizes that, socially, the United States is on the cusp of another shift in oppressive structural stratification. In reality it is already happening. The impending technocracy, which is currently taking shape, is mostly white and mostly male. It has the ability to reify socially oppressive structures through automation. Automating oppression adds another level of distance, further separating the benefactors of oppressive privilege from the technological re-enforcement of oppressive hierarchies. These added levels of distance make it easier for the benefactors of oppression to defend their goodness. So, regardless of whether automation leads to a complete social collapse, or not, the gradual reduction of people in the workforce is most likely to have the greatest impact on those from historically marginalized communities. Greater technology will undoubtedly extend the reach of surveillance. Police units, which may evolve into a combination of people, robots, computerized weaponry, facial recognition, emotional and artificial intelligence, will have an even greater potential to fill the prison industrial complex. Those who have been economically displaced due to an automation of the law will never be seen for the vitality which makes them people worthy of compassion or consideration. The racism maintained through biased algorithms might have less chance to persist if Black folks are leading the teams that implement technocratically automated processes.[28] Without Black biotechnology creating tech with Black folks in mind all context will be completely lost in the pursuit of a suspect (in the case of policing). Futuristic modes of law enforcement—automated or otherwise—will continue doing their "jobs" at rapid pace. Those who do not have the extended privileges of humanity, basic income, or basic assets will probably not see the leisure promised by the technocratic elite. So, while technocratic elites present an image of leisure and liberal pursuit (stemming from automation), the embodied remnants of the "Negro Problem" will probably be locked away in high security facilities, enslaved once again, but this time by robots. Although this section is filled with hypothetical dystopian postulation, the history between the United States government and Black biotech does not make this a far-fetched imagination.

Here is the most important thing to remember—God is not coming to liberate. Black transhuman liberation theology assumes that God is not coming to save Black folks from tyranny. There are too many instances in history where God did not intervene on the side of the oppressed—Egypt, Jewish conquest(s), Babylonian conquest(s), Rome, The Ottoman Empire, Persia, the Crusades, Colonialism, genocide (pick one), Antebellum Slavery, the Holocaust, Rwanda, Biko Haram, Libya, Sudan, etc. Now, there may be a significant contingent of Black folks that would attest to the demonstration of God's power in their individual lives. I do not contest that. I too have had countless instances where God has shown up in my life. I would compare these individual instances of

God's demonstrable power to act in the world to events that occur at the quantum level (using physics terminology). On the quantum level, physical anomalies occur that are not easily demonstrable or replicable at the level of perception. Likewise, while God has demonstrated God's ability on the individual level, the individual level is incommensurate to the level of whole societies, cultures, and the trajectory of history. God has not interrupted history on the larger levels that comprise societal relationality. One could argue that the Allied powers were an example of God showing up for a historicized group. Even if I were to go along with that, how many Jewish folks had to die before God could intervene? That still is not an instance of God saving Black folks from a regime. This is not to say God is not capable, or that God is unwilling. This is simply a rethinking of the way that God participates in the material world based on an honest assessment of history. And if that were the case, God has not shown up for the entirety of Black folks. We just "celebrated" 400 years of shitty tyranny in the United States. Anthony Pinn would suggest that the use of the term "God" is not even necessary in the conversation of liberation.[29] Some folks who embody the spirit of revolt may not even believe in God. That is perfectly fine. Let us remember that this theistic transhumanist approach accepts multiple iterations of belief. It affirms other terms for the word "God." The term "God," "Spirit," "Self," that which is beyond the Self, etc., is useful in this proposition because although the action of people are responsible for cultivating the condition of people, something has to be the thrust for biotechnological action. Here we reinsert the vitalistic qualities of the body's electrochemistry as the causal agent within human biotechnology. Theologically, there has to be a causal agent, or that which infuses action. Historically this causal agent has been understood through classical designations (God, Spirit, universe, community, vitality, etc.). For the sake of Black transhuman liberation theology, these blanket terms are classified as sacred entities. In this theistic transhumanism grounded in biology sacred entities, or the thrust behind embodied action, are defined as the electrochemical response of the body. Again, the electrochemical response of the body is the impetus for thought, action, intention, etc. In order for this vitalistic assertion to be maintained we must remember these entities are present through electrochemistry while enlivening biological systems. The panpsychic animism of this theistic transhumanism would still allow for these entities to manifest in other ways to maintain the integrity of nonbiological systems as they fight against entropy. Thus, as the bearer of various names which fall under the vitalist umbrella, sacred entities give space for bodies to be cultivated through social relationships and personal perception. So, even though the electrochemical response is a secondary action, it is entangled with vitality, previous personal responses, and experiences. The Spirit/God/that which is beyond the Self/any other sacred entity creates space for personally cultivated iterations of embodiment over time. This cultivation is based on an individual or community's experience with the combination of their sacred entity and the world—even if the self is their sacred entity. This is in recognition of the material aspects of divinity in nature and in biology. They are inseparable because sacred entities are not someone else or somewhere else.[30] They become incarnate within physical systems, and in this case Black biotechnological systems. Conceptualizing Black folks as biotechnology proposes that vitality (functioning as the body's electrical impulse) situates heart rhythms, sets neurons and muscles into motion, and initiates the body's biochemistry, while creating individual and communally transposed emotionality—the spiritual disposition. Black transhuman liberation theology claims that vitality is the indeterministic causal agent. Life is indeterminately vital. More plainly, Black life is vital. And for Black transhuman liberation theology, the origin of the vitalistic spring which creates space for the electrical pulse grounding Black biotechnological life is not a major concern. Because for this theology, what someone does with their life is much more important than where that life originates. However, some might argue that life's origin matters because people may want to pay homage to the giver of life. To that I would say that due to concepts of relationality, it may be best to live in a way that brings honor to those who are directly responsible for your life—such as parents and grandparents. This would also speak to one's identity (community, ethnicity, gender, etc.). Some might even suggest that a declaration of futility regarding the need to search for causality is problematic. However, I would suggest that the need for a declaration of causality is an attempt to assert control over questions whose answers are not readily available. More specifically, I would propose that whatever belief system someone chooses is constructed according to the parameters of satisfaction that coincide with their cognitive operators which situate reality for them. Essentially, belief systems represent the collection of internally cohesive intellectual systematics that help one self-identify in the midst of a complex and often unintelligible/ineffable world.

So, as the causal agent, the body's electricity becomes the materialization of the vital presence giving life to all on earth. As alluded to earlier, electricity bound to Black biotechnology carries transmitters and hormones. It transports feelings and thoughts that influence perception and subsequent action. The biological undercurrent of electricity is the primary characteristic of the central nervous system (CNS), whether it is fully functioning or not. Black transhuman liberation theology understands the influential capacity of electricity in the body and the influence of spirituality on its electrical rhythms. This theology works to actively merge Black spirituality and technology for the enhanced synchrony of Black biotechnology—as it undertakes its freedom work. It asserts that biological synchrony is a necessary component for cultivating one's spiritual disposition. Black transhuman liberation theology also recognizes the importance of intentionality in the task of sustaining the spiritual disposition of biotechnological capital while undertaking the greater work of actualizing freedom.

The proliferation of access to information, education, and technology places the onus on Black folks to begin participating in the current cohort already shaping new technologically grounded governing bodies. Black transhuman liberation theology advocates for Black folks to partake in the technocratic formation of the future. If Black folks refuse to utilize Black biotechnology to learn the necessary prerequisites for participation in the technological accrual of power then Black folks will continue to be relegated to a constant status of fear, survival, and struggle. Black transhuman liberation theology takes seriously the genetic capacity of biotechnological embodiment to learn, adapt, create, and enhance both itself and the environment it inhabits. It employs spirituality to begin unlocking generative epigenetics inherent with Black collective memory which recalls ancestral capacities to innovate within STEM fields.[31] Drawing from extensive ancestral lines of STEM-based innovation, Black transhuman liberation theology encourages Black biotechnology to create technological advancements and organizations capable of employing other Black bodies. This tactic is meant to cultivate dignity while accumulating power. Black transhuman liberation theology calls upon scientific wisdom to generatively influence the genetic regulation of spiritual embodiment, which primes the body for the work of liberation.

I submit that the Black theology's history of deconstructing power/colonial systems is closely correlated to the inability of Black folks to assert their will against preexisting power structures. Challenging harmful theologies while asserting theological self-worth has been a radical way to face oppressive structures. The act of rethinking and redefining the world, which begins with an engagement of overarching epistemologies, is a valid approach to liberation. Black transhuman liberation theology owes its framework to the work of Black and decolonial scholars who precede its construction. However, the act of theoretically deconstructing power also falls within the realm of revolts, marches, and other attempts to engage oppression. I think if these creative and artistic ways of expression were actually capable of freedom making, then theological and sociological conversations would carry a different tenor.

History has shown time and again that radical acts of disobedience, nonviolent or violent, have very rarely created the kind of change that oppressed and marginalized people really want. Over the course of history, freedom has only come to oppressed peoples on the backs of violent resistance. The American Revolution, the French Revolution, and the Haitian Revolution are all examples in recent history where people were able to free themselves. Yet, two of these three revolutions are celebrated and viewed in the light of humanity and civility. The Haitian Revolution is demonized and vilified, evidenced by the manner in which other countries conduct business with Haiti, the threats of aggression made against it (i.e., the US occupation), and through the international sanctions it has received.[32] Haiti is ostracized because it burned its bridge to whiteness—its bridge to humanity.

Nevertheless, with the multitude of theoretical deconstructions of power, there are not many theories that reflect on ways for the oppressed to procure real power. This "real power" that I reference refers to the concrete political, economic, and social power that allows for consequential decision-making. "Power" is a difficult term to wrestle with. Since the oppressed are primarily the actors of theoretical deconstruction, power is mainly presented as an evil, and many theorize to empower the oppressed, which has a very different end.[33] Empowerment and power are not the same. Black transhuman liberation theology theorizes ways for the oppressed to secure power in this life. Critical theorists suggest that power acquisition only reproduces power structures, calcifying structurally oppressive components that uphold current forms of power.[34] The truth of this statement has been used within religious circles to justify letting God handle the situation. But since God is not coming to help, Black folks must assume the active role of freeing themselves through concrete means that are spiritually grounded. Even if there were a theology juxtaposing God's ability to help while maintaining the importance of embodied action, the dependence upon embodied action to predicate God's help presupposes some imaginative position. This imaginative position, or checkpoint, is one that would suddenly unlock God's helpfulness. The obscure nature surrounding the timing of when God might enter history to act on behalf of the oppressed is an extension of theological thought that insists upon the immaculate nature of the hereafter. It is also too reminiscent of the process by which justice and liberty are dispersed to Black folks in America—with an emphasis on waiting and right behavior (all limitations attached to what good humans do). A recognition of the nondeterministic nature of God's life force accounts for the weight of biotechnology to act in every facet of existence. It also provides intellectual congruity for concerns regarding the historical vantage point that does not see God as liberator. Liberation comes through intentional action from people, which is the very foundation of the Black transhumanist liberation theological perspective. Although God shows up in various ways on the individual level, people have to show up at the larger level of complex interpersonal geopolitical power systems.

Black transhuman liberation theology: An illustration

Revolt is revolt. Deconstructing American hierarchies in theory still leaves America intact. Deconstructing American structural hierarchies in reality leaves America in a different space. It could no longer be America. There are two strands of thought when it comes to America:

1. America is not living up to its standards of excellence set out by the founding fathers; or
2. America is working exactly how it was built to work.

Scholars have intensely debated these two strands of thought. However, I tend to subscribe to the second strand. Nevertheless, a successful revolution, one that is the result of revolt, would not leave America intact. America would be something very different. But if the first strand were taken seriously in this equation, a revolt would not only be American, but its result should lead America to a place of deeper authenticity.

So far this chapter has set the stage for a consolidation of ideas. This section considers what the spirituality of revolt might look like in the year 2030. It is a short sketch of a six-hour time frame in the day of a spiritual revolter. The main character is a young man who sees himself as one who combines the world of technology with his spirituality in an individual fight toward the communal freedom of Black folks. It envisions an ideology that understands that his actions will change the way America operates. Before moving forward, I believe it right to explain why I chose a male figure for the main character. Being a man, I did not want to appropriate or project onto someone else's experience. I do not want to assume that I know what it is like to be a Black woman. I have only been a Black baby boy, little boy, teenager, young man, and Black man. So, I will tell this short story from that perspective.

It's 5:32 a.m. This is my usual wake up time: 28 minutes before 6 a.m. The nanobots in my bloodstream gently awaken me. The sensors in my home are alerted to my presence. My holographic SUHD television monitor and the shades on my windows rise with me. The television greets me with the news that I missed while asleep. It recaps my emails, goes over my schedule for the day, and plays my favorite tech podcast "The Future of Everything" all while I complete my morning workout. The news tells the story of "a series of attacks by an unknown source on various individuals who were responsible for killing unarmed Black men and women." There were no traces left at any scene. I get an eerie feeling in the pit of my stomach.

At 6:30 a.m., I make breakfast paying special attention to my ingredients. Then I eat; carefully aware of the flavors in each bite as I ground myself in the present moment. With every breath I take I am intentionally becoming aware that I posses the peace that I will need for the day ahead. By 7:15 a.m., I am on my way to work.

I am the Chief Technical Officer at my firm. We are an all-Black cast of misfits. Displaced by much of the industry in 2022, we banded together and formed a small team with a mission to change the game. Over the past eight years we have worked to give Black people control over how their data is bought and sold, secured several significant defense contracts, patented decentralized surveillance technologies and most importantly we've achieved quantum supremacy. We now employ a workforce of over 350 people.

I arrive to our city office by 8:30 a.m. The intelligent work environment of my lab overlooking the beach synchs with my nanobots as I enter the room. It allows me to continue working right where I left off. The nanobots link my current physiology with the one I embodied in the lab the night before. It's almost like re-establishing the same head space! For this contract we have developed hand weapons without triggers that require fingerprint and neurological signatures. Once synched, only the owner can pick up and fire them. I am presenting the latest versions at our board meeting at 9:45 a.m. I contact my CFO, Audre Stephens through a secure line on our integrated neural devices. She is directing the budget on this project, and I need to make sure we are on the same page. Our meeting begins with five deep breaths . . . in . . . and out . . . then we check in, to see how each of us are doing before starting our discussion. At 9:15 a.m., I discretely send a message to an undisclosed recipient on a quantum encrypted line: "Do we have the lists configured? Are we ready to move?" At 9:30 a.m., I head to the lobby and greet our guests. Hand shakes and smiles all around. I bring them up to the boardroom.

At 9:45 a.m. sharp, I begin the meeting. A few of our guests present some pushback in the meeting. They wonder about the ramifications of using neurological signatures in hand weapons. One asks, "What about culpability? What about biological integrity?" I remind everyone present of the weapons employed by other nations and how they do not sleep in their attempts to catch up with "us". China has just broken the code to multi-dimensional travel. If I am honest, our company has for quite some time, but while we explore these new dimensions we're not willing to present this technology to the government. At 10:45 a.m., I lead everyone up to the helipad. The testing ground is roughly a twenty-minute ride inland. We should arrive around 11:15 a.m. We're going to let them examine the new weapons for themselves. Get a real feel for them. I want everyone to experience how they operate.

We arrive to the testing ground on time. I inform them that our firm has already connected their fingerprints to their respective machines. It took them a few moments to get over their surprise. Just enough time for each weapon to familiarize itself with its user's neuro-signature. At 11:19 a.m., notifications come through to everyone's phone. At least fifty people associated with the unarmed killing of Black men and women have either disappeared or died. More are continuing to be discovered.

The country is in an uproar. I can feel that mass hysteria is creeping up on the brink. But I remind our guests why they are with us, and with arms spread wide I smile and encourage everyone to continue with the testing exercise.

"Don't these fit like a glove?" I say. They all nod and continue.

One says, "It feel like it's an extension of me. An extension of my own mind." *I chuckle.*

At 11:30 a.m., President Obama calls for an emergency press conference. She mourns the lives lost, and vows to bring justice. She then concludes the conference with a call to nonviolence and American unity. At 11:32 a.m., I get back onto my quantum encrypted network and check my messages. The latest one reads, "The crows have come home." That eerie feeling I had this morning is replaced with something else completely.

Fully immersed in the technological

A full immersion in the technological suggests a liberation into technology. This is not freedom through an abandonment of reality. It is freedom that is grounded in the natural world. Black transhuman liberation theology sees liberation as a full immersion into the technological, which is a reinterpretation of nature itself. So, a technologically immersed theology requires equity in the ability to access technology. Full immersion of one particular individual or group of people does not equate to full immersion. Full immersion happens when everyone around the globe can access the technological. This is where Black transhuman liberation extends to the third world and the global south. Access to the technological for Black folks in the North American context is not enough. Access in the North American context implies culpability in the disproportionate mistreatment of persons who are considered cogs and not people in the capitalist machine. The final section of this chapter will break down the illustration of the previous section to demonstrate what it means to be fully immersed, and how it extends to the global society. There will be allusion to parts of the story that went unmentioned above. The point is to provide more depth for the story, while demonstrating the assumptions of full technological immersion.

The Chief Technical Officer, who is the main character of the story, is heavily embedded within the technology industry. Everyone does not need to be part of the tech industry to achieve full immersion in the technological. Black folks who actively participate in the IoT can easily begin to claim a form of full immersion. I highlight the fact that the CTO worked at a tech firm because the tech firm he worked for made steps to negotiate fair wages for the African mineral workers they work with. Their workers have access to the same technology that they help to make. The firm owns the land and the company works the land, which supplies the necessary materials for their technologies. Likewise, his firm has structured deals with the eastern companies that run their factories. They do not employ children. They have air conditioning, fair wages, and safe working conditions. The automation that they helped to usher in creates a sustainable workforce, basic income requirements, and innovation quotas for people of African descent and their communities.

He is an active participant in the IoT. His television wakes up with him. It is triggered by the nanobots in his bloodstream that wakes him. His blinds are connected to his watch. His biorhythms (cardiac) are connected to his nanobots in his bloodstream that detect the release of NE, dopamine, serotonin, oxytocin, etc., and are matched in the cloud that holds his emails, reports his news and favorite podcast while he works out. Because technology has become an active participant in his reality, increasing his quality of life, it works alongside his intentional effort to cultivate his spiritual disposition. Even the messaging line that is guarded by quantum encryption is something that allows for communication with exactly who he wants to with the kind of privacy he needs—the epitome of intentionality!

At work, the care for his own spiritual disposition and the spiritual disposition of those around him is seen in action. He carefully engages his colleague and is mindful of the guests that he hosts while maintaining a connection to the technology he uses. His life requires an intersectional recognition of who he is, who he shares community with, his responses to himself and those with whom he shares community, and his location to the technological components he engages. The entire time he is at work, he has not interrupted his connection to the IoT. His employment of technology, in combination with his own spirituality, helps keep him spiritually grounded as a form of technological immersion. The manner in which he submerges himself into his work suggests a particular positive psychology (flow) or mystical unity (unio mystica) as evidenced in the joy and pride he takes in his work. One can imagine the high level of satisfaction and immersion he feels being on an all-Black team that has unearthed the mysteries of inter-dimensional travel, neurological signature application, and success in a field historically dominated by white males. The amalgam presented in the care he takes for his transhuman approach to life and work illustrates the potential to live in plain sight while practicing a spirituality of revolt.

A full immersion into the technological requires intention. Technology is a tool, regardless of whether it is paired with spirituality or not. As the advancement of people pushes society further along the immersion spectrum into the technological, intentionality and awareness will be necessary to cultivate the spirituality of revolt. Intentionality prepared the main character for the news he heard in the morning and the encrypted messages he sends and receives. Readers do not know whether he was part of the plan that took out the murderers of the unarmed Black men and women or not, but readers do know that he has a plan for something.

Full immersion in the technological is a purposeful commitment of the senses, which opens physiology to all of nature. It requires a desire to ethically engage the business practices and social predicaments that the technological presents through its progressive manifestation. It requires a plan, whether nonviolent or not, to engage injustice in a thoughtful and careful manner. The neurophysiological emphasis of technological immersion is a recognition of the important role individuals play within this liberative transhumanist endeavor. Individuals decide whether to participate. Individuals decide to join certain communities or utilize a particular technological apparatus to enhance their abilities. But, technologically immersed individuals must intentionally cultivate their personal awareness and spirituality which, in Black transhuman liberation theology, can be used to activate and employ an individual's own spirituality of revolt. An emphasis on neurophysiology acknowledges that individual biochemistry results in different responses to, and an attraction toward, specific types of spiritual expression, community involvement, and technological buy in. So, an integral piece to imagining practical demonstrations of full immersion in the technological is personal authenticity. Authenticity in practice leads to the greatest biologically affirmative affect or effectiveness. A recognition of the complex biotechnological representations that result from convergent biocultural influences suggests that there is no "right" way to embody one's revolt spirituality; however, what is needed is an affirmation of the importance of converging subversive perspectives on societal structures. Tactically speaking, when revolt puts all of its hope in one form of rebellion, oppressive structures may recognize its approach and spoil it. But, a multilayered, intersectional strategy, that spans generations and creates space for both violent and nonviolent action, is necessary to allow for various iterations of freedom fighting to converge on the focal point of liberation in order to ultimately dismantle the oppressive structures disproportionately effecting Black folks in the world. Black transhuman liberation theology requires an infiltration of the technocracy. It necessitates an accumulation of its power and a utilization of its arsenal. For Black transhuman liberation theology, these characteristics are essential to actualizing the kind of transhumanism necessary for making an immediate and lasting impact on the desired outcome Black folks seek in the fight to materialize liberating realities.

Glossary of Terms

Directed evolution The intentional method of protein engineering that mimics the process of Darwin's natural selection with a specific goal. Directed evolution has normatively been talked about at the cellular level. However, I will add that any change in a particular direction of progress can be seen as a form of directing the evolutionary process. So, with the use of medicine, supplementation, machinery, virtual reality, and interactive technology there is a neurological/physiological change that takes place through form of practices and education that allow for a directed evolution based on the goal of the technology on the human.

Epigenetic Epigenetics have been theorized as genetic memory. In the case of this project they are also associated with the nonheritable transgenerational genetic traits that pass through families and people of similar cultural and geographic histories. Epigenetics are environmentally influenced genetic traits that are not included in the process of DNA transcription. Yet, are still passed from parent to offspring. In reference to Black people, it can be thought of in terms of a meta-narrative or collective memor(ies). In the example of memory, it is a term that refers to genetic expression that is both the response to and result of implicit memory's association with the inner regions of the brain's relationship to environmental stimuli. Implicit memory is primarily found in the collective operation of the limbic system. The limbic system is comprised of the hippocampus, thalamus, hypothalamus, and amygdala. It is most often associated with the fight or flight response most closely related to one's survival.

Liberation A term used to denote the concrete materialization of dismantled oppressive structures, be they sociological, economic, gendered, sexed, ethical, racial, etc. It has tactile qualities: perceptible through touch, taste, smell, sight, vibes, and hearing. It goes beyond spiritual liberation even though it encompasses spiritual liberation. It is spiritual liberation coupled with a radical awareness and redistribution of power that is embodied through spiritual connectedness with the natural world. It assumes others, and what may be understood as the self are one (inextricably entwined) with the natural world. It dismisses notions that others the natural world.

Material This term refers to the matter of natural science, and the material universe. It is comprised of objects with tactile properties. This is not a reference to prosperity or monetary gain. It is a reference to the physical through that which can be manifested in the natural world.

Neurophysiology A term used to define the interaction of the central nervous system on the electoral and chemical reactions within the brain and body.

Neuroscience A term used when referencing the study of the central nervous system.

Potency The power felt by the spiritual practitioner based on their perceived importance of the practice.

Religious/osity The rigid adherence to a particular set of faith practices as opposed to another.

Satisfaction In terms of spirituality, satisfaction is based on the resulting emotional affect, physiological half-life/biologically sustainable capacity, and intellectual consistency associated with the participation of a particular spiritual practice.

Self I choose to utilize Dick Schwartz's definition of the self. It is the most authentic version of the person—psychologically and spiritually—capable of clear perspective, confidence, compassion, and acceptance.

Soul The totality of the central nervous system and its extended afferent/efferent connections; the living and breathing individual.

Spirit The energy that excites a person or group of people. In terms of a group of people it can be a unifying notion. It can reference God's Spirit, a person (as in an individual's spirit or the human spirit), aśe, ntu, or the human Spirit or external influencing spirits. This term can also be seen as breath. For each context I will sure to explicate how I am using it in that particular instance.

Spiritual The fluid adherence to a set of practices that effect one's spiritual development.

Spiritual liberation Liberation that happens internally. In most cases it is a liberation of the mind regarding a particular aspect of oppression or limitation. It does not always denote a complete internal freedom. One aspect of the self can be liberated while another is still oppressed. It does not denote any physical manifestation other than in an individual's physiology or close circle of affiliation. In Black theology spiritual liberation has become what Black folks have settled for in lieu of liberation. Spiritual liberation is what white slave owners determined to be the freedom of the soul. It does not include material freedom whereby the body and its surroundings reflect the release from oppressive structures. Many Black folks, preachers included, seem to struggle to free their minds from the deleterious effects of Christocentric sociality. It is indicative of the struggle to usurp lasting influences of the legend of Willy Lynch. However, for me it is simply what it is, spiritual. It is internal. It is essential for the path toward liberation, but spiritual liberation is not complete liberation.

Spirituality The felt and unfelt connection one has with God or that which is beyond the self through the physical/perceptible world (seen and unseen). I chose to incorporate the seen and unseen within the bounds of the physical world as a means to introduce the importance of the body's biology to this spiritual proposition. The body, although visible, is the only space that humans experience spirituality. The physical world is the setting that the body interacts with which help to form the basis of any experience. The body's underlying processes (of the brain or heart) are not immediately visible, but do exist. In this instance, spirituality is an inclusive term, even within the context of Blackness. It covers more than Black Christian spirituality in an attempt to discontinue the cycle of reifying an ontology of monolithic Black spiritual experience. So even though this project does focus on Black spirituality in the North American context, it is not limited to one Black Christian experience in the North American context. Furthermore, in terms of Blackness, spirituality cannot be separated from identity. Black identity is commensurate with spirituality. Black scholars have laid out countless examples of how when someone Black acknowledges their spiritual practices it not only denotes what is at the essence of that person's self-identifying nature, but is also a recognition that spirituality is the identity forming and life giving component of the Black personal life.

Technocracy A term used to define the governing of society by the technically elite.

Technorganics The convergent evolution of living organisms and technology at the cellular level.

Transhuman Anyone who uses technology to enhance their physical, psychological, and intellectual ability. Malleable forms of personal physicality and social operation.

Notes

Introduction and Overview

1 Cary Wolfe, *What Is Posthumanism* (Minneapolis: University of Minnesota Press, 2009), xv.

2 Nick Bostrom, "Human Genetic Enhancements: A Transhumanist Perspective," *The Journal of Value Inquiry* 37, no. 4 (2003): 493–506.

3 Alane Daugherty, *From Mindfulness to Heartfulness* (Bloomington, IN: Archway Publishing, 2014), 18.

4 George G. M. James, *Stolen Legacy*, Vol. 1 (Sauk Village, IL: Library of Alexandria, 1954), 131.

5 Victor Anderson, *Beyond Ontological Blackness: An Essay on African American Religious and Cultural Criticism* (New York: Continuum, 1995), 56.

6 "Nomophobia" is the fear of being without a cell phone.

7 Lee Rainie and Barry Wellman, *Networked: The New Social Operating System* (Cambridge, MA: MIT Press, 2012), 12.

8 Black Lives Matter movement (BLM) and Black Twitter are spaces and organizations that utilize social media very heavily for the purpose of raising awareness of various issues that are important to Black and Brown people that often involve oppression. It is important to note that BLM does perform various on the ground efforts and emphasizes the importance of a physical presence. However, the #BLM hashtag has been appropriated and misunderstood as a means of activism that only needs to happen via social media, negating the importance of follow-up actions; David Carr, "Hashtag Activism, and Its Limits," *The New York Times*, 25 (2012); Caitlin Dewey, "# Bringbackourgirls,# Kony2012, and the Complete, Divisive History of 'Hashtag Activism,'" *The Washington Post*, 8 (2014); Sherri Williams, "Digital Defense: Black Feminists Resist Violence with Hashtag Activism," *Feminist Media Studies* 15, no. 2 (2015): 341–44.

9 Herbert Marcuse, *One-Dimensional Man* (Boston, MA: Beacon Press, 1964), 11.

10 Min Chen, Shiwen Mao, and Yunhao Liu, "Big Data: A Survey," *Mobile Networks and Applications* 19, no. 2 (2014): 171–209.

11 Zeynep Tufekci, "Engineering the Public: Big Data, Surveillance and Computational Politics," *First Monday* 19, no. 7 (2014). doi: http://dx.doi.org/10.5210/fm.v19i7.4901.

12 Jane E. Fountain, "On the Effects of e-Government on Political Institutions," in *Routledge Handbook of Science, Technology, and Society*, eds. Daniel Lee Kleinman and Kelly Moore (NewYork: Routledge, 2014), 471.

13 Path dependence is essentially the use of long-term implementation to test and determine the accuracy of a newly implemented governmental policy. It justifies the keeping of policies and procedures in place for its need to determine longitudinal efficiency, often overlooking initial setback, but it does applaud early stage success. Fountain, "On the Effects of e-Government," 473.

14 A theoretical sketch of the added layers of becoming digital ontologies might assume this structure: Environment (where everything happens), People (that are governed and live in the environment), Data (contains raw info from real-world interactions between people, other people, and the environment), Technical specialists (who process data), Democratic Process (If this is the structure of the government, it includes the legislative process—legislators, voters, etc.), Programmers (writers of code), Hardware (components that are run on previously written software that allow for the creation of new code to write new software geared toward legislation), Storage (multiple hardware units that together maintain the relationship between data, hardware, and software for the continual running of the system), Code (in the specific case of digital ontologies, is the logic used to run contingency models. It is based on the processes created by technical specialists; however programmers can also serve as technical specialists through the structure of a particular programming language to create a functioning software program used to determine outcomes and the implementation of laws, Media (websites, phones, digital applications, etc.), and People. It could be argued that these structures already mimic previous governmental modes of layering (legislative process, paper, storage, people), but the added layering of technology, technical experts, and technologically mediated storage units (which can be backed up in a cloud) make it an incredibly more buttressed system. This is admittedly a very linear approach. It does not begin to include the added variables of the inverse parallel process of the order I have created, or most importantly the invariable way that these layers can be by passed. For example, the communality of personhood needs to be accounted for as to how someone who is governed can either influence another person in the order or have the ability to become one of those role or not based on socioeconomic status or other marginalizations (i.e., legislator, technical specialist of programmer).

15 Suzanne Mettler and Joe Soss, "The Consequences of Public Policy for Democratic Citizenship: Bridging Policy Studies and Mass Politics," *Perspectives on Politics* 2, no. 1 (2004): 60.

16 Michelle Alexander, *The New Jim Crow: Mass Incarceration in the Age of Colorblindness* (New York: The New Press, 2012), 20–57; 173–208.

17 Kelly Brown Douglas, *Black Bodies and the Black Church: A Blues Slant* (New York: Palgrave MacMillan, 2012), xv.
18 Anthony B. Pinn, ed. *Black Religion and Aesthetics: Religious Thought and Life in Africa and the African Diaspora* (New York: Palgrave MacMillan, 2009), 1.
19 "Statement by the National Committee of Negro Churchmen, July 31, 1966," *New York Times*, July 31, 1966; reprinted in James H. Cone and Gayraud Wilmore, *Black Theology: A Documentary History, Vol. 1: 1966–1979*, 2nd ed., rev. (Maryknoll, NY: Orbis, 1993), 19.
20 James Cone and Cornel West, "The Marty Forum: James H Cone SD," in *American Academy of Religion Annual Meeting, Montreal Quebec*, published on June 26, 2015, original recording Sunday November 8, 2009, posted to American Academy of Religion YouTube Channel, 35:49, https://www.youtube.com/watch?v=28egmRyaInw.
21 Anthony Pinn, "Black Theology," in *Liberation Theologies in the United States: An Introduction*, eds. Stacey Flody-Thomas and Anthony Pinn (New York: New York University Press, 2010), 17.
22 Benjamin Wormald, "2014 Religious Landscape Study," *Pew Research Centers Religion & Public Life Project*, accessed May 16, 2016, http://goo.gl/OIvdCx.
23 Stephen D. Edwards, "HeartMath: A Positive Psychology Paradigm for Promoting Psychophysiological and Global Coherence," *Journal of Psychology in Africa* 25, no. 4 (2015): 367–74.
24 Wormald, "2014 Religious Landscape Study."
25 Luis Lugo, "U.S. Religious Landscape Survey Religious Affiliation: Diverse and Dynamic February 2008," *Pew Research Centers Religion & Public Life Project*, accessed February 19, 2017, https://goo.gl/KkoTyQ; Wormald, "2014 Religious Landscape Study."
26 Technorganic: A being composed of both technological and biological components at the cellular level.
27 James H. Cone, *A Black Theology of Liberation* (Maryknoll, NY: Orbis Books, 2010), 64.
28 Example can be found in the fictitious feminist narrative outlined by Mary Daly, in Quintessence, or Rosemary Radford's ecofeminist theology. Mary Daly, *Quintessence . . . Realizing the Archaic Future: A Radical Elemental Feminist Manifesto* (Boston, MA: Beacon Press, 1999); Rosemary Radford Ruether, *Gaia & God: An Ecofeminist Theology of Earth Healing* (San Francisco, CA: HarperSanFrancisco, 1992).
29 Anthony B. Pinn, *Terror and Triumph: The Nature of Black Religion* (Minneapolis, MN: Fortress Press, 2003); Barbara A. Holmes, *Race and the Cosmos: An Invitation to View the World Differently* (London: A&C Black, 2002); Mary Shawn Copeland, *Enfleshing Freedom: Body, Race, and Being* (Minneapolis, MN: Fortress Press, 2010);

Alton B. Pollard and Carol B. Duncan, eds. *The Black Church Studies Reader* (New York: Springer, 2016); Kelly Brown Douglas, *What's Faith Got to Do With It?: Black Bodies/Christian Souls* (New York: Orbis Books, 2005); Kelly Brown Douglas, *Stand Your Ground: Black Bodies and the Justice of God* (New York: Orbis Books, 2015). These are examples of Black theologies that address the discursive body.

30 Barbara Ann Holmes, *Joy Unspeakable: Contemplative Practices of the Black Church* (Minneapolis, MN: Fortress Press, 2004), 11.

31 Diana L. Hayes, *Forged in the Fiery Furnace: African American Spirituality* (Maryknoll, NY: Orbis Books, 2012), 46.

32 Gloria T. Hull, *Soul Talk: The New Spirituality of African American Women* (Rochester, VT: Inner Traditions, 2001), 69.

33 Charles H. Long, *Significations: Signs, Symbols, and Images in the Interpretation of Religion* (Philadelphia, PA: Fortress Press, 1986), 153.

34 Hull, *Soul Talk*, 102.

35 Paul Lehrer, Yuji Sasaki, and Yoshihiro Saito, "Zazen and Cardiac Variability," *Psychosomatic Medicine* 61, no. 6 (1999): 812–21.

36 Andrew B. Newberg and Jeremy Iversen, "The Neural Basis of the Complex Mental Task of Meditation: Neurotransmitter and Neurochemical Considerations," *Medical Hypotheses* 61, no. 2 (2003): 282–91.

37 Brick Johnstone, Angela Bodling, Dan Cohen, Shawn E. Christ, and Andrew Wegrzyn, "Right Parietal Lobe-Related 'Selflessness' as the Neuropsychological Basis of Spiritual Transcendence," *International Journal for the Psychology of Religion* 22, no. 4 (2012): 267–84.

38 Nick Bostrom, "In Defense of Posthuman Dignity," *Bioethics*, 19, no. 3 (2005): 202–14.

39 Gregory Stock, "Germinal Choice Technology and the Human Future," *Reproductive Biomedicine Online* 10 (2005): 27, 34.

40 Leon Kass, "Ageless Bodies, Happy Souls: Biotechnology and the Pursuit of Perfection," *New Atlantis* 1 (2003): 9–28.

41 Maxwell J. Mehlman, *Transhumanist Dreams and Dystopian Nightmares: The Promise and Peril of Genetic Engineering* (Baltimore, MD: JHU Press, 2012), 8.

42 Mehlman, *Transhumanist* Dreams, 13.

43 Dwight N. Hopkins, ed. *Black Faith and Public Talk: Critical Essays on James H. Cone's Black Theology and Black Power* (Waco, TX: Baylor University Press, 1999), 97.

44 William David Hart, *Afro-Eccentricity: Beyond the Standard Narrative of Black Religion,* (Basingstoke: Palgrave Macmillan, 2011), 15.

45 Pinn, *The End of God-Talk*, 140.

46 Ibid., 150.

47 Roland Faber and Brian G. Henning, "Whitehead's Other Copernican Turn," in *Beyond Metaphysics: Explorations in Alfred North Whitehead's Late Thought*, eds. Roland Faber, Brian G. Henning, and Clinton Combs (New York: Rodopi, 2010), 2.

48 David A. Hogue, "Sometimes It Causes Me to Tremble: Fear, Faith, and the Human Brain," *Pastoral Psychology* 63, no. 5–6 (2014): 659–71.
49 Andrew B. Newberg and Eugene G. D'Aquili, *Mystical Mind* (Minneapolis, MN: Fortress Press, 1999), 52.

Chapter 1

1 Fanon initially said that the Black man "is not a man." While he was drawing from his own experience, the language he utilized while theorizing throughout this work was not gender inclusive. So, I will be using human instead of man when referencing him; Frantz Fanon, *Black Skin White Masks* (New York: Grove Press, 2008), xii.
2 Darwin's theory of evolution posits the human form as fluid. Evolution is change over time which does not allow for a static iteration of human biology.
3 Fanon, *Black Skin*, xii.
4 Frantz Fanon, *The Wretched of the Earth* (New York: Grove Press, 1963), 315–16.
5 Holly Randell-Moon and Ryan Tippet, eds. *Security, Race, Biopower: Essays on Technology and Corporeality* (New York: Springer, 2016), v.
6 There is a very real danger to this classification as well. Since transhumanists maintain humanistic assumptions the proposition of what "is" human does pass into transhumanism. Although transhumanists ascribe to an anti-racist philosophy, placing Black folks under this umbrella could lead to white males morphing into anything, including Blackness, whenever they would like. Still the manner in which the term functions as a declension of morphology allows for Blackness to explore the possibility of transformative morphologies for Black bodies.
7 Glenn Rikowski, "Education, Capital and the Transhuman," in *Marxism against Postmodernism in Educational Theory*, eds. Dave Hill, Peter McLaren, and Glenn Rikowski (Lanham, MD: Lexington Books, 2002), 111–43.
8 Nick Bostrom, "The Transhumanist FAQ: v 3.0," *Humanity+*, 2018. https://web.archive.org/web/20180604232220/https://humanityplus.org/philosophy/transhumanist-faq/
9 This is not to be confused with posthumanism. Posthumanism, or critical posthumanism, is a growing discipline that engages in critical discourse through a decentering of the human, or "man." It places nonhuman animals, plants, and the natural environment on the same level as humanity. It incorporates critical theory, cultural studies, animal studies, gender studies, and ecology studies (among other disciplines to explore a reconfiguration of the posthuman and its future). The posthuman future is a re-imaging of the relationship of the human entity with the infinitely complex (and oft-times sentient) natural environment. Transhumanism is concerned with directing evolution through scientific and technological progress. Posthumanism has the potential to lead to technological progress, but is more

concerned with shifting epistemologies through philosophical explorations; Philip Butler, "Making Enhancement Equitable: A Racial Analysis of the Term Human-Animal and the Inclusion of Black Bodies in Human Enhancement," *Journal of Posthuman Studies* 2, no. 1 (2018): 106–21.

10 Bostrom, "The transhumanist FAQ"; Bostrom, "Human Genetic Enhancements"; Bostrom, "In Defense of Posthuman Dignity"; Robert Ranisch and Stefan Lorenz Sorgner, eds. *Post-and Transhumanism: An Introduction.* (Bern: Peter Lang Edition, 2014).

11 Ranisch and Sorgner, *Post-and Transhumanism.*

12 Ray Kurzweil, *The Singularity Is Near* (London: Gerald Duckworth & Co, 2010).

13 Craig T. Nagoshi and Julie L. Nagoshi, "Being Human versus Being Transhuman: The Mind–Body Problem and Lived Experience," in *Beyond Humanism: Trans- and Posthumanism: Building Better Humans? Refocusing the Debate on Transhumanism*, eds. Stefan Lorenz Sorgner, Hava Tirosh-Samuelson, and Kenneth L. Mossmaned (Frankfurt: Peter Lang, 2011), 303–20.

14 Thomas D. Philbeck, "Ontology," In *Post-and Transhumanism: An Introduction*, eds. Robert Ranisch and Stefan Lorenz Sorgner (Bern: Peter Lang Edition, 2014), 175.

15 Nick Bostrom, "A History of Transhumanist Thought," in *Academic Writing across the Disciplines*, eds. Michael Rectenwald and Lisa Carl (New York: Pearson Longman, 2011), 2.

16 Immanuel Kant, *Observations on the Feeling of the Beautiful and Sublime* (Cambridge: Cambridge University Press, 2006), 58–69, 61.

17 Pauline Kleingeld, "Kant's Second Thoughts on Race," *The Philosophical Quarterly* 57, no. 229 (2007): 573–92.

18 Immanuel Kant, *Anthropology from a Pragmatic Point of View*, trans. Victor Lyle Dowdell (Carbondale/Edwardsville: Southern Illinois University Press), 119.

19 David Hume, *Essays Moral, Political and Literary* (Oxford: Oxford University Press, 1963), 213.

20 Julian Huxley, "Knowledge, Morality, and Destiny: I," *Psychiatry* 14, no. 2 (1951): 129–40; Joseph Wolyniak in "The Relief of Man's Estate" mentions that transhumanists like Bostrom credit Huxley's 1927 essay "Religion Without Revelation" for the first appearance of the term. But Wolyniak attempts to right this inaccuracy pointing to Huxley's aforementioned 1951 essay and his 1957 essay, "New Bottles for New Wine"; Wolyniak Joseph, "The Relief of Man's Estate: Transhumanism, the Baconian Project, and the Theological Impetus for Material Salvation," *Religion and Transhumanism: The Unknown Future of Human Enhancement*, eds. C. Mercer and T. J. Trothen (Santa Barbara, CA: Praeger, 2014): 53–70.

21 Julian Huxley, "The Negro Mind," Typescript 1918. JSHP Box 58:6.

22 Julian Huxley, "America Revisited. V. 'The Quota,'" *The Spectator*, December 20, 1924, 980–82.

23 Julian Huxley, "America Revisited. III. 'The Negro Problem,'" *The Spectator*, November 29, 1924, 821.
24 Huxley, "America Revisited," 980–82.
25 Julian Huxley, Alfred Cort Haddon, and Alexander Morris Carr-Saunders, *We Europeans: A Survey of "Racial" Problems* (London: Harper, 1936), 122–28.
26 Julian Huxley, "The Vital Importance of Eugenics," *Harpers Monthly*, 163 (1931), 324.
27 Joanne Woiak, "Designing a Brave New World: Eugenics, Politics, and Fiction," *The Public Historian* 29, no. 3 (2007): 105–29.
28 Paul Weindling, "Julian Huxley and the Continuity of Eugenics in Twentieth-Century Britain," *Journal of Modern European History= Zeitschrift fur Moderne Europaische Geschichte= Revue D'histoire Europeenne Contemporaine* 10, no. 4 (2012): 480–99.
29 Aubrey de Grey, "The Curate's Egg of Anti-Anti-Aging Bioethics," in *The Transhumanist Reader: Classical and Contemporary Essays on the Science, Technology, and Philosophy of the Human Future*, eds. Max More and Natasha Vita-More (West Sussex: Wiley-Blackwell, 2013), 215–19.
30 James Q. Whitman, *Hitler's American Model: The United States and the Making of Nazi Race Law* (Princeton, NJ: Princeton University Press, 2017), 9.
31 Bostrom, "A History of Transhumanist Thought."
32 Robert Nozick, *Anarchy, State, and Utopia* (New York: Basic Books, 1974), 315; Jonathan Glover, *What Sort of People Should There Be?* (New York: Penguin, 1984); Michael H. Shapiro, "Performance Enhancement and Legal Theory," in *The Transhumanist Reader: Classical and Contemporary Essays on the Science, Technology, and Philosophy of the Human Future*, eds. Max More and Natasha Vita-More (West Sussex: Wiley-Blackwell, 2013), 215–19.
33 Huxley, *We Europeans*, 122–28; Martine Rothblatt, "Mind Is Deeper Than Matter: Transgenderism, Transhumanism, and the Freedom of Form," in *The Transhumanist Reader: Classical and Contemporary Essays on the Science, Technology, and Philosophy of the Human Future*, eds. Max More and Natasha Vita-More (Oxford: Wiley-Blackwell, 2013), 317–26.

Chapter 2

1 Achille Mbembe,"Necropolitics," in *Foucault in an Age of Terror*, eds. Morton, Stephen, and Stephen Bygrave (London: Palgrave Macmillan, 2008), 152–82.
2 Stephanie L. Batiste, "Dunham Possessed: Ethnographic Bodies, Movement, and Transnational Constructions of Blackness," *Journal of Haitian Studies* (2007): 8–22.
3 Tina Beattie, *Theology after Postmodernity: Divining the Void: A Lacanian Reading of Thomas Aquinas* (Oxford: Oxford University Press, 2013).

4 Agustín Fuentes, *Race, Monogamy, and Other Lies They Told You: Busting Myths about Human Nature* (Berkeley: University of California Press, 2015), 81.

5 Kazutoyo Osoegawa, Aaron G. Mammoser, Chenyan Wu, Eirik Frengen, Changjiang Zeng, Joseph J. Catanese, and Pieter J. de Jong, "A Bacterial Artificial Chromosome Library for Sequencing the Complete Human Genome," *Genome Research* 11, no. 3 (2001): 483–96.

6 Rachel M. Sherman, Juliet Forman, Valentin Antonescu, Daniela Puiu, Michelle Daya, Nicholas Rafaels, Meher Preethi Boorgula et al., "Assembly of a Pan-genome from Deep Sequencing of 910 Humans of African Descent," *Nature Genetics* 51, no. 1 (2019): 30–35.

7 Ibid.,35.

8 Gayraud S. Wilmore, *Black Religion and Black Radicalism: An Interpretation of the Religious History of Afro-American* People, 2nd ed., Rev. (Maryknoll, NY: Orbis Books, 1983).

9 Physicalism suggests that there is not quite a 1:1 correlation of material to concept. For instance, mind does not equal brain. This is in contrast to a completely materialist notion which suggests there is an exact 1:1 correlation between material and concept. Materialism not only asserts there is an exact 1:1 correlation, it also reduces experience to these material processes. Still, both remain forms of monism, which denounce dualistic claims of mind and body. In fact, physicalism maintains the complex nature of the world and therefore does not look to simply resort to reductive materialism, negating the many levels of existence for the description of the atomic; Kenji Kansaku, Leonardo G. Cohen, and Niels Birbaumer, eds. *Clinical Systems Neuroscience* (Tokyo, Japan: Springer, 2015), vii.

10 John Searle, *The Rediscovery of the Mind* (Cambridge, MA: MIT Press, 1992); Nancey Murphy, "Nonreductive Physicalism," in *Encyclopedia of Sciences and Religions* (Dordrecht: Springer, 2013), 1533–39.

11 Daniel L. Schacter, "Priming and Multiple Memory Systems: Perceptual Mechanisms of Implicit Memory," *Journal of Cognitive Neuroscience* 4, no. 3 (1992): 244–56.

12 Placide A. Tempels, A. Rubbens, and Colin King, *Bantu Philosophy* (Paris: Présence Africaine, 1959), 37.

13 Tempels, *Bantu Philosophy*.

14 Celestine Chukwuemeka Mbaegbu, "The Mind Body Problem: The Hermeneutics of African Philosophy," *Journal of Religion and Human Relations* 8, no. 2 (2016): 2–18.

15 Valentin Y. Mudimbe, "African Gnosis Philosophy and the Order of Knowledge: An Introduction," *African Studies Review* 28, no. 2–3 (1985): 149–233.

16 Tempels recognized that ancestors had vital force, but did not acknowledge that ancestors were people. He referred to them as either bavidye (ancestral elders) or "manes" (regular ancestors). This further highlights Tempels refusal to communicate Bantu culture for what it was, and not what he wanted it to be.

17 Mudimbe, "African Gnosis," 149–233.
18 E. N. C. Mujynya, *L'Homme dans l'Univers des Bantu* (Lubumbashi: Presses Universitairs du Zaire, 1972), 21–22.
19 V. Mulago, *Un Visage Africaine du Christianisme* (Paris: Presence Africaine, 1965), 155–56.
20 Didier N. Kaphagawani, "African Conceptions of a Person: A Critical Survey," in *A Companion to African Philosophy*, eds. Kwasi Wiredu (Malden, MA: Blackwell Publishing, 2004), 332–42.
21 Leke Adeofe, "Personal Identity in African Metaphysics," in *African Philosophy: New and Traditional Perspectives*, eds. Lee M. Brown (New York: Oxford University Press, 2004). Oxford Scholarship Online, 2006. doi: 10.1093/019511440X.003.0005.
22 Adeofe, "Personal Identity in African Metaphysics," 45.
23 Asaresu Imhotep, "Understanding Ase and Its Relation to Esu Among the Yoruba and Ase. T in Ancient Egypt," in *The MOCHA-Versity Institute of Philosophy and Research* Part 1 (January 2012): 20.
24 Mambo Ama Mazama, "Afrocentricity and African Spirituality," *Journal of Black Studies* 33, no. 2 (2002): 218–34.
25 Didier Njirayamanda Kaphagawani, "African Conceptions of a Person: A Critical Survey," in *A Companion to African Philosophy* Kwasi Wiredu, ed. (Malden, MA: Blackwell Publishing, 2004), 332–42.
26 Wilfred Lajul cites D. Fred Miller, Jr, *Nature, Justice, and Rights in Aristotle's Politics* (New York: Clarendon Press, 1997), "African Metaphysics: Traditional and Modern Discussions," in *Themes, Issues and Problems in African Philosophy* (New York: Palgrave Macmillan, Cham, 2017), 9–48.
27 Lajul, "African Metaphysics," 44.
28 Emmanuel Bueya, *Stability in Postcolonial African States* (Lanham, MD: Lexington Books, 2017), 20.
29 Bueya, *Stability*, 20.
30 Tempels, *Bantu Philosophy*, 18.
31 F. Abiola Irele, *The African Experience in Literature and Ideology* (London: Heinemann, 1981).
32 Donna V. Jones Cites Henri Bergson, *The Two Sources of Morality and Religion*, 136–37. In *The Racial Discourses of Life Philosophy: Negritude, Vitalism, and Modernity*, Vol. 45 (New York: Columbia University Press, 2010), 125–27.
33 Philip Clayton, *Mind and Emergence* (New York: Oxford University Press, 2005), 6.
34 Alfred North Whitehead, *Process and Reality* (New York: The Free Press, 1979), xiii.
35 Alfred North Whitehead, *An Enquiry Concerning the Principles of Natural Knowledge* (Cambridge: Cambridge University Press, 2011), 61–62.

36 Barbara Herrnstein Smith and E. Roy Weintraub, *Emergence and Embodiment: New Essays on Second-Order Systems Theory* (Durham, NC: Duke University Press, 2009), 85.

37 George Dvorsky, "Rights of Non-Human Persons," *The Institute for Ethics and Emerging Technologies (IEET).* https://ieet.org/index.php/IEET2/RNHP. 2011

38 Donna Jones, trans. "*Ce Que L'homme Noir Apporte,*" *L'Homme De Couleur* (Paris: Librairie Plon, 1939), 24.

39 Léopold Sédar Senghor, "Negritude: A Humanism of the Twentieth Century," in *Postcolonialisms: An Anthology of Cultural Theory and Criticism*, eds. Gaurav Gajanan Desai and Supriya Nair (New Brunswick: Rutgers University Press, 2005), 183–90.

40 Cornel West, "Philosophy and the Afro-American Experience," in *A Companion to African-American Philosophy*, eds. Tommy L. Lott and John P. Pittman (Hoboken, NJ: Blackwell Publishing, 2003), 7.

41 Eboni Marshall Turman, *Toward a Womanist Ethic of Incarnation: Black Bodies, the Black Church, and the Council of Chalcedon* (New York: Springer, 2013), 169.

42 Turman, *Womanist Ethics of Incarnation*, 170.

43 Trisha A. Jenkins, Jason C. D. Nguyen, Kate E. Polglaze, and Paul P. Bertrand, "Influence of Tryptophan and Serotonin on Mood and Cognition With a Possible Role of the Gut-Brain Axis," *Nutrients* 8, no. 1 (2016): 56.

44 Mandayam A. Srinivasan and Cagatay Basdogan, "Haptics in Virtual Environments: Taxonomy, Research Status, and Challenges," *Computers & Graphics* 21, no. 4 (1997): 393–404.

45 Blake Hannaford and Allison M. Okamura, "Haptics," in *Springer Handbook of Robotics*, eds. Siciliano and Oussama Khatib (New York: Springer, Cham, 2016), 1063–84.

46 Dee Unglaub Silverthorn, William C. Ober, Claire W. Garrison, Andrew C. Silverthorn, and Bruce R. Johnson, *Human Physiology: An Integrated Approach*, 7th edn. (San Francisco, CA: Pearson/Benjamin Cummings, 2016), 350.

47 Silverthorn et al., *Human Physiology*, 251.

48 Ibid., 315.

49 Bessel A. Van der Kolk, "The Body Keeps the Score: Memory and the Evolving Psychobiology of Posttraumatic Stress," *Harvard Review of Psychiatry* 1, no. 5 (1994): 253–65; Sarah Wilker, Thomas Elbert, and Iris-Tatjana Kolassa, "The Downside of Strong Emotional Memories: How Human Memory-Related Genes Influence the Risk for Posttraumatic Stress Disorder–A Selective Review," *Neurobiology of Learning and Memory* 112 (2014): 75–86.

50 Walter B. Cannon, "The James-Lange Theory of Emotions: A Critical Examination and an Alternative Theory," *The American Journal of Psychology* 39, no. 1/4 (1927): 106–24.

51 Stanley Schachter and Jerome Singer, "Cognitive, Social, and Physiological Determinants of Emotional State," *Psychological Review* 69, no. 5 (1962): 379.

52 Agnes Moors, "Theories of Emotion Causation: A Review," in *Cognition and Emotion: Reviews of Current Research and Theories*, eds. Jan De Houwer and Dirk Hermans (Florence, KY: Psychology Press, 2010), 13–14.

53 John G. Taylor, "The Perception-Conceptualisation-Knowledge Representation-Reasoning Representation-Action Cycle: The View from the Brain," in *Perception-Action Cycle*, eds. Vassilis Cutsuridis, Amir Hussain, and John G. Taylor (New York: Springer, 2011), 243–85.

54 Silverthorn et al., *Human Physiology*, 831.

55 Some interesting facts about melanin expression and evolution. "Bare skin is at risk from damage from ultraviolet (UV) radiation (UVR), in particular UV-B (wavelength 290–315 nm), the most energetic form of UVR that normally reaches the Earth's surface. Melanin has a twofold role in protecting us from UVR. First, it reduces the amount of radiation entering the deeper layers of the epidermis by absorbing or scattering it. Second, it acts as a filter, absorbing chemical by-products of UVR damage that would otherwise be toxic or carcinogenic. The immediate ancestors of all modern humans therefore must have developed dark skins, and the issue of skin color variation becomes a question of explaining the different degrees of subsequent loss of pigmentation"; Mark Jobling, Matthew Hurles, and Chris Tyler-Smith, *Human Evolutionary Genetics: Origins, Peoples & Disease* (New York: Garland Science, 2014), 487.

56 Wilker, Elbert, and Kolassa, "The Downside of Strong Emotional Memories," 75–86; Johannes M. H. M. Reul, "Making Memories of Stressful Events: A Journey Along Epigenetic, Gene Transcription, and Signaling Pathways," *Frontiers in Psychiatry* 5 (2014): 5; Moshe Szyf, "Nongenetic Inheritance and Transgenerational Epigenetics," *Trends in Molecular Medicine* 21, no. 2 (2015): 134–44.

57 Andrew P. Feinberg, "Phenotypic Plasticity and the Epigenetics of Human Disease," *Nature* 447, no. 7143 (2007): 433; Benjamin R. Carone, Lucas Fauquier, Naomi Habib, Jeremy M. Shea, Caroline E. Hart, Ruowang Li, Christoph Bock et al., "Paternally Induced Transgenerational Environmental Reprogramming of Metabolic Gene Expression in Mammals," *Cell* 143, no. 7 (2010): 1084–96; Michael J. Sheriff, Ben Dantzer, Oliver P. Love, and John L. Orrock, "Error Management Theory and the Adaptive Significance of Transgenerational Maternal-Stress Effects on Offspring Phenotype," *Ecology and Evolution* 8, no. 13 (2018): 6473–82.

58 Sylvia Wynter, "Human, Being as Noun? Or *Being Human* as Praxis? Towards the Autopoetic Turn/Overturn: A Manifesto," 2007. http://bit.ly/2I1A3Oj.

59 Spillers, Hortense J. Spillers, "Mama's Baby, Papa's Maybe: An American Grammar Book," *Diacritics* 17, no. 2 (1987): 65–81.

60 E. Patrick Johnson, "'Quare' Studies, or (Almost) Everything I Know about Queer Studies I Learned from My Grandmother," *Text and Performance Quarterly* 21, no. 1 (2001): 1–25.

61 Alexander Weheliye mentions Stuart Hall, "Race, Articulation, and Societies Structured in Dominance," in *Sociological Theories: Race and Colonialism* (Paris: Unesco, 1980), 303–45, *Habeas Viscus: Racializing Assemblages, Biopolitics, and Black Feminist Theories of the Human* (Durham, NC: Duke University Press, 2014), 48.

62 Fabrício Pontin, Laura Dick Guerim, Camila Palhares Barbosa, and Bruna Fernandes Ternus, "Sexual Identity and Neurosexism: A Critique of Reductivist approaches of Sexual Behavior and Gender," *Revista Dissertatio de Filosofia* (2017): 22–37.

63 Cordelia Fine, "Is There Neurosexism in Functional Neuroimaging Investigations of Sex Difference?" *Neuroethics* 6, no. 2 (2013): 369–409.

64 Frances M. Beal, "Double Jeopardy: To Be Black and Female," *Meridians: Feminism, Race, Transnationalism* 8, no. 2 (2008): 154.

65 A. F. Sanders, "Towards a Model of Stress and Human Performance," *Acta Psychologica* 53, no. 1 (1983): 61–97; Harris R. Lieberman, William J. Tharion, Barbara Shukitt-Hale, Karen L. Speckman, and Richard Tulley, "Effects of Caffeine, Sleep Loss, and Stress on Cognitive Performance and Mood During US Navy SEAL Training," *Psychopharmacology* 164, no. 3 (2002): 250–61.

66 Candace West and Don H. Zimmerman, "Doing Gender," *Gender & Society* 1, no. 2 (1987): 125–51.

67 Beal, "Double Jeopardy," 166–76.

68 Kara Keeling, "I = Another: Digital Identity Politics," in *Strange Affinities: The Gender and Sexual Politics of Comparative Racialization*, eds. Grace Kyungwon Hong and Roderick A. Ferguson (Durham, NC: Duke University Press, 2011), 53–75.

69 James G. Pfaus and Sherri L. Jones, "Central Nervous System Anatomy and Neurochemistry of Sexual Desire," *Textbook of Female Sexual Function and Dysfunction: Diagnosis and Treatment*, eds. Irwin Goldstein, Anita H. Clayton, Andrew T. Goldstein, Noel N. Kim, and Sheryl A. Kingsberg (Oxford: Wiley-Blackwell, 2018), 25–51.

70 Ivan Pavlov, *Conditioned Reflexes* (Mineola, NY: Courier Dover Publications, 1927).

71 Melanie Taziaux, Annemieke S. Staphorsius, Mohammad A. Ghatei, Stephen R. Bloom, Dick F. Swaab, and Julie Bakker, "Kisspeptin Expression in the Human Infundibular Nucleus in Relation to Sex, Gender Identity, and Sexual Orientation," *The Journal of Clinical Endocrinology & Metabolism* 101, no. 6 (2016): 2380–89.

72 Fanon, *The Wretched of the Earth*, 35.

73 George Ciccariello-Maher, "Jumpstarting the Decolonial Engine: Symbolic Violence from Fanon to Chavez," *Theory & Event* 13, no. 1 (2010).
74 Lewis R. Gordon, "Through the Hellish Zone of Nonbeing: Thinking Through Fanon, Disaster, and the Damned of the Earth," *Human Architecture: Journal of the Sociology of Self-Knowledge* 5, no. 3 (2007): 3.
75 Ciccariello-Maher, "Jumpstarting the Decolonial Engine."
76 Jan Fook and Gurid Aga Askeland, "Challenges of Critical Reflection:'Nothing Ventured, Nothing Gained,'" *Social Work Education* 26, no. 5 (2007): 520–33.
77 Stefan G. Hofmann, Paul Grossman, and Devon E. Hinton, "Loving-Kindness and Compassion Meditation: Potential for Psychological Interventions," *Clinical Psychology Review* 31, no. 7 (2011): 1126–32; Antoine Lutz, Julie Brefczynski-Lewis, Tom Johnstone, and Richard J. Davidson. "Regulation of the Neural Circuitry of Emotion by Compassion Meditation: Effects of Meditative Expertise," *PloS One* 3, no. 3 (2008): e1897.

Chapter 3

1 Felt and unfelt components of spirituality operate on a three-dimensional axis that includes psychological, emotional, and somatic awareness. Awareness ranges from conscious to subconscious awareness, inclusive of neutral awareness. Felt and unfelt spiritual experiences are only mediated through the body. No matter how felt, neutral, unfelt, or out of body a particular experience may be perceived, there are always biological structures at work, facilitating that spiritual experience.
2 Ann Taves, *Religious Experience Reconsidered: A Building-Block Approach to the Study of Religion and Other Special Things* (Princeton, NJ: Princeton University Press, 2009), 26.
3 Elaine Pagels, *Beyond Belief: The Secret Gospel of Thomas* (New York: Random House, 2003); Jeffrey J. Kripal, *The Serpent's Gift: Gnostic Reflections on the Study of Religion* (Chicago, IL: University of Chicago Press, 2008), 11–12.
4 Kripal, *Serpent*, 12.
5 Courtney Bender, *The New Metaphysicals: Spirituality and the American Religious Imagination* (Chicago, IL: University of Chicago Press, 2010), 5, 183.
6 Long, *Significations*, 6.
7 Benedicta Ward, *The Sayings of the Desert Fathers: The Alphabetical Collection, No. 59* (Kalamazoo, MN: Cistercian Publications, 1984), xxi.
8 Chris J. Boyatzis, "A Critique of Models of Religious Experience," *International Journal for the Psychology of Religion* 4 (2001): 247–58.
9 Bender, *New Metaphysicals*, 62.
10 Long, *Significations*, 32.

11 Amanda C. Marshall, Antje Gentsch, Valentina Jelinčić, and Simone Schütz-Bosbach, "Exteroceptive Expectations Modulate Interoceptive Processing: Repetition-suppression Effects for Visual and Heartbeat Evoked Potentials," *Scientific Reports* 7, no. 1 (2017): 16525; Claudio Zampin, Roberta Ficacci, Miriam Checcacci, Fabio Franciolini, and Luigi Catacuzzeno, "Pain Control by Proprioceptive and Exteroceptive Stimulation at the Trigeminal Level," *Frontiers in Physiology* 9 (2018); Xiao Yang, J. Richard Jennings, and Bruce H. Friedman, "Exteroceptive Stimuli Override Interoceptive State in Reaction Time Control," *Psychophysiology* 54, no. 12 (2017): 1940–50.

12 Daugherty, *From Mindfulness to Heartfulness*, 52.

13 Agnes Moors, Phoebe C. Ellsworth, Klaus R. Scherer, and Nico H. Frijda, "Appraisal Theories of Emotion: State of the Art and Future Development," *Emotion Review* 5, no. 2 (2013): 119–24.

14 Taves, *Religious Experience Reconsidered*, 38; Owen Flanagan, *The Really Hard Problem: Meaning in a Material World* (Cambridge: MIT Press, 2007).

15 Agnes Moors, "Flavors of Appraisal Theories of Emotion," *Emotion Review* 6, no. 4 (2014): 303–7.

16 Meuleman et al. reference several studies that have outlined the five components of appraisal on their way to affirming the multi-componential model of emotion; Ben Meuleman, Agnes Moors, Johnny Fontaine, Olivier Renaud, and Klaus Scherer, "Interaction and Threshold Effects of Appraisal on Componential Patterns of Emotion: A Study Using Cross-cultural Semantic Data," *Emotion* 19, no. 3 (2019): 425.

17 Jennifer K. MacCormack and Kristen A. Lindquist, "Bodily Contributions to Emotion: Schachter's Legacy for a Psychological Constructionist View on Emotion," *Emotion Review* 9, no. 1 (2017): 36–45.

18 Daugherty, *Mindfulness to Heartfulness*, 86–88; Alane Daugherty, *The Power Within: From Neuroscience to Transformation* (Dubuque, IA: Kendall Hunt Publishing Company, 2008), 95.

19 Daugherty, *Mindfulness to Heartfulness*, 54.

20 James E. Darnell Lodish, Arnold Berk, Chris A. Kaiser, Monty Krieger, Matthew P. Scott, Anthony Bretscher, Hidde Ploegh, and Paul Matsudaira, *Molecular Cell Biology* (New York: Macmillan, 2008), 16.1.

21 Daugherty, *Mindfulness to Heartfulness*, 92.

22 Eva Bianconi, Allison Piovesan, Federica Facchin, Alina Beraudi, Raffaella Casadei, Flavia Frabetti, Lorenza Vitale et al., "An Estimation of the Number of Cells in the Human Body," *Annals of Human Biology* 40, no. 6 (2013): 463–71.

23 Newberg, *Mystical Mind*, 52.

24 Ibid., 157–61.

25 Ibid., 172.

26 Kristen Brown Golden, *Nietzsche and Embodiment: Discerning Bodies and Non-Dualism* (Albany, NY: SUNY Press, 2012), 35.

27 Newberg, *Mystical Mind*, 81–85.

28 Andrea Hollingsworth, "Implications of Interpersonal Neurobiology for a Spirituality of Compassion," *Zygon®* 43, no. 4 (2008): 837–60.

29 Aurélie Ernst and Jonas Frisén, "Adult Neurogenesis in Humans-Common and Unique Traits in Mammals," *PLoS Biology* 13, no. 1 (2015): e1002045.

30 Jayaram Thimmapuram, Robert Pargament, Kedesha Sibliss, Rodney Grim, Rosana Risques, and Erik Toorens, "Effect of Heartfulness Meditation on Burnout, Emotional Wellness, and Telomere Length in Health Care Professionals," *Journal of Community Hospital Internal Medicine Perspectives* 7, no. 1 (2017): 21–27; Shailesh M. Varu, "Heart Based Meditation: Panacea for Today's Youth," *European Journal of Multidisciplinary Studies* 2, no. 6 (2017): 180–83.

31 Madeline Lee Pe, Filip Raes, and Peter Kuppens, "The Cognitive Building Blocks of Emotion Regulation: Ability to Update Working Memory Moderates the Efficacy of Rumination and Reappraisal on Emotion," *PloS One* 8, no. 7 (2013): e69071; Selene Nasso, Vanderhasselt Marie-Anne, Demeyer Ineke, and Rudi De Raedt, "Autonomic Regulation in Response to Stress: The Influence of Anticipatory Emotion Regulation Strategies and Trait Rumination," *Emotion* 19, no. 3 (2019): 443.

32 Charlotte vanOyen Witvliet, Ross W. Knoll, Nova G. Hinman, and Paul A. DeYoung, "Compassion-focused Reappraisal, Benefit-focused Reappraisal, and Rumination after an Interpersonal Offense: Emotion-Regulation Implications for Subjective Emotion, Linguistic Responses, and Physiology," *The Journal of Positive Psychology* 5, no. 3 (2010): 226–42.

33 Daugherty, *Mindfulness to Heartfulness*, 18.

34 Andrew B. Newberg, Nancy A. Wintering, Donna Morgan, and Mark R. Waldman, "The Measurement of Regional Cerebral Blood Flow During Glossolalia: A Preliminary SPECT Study," *Psychiatry Research: Neuroimaging* 148, no. 1 (2006): 67–71.

35 Lutz, Brefczynski-Lewis, Johnstone, and Davidson, "Regulation of the Neural Circuitry of Emotion by Compassion Meditation," e1897.

36 Robin L. Carhart-Harris, David Erritzoe, Tim Williams et al., "Neural Correlates of the Psychedelic State as Determined by fMRI Studies With Psilocybin," *Proceedings of the National Academy of Sciences* 109, no. 6 (2012): 2138–43.

37 Mario Beauregard and Vincent Paquette, "Neural Correlates of a Mystical Experience in Carmelite Nuns," *Neuroscience Letters* 405, no. 3 (2006): 186–90.

38 Mark R. Gover, "The Embodied Mind: Cognitive Science and Human Experience (Book)," *Mind, Culture, and Activity* 3, no. 4 (1996): 295–99.

39 Newberg, "Glossolalia, SPECT," 67–71.

40 Brick Johnstone, Angela Bodling, Dan Cohen, Shawn E. Christ, and Andrew Wegrzyn, "Right Parietal Lobe-Related 'Selflessness' as the Neuropsychological Basis of Spiritual Transcendence," *International Journal for the Psychology of Religion* 22, no. 4 (2012): 267–84.

41 Jacqueline Lutz, Uwe Herwig, Sarah Opialla et al., "Mindfulness and Emotion Regulation—An fMRI Study," *Social Cognitive and Affective Neuroscience* 9, no. 6 (2014): 776–85; Megan M. Short, Dwight Mazmanian, Lana J. Ozen, and Michel Bédard, "Four Days of Mindfulness Meditation Training for Fraduate Students: A Pilot Study Examining Effects on Mindfulness, Self-Regulation, and Executive Function," *The Journal of Contemplative Inquiry* 2, no. 1 (2015); Sam Harris, Sameer A. Sheth, and Mark S. Cohen, "Functional Neuroimaging of Belief, Disbelief, and Uncertainty," *Annals of Neurology* 63, no. 2 (2008): 141–47.

42 Newberg and Iversen, "The Neural Basis of the Complex Mental Task of," 282–91.

43 T. W. Chow and J. L. Cummings, "Frontal Subcortical Circuits," in *The Human Frontal Lobes*, eds. B. L. Miller and J. L. Cummings (New York: Guilford Press, 1999); J. Newman and A. A. Grace, "Binding across Time: The Selective Gating of Frontal and Hippocampal Systems Modulating Working Memory and Attentional States," *Conscious Cognition* 8 (1999): 196–212.

44 M. Davis, "The Role of the Amygdala in Fear and Anxiety," *Annual Review of Neuroscience* 15 (1992): 353–75.

45 S. Foote, "Extrathalamic Modulation of Cortical Function," *Annual Review of Neuroscience* 10 (1987): 67–95.

46 E. Davies, C. J. Keyon, and R. Fraser, "The Role of Calcium Ions in the Mechanism of ACTH Stimulation of Cortisol Synthesis," *Steroids* 45 (1985): 551–60.

47 R. Pietrowsky et al., "Vasopressin and Oxytocin Do Not Influence Early Sensory Processing but Affect Mood and Activation in Man," *Peptides* 12 (1991): 1385–91.

48 J. Kiss, J. K. Kocsis, A. Csaki et al., "Metabotropic Glutamate Receptor in GHRH and b-endorphin Neurons of the Hypothalamic Arcuate Nucleus," *Neuroreport* 8 (1997): 3703–7.

49 M. Janal, E. Colt, W. Clark et al., "Pain Sensitivity, Mood and Plasma Endocrine Levels in Man Following Long-Distance Running: Effects of Naxalone," *Pain* 19 (1984): 13–25.

50 R. Albin and J. Greenamyre, "Alternative Excitotoxic Hypotheses," *Neurology* 42 (1992): 733–38.

51 F. X. Vollenweider, K. L. Leenders, C. Scharfetter et al., "Metabolic Hyperfrontality and Psychopathology in the Ketamine Model of Psychosis Using Positron Emission Tomography (PET) and [18F]Fluorodeoxyglucose (FDG)," *Eur Neuropsychopharmacol* 7 (1997): 9–24.

52 Gao-Xia Wei, Ting Xu, Feng-Mei Fan et al., "Can Tai Chi Reshape the Brain? A Brain Morphometry Study," *PLoS One* 8, no. 4 (2013): e61038.

53 Gao-Xia Wei, Hao-Ming Dong, Zhi Yang et al., "Tai Chi Chuan Optimizes the Functional Organization of the Intrinsic Human Brain Architecture in Older Adults," *Frontiers in Aging Neuroscience* 6 (2014): 74.

54 Jing Tao, Jiao Liu, Natalia Egorova et al., "Increased Hippocampus–Medial Prefrontal Cortex Resting-State Functional Connectivity and Memory Function after Tai Chi Chuan Practice in Elder Adults," *Frontiers in Aging Neuroscience* 8 (2016): 1–9.

55 Francesco Taddei, Alessandro Bultrini, Donatella Spinelli, and Francesco Di Russo, "Neural Correlates of Attentional and Executive Processing in Middle-Age Fencers," *Medicine & Science in Sports & Exercise* 44, no. 6 (2012): 1057–66.

56 Adrienne A. Taren, J. David Creswell, and Peter J. Gianaros, "Dispositional Mindfulness Co-Varies with Smaller Amygdala and Caudate Volumes in Community Adults," *PLoS One* 8, no. 5 (2013): e64574.

57 Carhart-Harris, "Neural Correlates of the Psychedelic State . . . " 2138–43.

58 E. Baron Short, Samet Kose, Qiwen Mu et al., "Regional Brain Activation during Meditation Shows Time and Practice Effects: an Exploratory FMRI Study," *Evidence-Based Complementary and Alternative Medicine* 7, no. 1 (2010): 121–27.

59 Hull, *Soul Talk*, 102.

60 Barbara Holmes references the portal as that which opens one up to enter the spiritual or contemplative realm in *Joy Unspeakable*, 6, 32, 50, 66.

61 Holmes, *Joy Unspeakable*, 82.

62 Hull, *Soul Talk*, 64.

63 Stephanie Rose Bird, *The Big Book of Soul: The Ultimate Guide to the African American Spirit* (Newburyport, MA: Hampton Roads Publishing, 2010), 19–32, 64–98.

64 Randy L. Buckner, Jessica R. Andrews-Hanna, and Daniel L. Schacter, "The Brain's Default Network," *Annals of the New York Academy of Sciences* 1124, no. 1 (2008): 1–38.

65 Wudū (ablution) is the Islamic practice of ritual purification through washing before prayer. It is practiced several times a day. Wudū incorporates washing bodily extremities. Specifically, it entails washing the hands and arms, up to the elbows, the face and head, and the feet and ankles; Marion H. Katz, "The Study of Islamic Ritual and the Meaning of Wuḍūʾ," *Der Islam* 82, no. 1 (2005): 106–45.

66 Holmes, *Joy Unspeakable*, 45.

67 Doug McAdam, "Tactical Innovation and the Pace of Insurgency," *American Sociological Review* (1983): 735–54; Gregg Lee Carter, "In the Narrows of the 1960s US Black Rioting," *Journal of Conflict Resolution* 30, no. 1 (1986): 115–27; William J. Collins and Robert A. Margo, "The Economic Aftermath of the 1960s Riots in American Cities: Evidence from Property Values," *The Journal of Economic History* 67, no. 4 (2007): 849–83; Sam Forman and Dr. Joseph Warren, "The Way to War,"

in *The Boston Tea Party, Bunker Hill, and the Birth of American Liberty* (Gretna, LA: Pelican Publishing Company, Inc., 2011), 237–49.

68 Elif Özdemir, Andrea Norton, and Gottfried Schlaug, "Shared and Distinct Neural Correlates of Singing and Speaking," *Neuroimage* 33, no. 2 (2006): 628–35.

69 Pranjal H. Mehta, Stefan M. Goetz, and Justin M. Carré, "Genetic, Hormonal, and Neural Underpinnings of Human Aggressive Behavior," in *Handbook of Neurosociology*, eds. David D. Franks, and Jonathan H. Turner (New York: Springer, 2013), 47–65.

70 C. K. W. De Dreu, L. L. Greer, M. J. Handgraaf et al., "The Neuropeptide Oxytocin Regulates Parochial Altruism in Intergroup Conflict among Humans," *Science* 328, (2010): 1408–11.

71 Holmes, *Joy Unspeakable*, 61–62.

72 These dances are often tied to more indigenous forms of Black religion. For instance, dances connected to the Kun people work to provide healing from the day and are practiced daily to increase the spirit, or num, of the individual. Dances performed to the Gran Bwa seek to have its energy enter the person's arms, legs, and heart; Bird, *Big Book of Soul*, 114. Dances were also seen as a way to connect with ancestors, giving credence to their immortality, through spirit possession as a means to acknowledge the ancestor's awareness of the current temporality and their influence over it; Monica A. Coleman, *Making a Way Out of No Way* (Minneapolis, MN: Fortress Press, 2008), 114.

73 Newberg, *Mystical Mind*, 24.

74 Angel Kyodo Williams, *Being Black: Zen and the Art of Living with Fearlessness and Grace* (London: Penguin, 2002), 129–41.

75 Daniel J. Siegel, "Mindfulness Training and Neural Integration: Differentiation of Distinct Streams of Awareness and the Cultivation of Well-being," *Social Cognitive and Affective Neuroscience* 2, no. 4 (2007): 259–63.

76 Taren, "Dispositional Mindfulness . . . ," e64574.

77 Ravinder Jerath, Vernon A. Barnes, David Dillard-Wright, Shivani Jerath, and Brittany Hamilton, "Dynamic Change of Awareness during Meditation Techniques: Neural and Physiological Correlates," *Frontiers in human neuroscience* 6 (2012): 131.

78 Lehrer, "Zazen and Cardiac Variability," 812–21.

79 Pierre Jacob, "What Do Mirror Neurons Contribute to Human Social Cognition?" *Mind & Language* 23, no. 2 (2008): 190–223.

80 Roy Mukamel, Arne D. Ekstrom, Jonas Kaplan, Marco Iacoboni, and Itzhak Fried, "Single-Neuron Responses in Humans during Execution and Observation of Actions," *Current Biology* 20, no. 8 (2010): 750–56.

81 Christian Keysers and Valeria Gazzola, "Social Neuroscience: Mirror Neurons Recorded in Humans," *Current Biology* 20, no. 8 (2010): R353–54.

82 James J. Knierim, Joshua P. Neunuebel, and Sachin S. Deshmukh, "Functional Correlates of the Lateral and Medial Entorhinal Cortex: Objects, Path Integration and Local–Global Reference Frames," *Philosophical Transactions of the Royal Society of London. Series B* 369, no. 1635 (2014): 20130369.

83 Holmes, *Joy Unspeakable*, 81.

84 Ibid., 82.

85 Darnise C. Martin, "The Self Divine: Know Ye Not that Ye are Gods?" in *Esotericism in African American Religious Experience*, eds. Stephen Finley, Margarita Guillory, and Hugh Page Jr. (Boston: Brill, 2014), 59.

86 Emily B. Falk, Matthew Brook O'Donnell, Christopher N. Cascio et al., "Self-Affirmation Alters the Brain's Response to Health Messages and Subsequent Behavior Change," *Proceedings of the National Academy of Sciences* 112, no. 7 (2015): 1977–82; Uffe Schjoedt, Hans Stødkilde-Jørgensen, Armin W. Geertz, and Andreas Roepstorff, "Highly Religious Participants Recruit Areas of Social Cognition in Personal Prayer," *Social Cognitive and Affective Neuroscience* 4, no. 2 (2009): 199–207.

87 Kyungmi Kim and Marcia K. Johnson, "Activity in Ventromedial Prefrontal Cortex during Self-Related Processing: Positive Subjective Value or Personal Significance?" *Social Cognitive and Affective Neuroscience* 10, no. 4 (2015): 494–500.

88 Schjoedt, "Highly Religious Participants . . . ," 199–207.

89 D. A. Gurnard and M. E. Raichle, "Searching for a Baseline: Functional Imaging and the Resting Human Brain," *Nature* 2, (2001): 685–94.

90 Kemetic yoga: Bird, *The Big Book of Soul*, 118.

91 Williams, *Being Black*, 148.

Chapter 4

1 Yvonne Harris, Philip B. Gorelick, Patricia Samuels, and Isaac Bempong, "Why African Americans May Not Be Participating in Clinical Trials," *Journal of the National Medical Association* 88, no. 10 (1996): 630.

2 Harriet A. Washington, *Medical Apartheid: The Dark History of Medical Experimentation on Black Americans from Colonial Times to the Present* (New York: Broadway, 2007); Dorothy Roberts, "Black Women and the Pill," *Perspectives on Sexual and Reproductive Health* 32, no. 2 (2000): 92.

3 Wilmore, *Black Radicalism*, 198–202.

4 James H. Cone, *The God of the Oppressed* (Maryknoll, NY: Orbis, 1977), 11–12, 32–33, 114, 141–42.

5 Cary Funk and Becka A. Alper, "Perception of Conflict Between Science and Religion," *Pew Research*, https://pewrsr.ch/1QXYU0B

6 George Deane, "Technological Unemployment: Panacea or Poison?" *Institute of Ethics and Emerging Technologies blog*, March 5, accessed October 7, 2016, http: //ieet.org/index.php/IEET/more/deane20130305; Gary E. Marchant, Yvonne A. Stevens, and James M. Hennessy, "Technology, Unemployment & Policy Options: Navigating the Transition to a Better World," *Technology* 24, no. (2014): 26–44.

7 National Academy of Sciences, *Technology and Employment: Innovation and Growth in the U.S. Economy* (Washington DC: National Academy Press, 1987).

8 Dean, "Technological Unemployment..." http://ieet.org/index.php/IEET/more/deane20130305

9 Aaron Smith, "Public Predictions for the Future of Workforce Automation," *Pew Research*, https://bit.ly/2LCiLp6

10 Jerome Bonnet, Pakpoom Subsoontorn, and Drew Endy, "Rewritable Digital Data Storage in Live Cells Via Engineered Control of Recombination Directionality," *Proceedings of the National Academy of Sciences* 109, no. 23 (2012): 8884–89.

11 Sadhbh Walshe, "How US Prison Labour Pads Corporate Profits at Taxpayers' Expense," *The Guardian*, July 6, 2012, accessed January 7, 2017, goo.gl/fElUje.

12 Alexander, *The New Jim Crow*, 32.

13 Sam Altman, "Moving Forward On Basic Income," *The Y-Combinator Blog*, May 31, 2016, https://web.archive.org/web/20161008005352/, https://blog.ycombinator.com/moving-forward-on-basic-income

14 Bureau of Labor Statistics, "Labor Force Statistics from the Current Population Survey," August 6, 2019. http://bit.ly/2OCdHrG

15 Lee M. Silver, "Biotechnology in a World of Spiritual Beliefs," in *Biotechnology: Our Future as Human Beings and Citizens*, ed. Sean D. Sutton (Albany, NY: State University of New York Press, 2009), 67–79.

16 Silver, "Biotechnology in a World of Spiritual Beliefs," 67–79.

17 Scientists would not know about this relationship had it not been for genetic reverse engineering.

18 A breeding technique applied during slavery.

19 A. Beja-Pereira and G. Luikart et al., "Gene-Culture Co-Evolution Between Cattle Milk Protein Genes and Human Lactase Genes," *Nature Genetics* 35 (2003): 311–13.

20 "The Fitness Model Without a Pulse," *Great Big Story*, https://web.archive.org/web/20161012030340/, http://www.greatbigstory.com/stories/living-on-an-artificial-heart

21 Andy Palma, "Meet Andrew Jones, The Bodybuilder Without a Pulse" *Futurism*, https://web.archive.org/web/20161012031029/, http://futurism.com/meet-andrew-jones-the-bodybuilder-without-a-pulse/

22 Gianluca Torregrossa, Michiel Morshuis, Robin Varghese et al., "Results with SynCardia Total Artificial Heart Beyond 1 Year," *ASAIO Journal* 60, no. 6 (2014): 626–34.

23 Anthony Pinn, "Sweaty Bodies in a Circle: Thoughts on the Subtle Dimensions of Black Religion as Protest," *Black Theology*, 4, no 1 (2015): 11–26; Anthony G. Reddie, ed. *Black Theology, Slavery and Contemporary Christianity: 200 Years and No Apology* (Abingdon: Routledge, 2016); Anthony G. Reddie, *Working Against the Grain: Re-Imaging Black Theology in the 21st Century* (Abingdon: Routledge, 2014).

24 Bill McKibben, *Enough: Staying Human in an Engineered Age* (New York: Times Books, 2003), 44–65.

25 Scott A. Huettel, Allen W. Song, and Gregory McCarthy, *Functional Magnetic Resonance Imaging*, 2nd edn. (Sunderland, MA: Sinauer Associates, 2009), 26.

26 Huettel, *Functional Magnetic Resonance Imaging*, 220.

27 Miles N. Wernick and John N. Aarsvold, *Emission Tomography: The Fundamentals of PET and SPECT* (San Diego: Elsevier Academic Press, 2004), 17.

28 Wernick and Aarsvold, *Emission Tomography*, 11.

29 Ibid., 15.

30 Ibid., 16.

31 Akira Date, "An Information Theoretic Analysis of 256-channel EEG Recordings: Mutual Information and Measurement Selection Problem," *Proceedings of the International Conference on Independent Component Analysis and Blind Signal Separation (ICA2001)* (2001): 85–188.

32 Michal Teplan, "Fundamentals of EEG Measurement," *Measurement Science Review* 2, no. 2 (2002): 1–11.

33 Teplan, "Fundamentals of EEG Measurement," 1–11.

34 Brouwer et al., "Using Neurophysiological Signals That Reflect Cognitive or Affective State: Six Recommendations to Avoid Common Pitfalls," *Frontiers in Neuroscience* 9 (2015); 136.

35 Payne et al., "Pulse Transit Time Measured from the ECG: An Unreliable Marker of Beat-To-Beat Blood Pressure," *Journal of Applied Physiology* 100, no. 1 (2006): 136–41.

36 Edwards, "HeartMath," 367–74.

37 Bradley M. Appelhans and Linda J. Luecken, "Heart Rate Variability as an Index of Regulated Emotional Responding," *Review of General Psychology* 10, no. 3 (2006): 229.

38 Aaron S. Heller et al., "Simultaneous Acquisition of Corrugator Electromyography and Functional Magnetic Resonance Imaging: A New Method for Objectively Measuring Affect and Neural Activity Concurrently," *Neuroimage* 58, no. 3 (2011): 930–34.

39 Ayla Kruis et al., "Effects of Meditation Practice on Spontaneous Eyeblink Rate," *Psychophysiology* 53, no. 5 (2016): 749–58.

40 Fatima Ibrahim and Siti A. Ahmad, "Investigation of Electromyographic Activity during Salat and Stretching Exercise," in *Biomedical Engineering and Sciences (IECBES), 2012 IEEE EMBS Conference*, 335–38 (IEEE, 2012).

41 Yu Shi, Natalie Ruiz, Ronnie Taib, Eric Choi, and Fang Chen, "Galvanic Skin Response (GSR) as an Index of Cognitive Load," in *CHI'07 Extended Abstracts on Human Factors in Computing Systems* (ACM: 2007), 2651–56.

42 Shi, "Galvanic Skin Response . . . " 2651–56.

43 Jorge A. Barraza et al., "The Heart of the Story: Peripheral Physiology during Narrative Exposure Predicts Charitable Giving," *Biological Psychology* 105 (2015): 138–43.

44 Harvey Lodish, Arnold Berk, and S. L. Zipursky, *Molecular Cell Biology*, 4th edn. (New York: W. H. Freeman, 2000), Section 20.2 https://www.ncbi.nlm.nih.gov/books/NBK21553/

45 V. A. Coenen et al., "Diffusion Tensor Imaging and Neuromodulation: DTI as Key Technology for Deep Brain Stimulation," *International Review of Neurobiology* 107 (2012): 207–34.

46 K. J. Boggio et al., "Recent Advances in Single-Cell MALDI Mass Spectrometry Imaging and Potential Clinical Impact," *Expert Review of Proteomics* 8, no. 5 (2011): 591–604.

47 Kubo Akiko, Mayumi Kajimura, and Makoto Suematsu, "Matrix-Assisted Laser Desorption/Ionization (MALDI) Imaging Mass Spectrometry (IMS): A Challenge for Reliable Quantitative Analyses," *Mass Spectrometry* 1, no. 1 (2012): A0004.

48 Robert Farra, Norman F. Sheppard, Laura McCabe et al., "First-In-Human Testing of a Wirelessly Controlled Drug Delivery Microchip," *Science Translational Medicine* 4, no. 122 (2012): 122ra21.

49 Günther Deuschl, Carmen Schade-Brittinger, Paul Krack, Jens Volkmann, Helmut Schäfer, Kai Bötzel, Christine Daniels et al., "A Randomized Trial of Deep-Brain Stimulation for Parkinson's Disease," *New England Journal of Medicine* 355, no. 9 (2006): 896–908.

50 Jörg Daniel Fischer, "The Braincon Platform Software-a Closed-Loop Brain-Computer Interface Software for Research and Medical Applications," PhD diss., University of Freiburg, Germany, 2015.

51 Grigori Guitchounts, Jeffrey E. Markowitz, William A. Liberti, and Timothy J. Gardner, "A Carbon-Fiber Electrode Array for Long-Term Neural Recording." *Journal of Neural Engineering* 10, no. 4 (2013): 046016.

52 S. H. Jung, W. Song, S. I. Lee et al., "Synthesis of Graphene and Carbon Nanotubes Hybrid Nanostructures and Their Electrical Properties," *Journal of Nanoscience and Nanotechnology* 13 (2013): 6730–34.

53 A. S. Bhat, "Nanobots: The Future of Medicine," *International Journal of Engineering and Management Sciences* 5, no. 1 (2014): 44–49; F. Lan and G. Li, "Direct Observation of Hole Transfer from Semiconducting Polymer to Carbon Nanotubes," *Nano Letters* 13 (2013): 2086–91.

54 Hugh M. Herr and Alena M. Grabowski, "Bionic Ankle–Foot Prosthesis Normalizes Walking Gait for Persons With Leg Amputation," *Proceedings of the Royal Society B* 279, no. 1728 (London: The Royal Society, 2012): 457–64.

55 Matthew S. Fifer, Soumyadipta Acharya, Heather L. Benz, Mohsen Mollazadeh et al., "Towards Electrocorticographic Control of a Dexterous Upper Limb Prosthesis," *IEEE Pulse* 3, no. 1 (2012): 38.

56 Chengzhi Zong and Roozbeh Jafari, "Robust Heart Rate Estimation Using Wrist-Based PPG Signals in the Presence of Intense Physical Activities," in *2015 37th Annual International Conference of the IEEE Engineering in Medicine and Biology Society (EMBC)* (Milan, Italy: IEEE Conference Publications, 2015), 8078–82, 10.1109/EMBC.2015.7320268.

57 Lehrer, Sasaki, and Saito, "Zazen and Cardiac Variability."

58 Berkan Guleyupoglu, Pedro Schestatsky, Felipe Fregni, and Marom Bikson, "Methods and Technologies for Low-Intensity Transcranial Electrical Stimulation: Waveforms, Terminology, and Historical Notes," in *Textbook of Neuromodulation*, eds. Helena Knotkova and Dirk Raschepp (New York: Springer, 2015), 7–16.

59 Sheena Waters-Metenier, Masud Husain, Tobias Wiestler, and Jörn Diedrichsen, "Bihemispheric Transcranial Direct Current Stimulation Enhances Effector-Independent Representations of Motor Synergy and Sequence Learning," *The Journal of Neuroscience* 34, no. 3 (2014): 1037–50.

60 A. St Clair Gibson and T. D. Noakes, "Evidence for Complex System Integration and Dynamic Neural Regulation of Skeletal Muscle Recruitment during Exercise in Humans," *British Journal of Sports Medicine* 38, no. 6 (2004): 797–806.

61 David J. Diehl and Samuel Gershon, "The Role of Dopamine in Mood Disorders," *Comprehensive Psychiatry* 33, no. 2 (1992): 115–20.

62 Boris D. Heifets and Robert C. Malenka, "MDMA as a Probe and Treatment for Social Behaviors," *Cell* 166, no. 2 (2016): 269–72; Ana Rubio-Araiz, Mercedes Perez-Hernandez, Andrés Urrutia et al., "3, 4-Methylenedioxymethamphetamine (MDMA, Ecstasy) SDsrupts Blood-Brain Barrier Integrity Through a Mechanism Involving P2X7 Receptors," *International Journal of Neuropsychopharmacology* 17, no. 8 (2014): 1243–55.

63 Tim Outhred, Brittany E. Hawkshead, Tor D. Wager et al., "Acute Neural Effects of Selective Serotonin Reuptake Inhibitors Versus Noradrenaline Reuptake Inhibitors on Emotion Processing: Implications for Differential Treatment Efficacy," *Neuroscience & Biobehavioral Reviews* 37, no. 8 (2013): 1786–800.

64 Caroline D. Rae and Stefan Bröer, "Creatine as a Booster for Human Brain Function: How Might It Work?" *Neurochemistry International* 89 (2015): 249–59; Sergej M. Ostojic, Jelena Ostojic, Patrik Drid, and Milan Vranes, "Guanidinoacetic Acid Versus Creatine for Improved Brain and Muscle Creatine Levels: A Superiority Pilot Trial in Healthy Men," *Applied Physiology, Nutrition, and Metabolism* 41, no. 9 (2016): 1005–7.

65 A majority of religious Americans see technological augmentation as morally and theologically wrong: Michael Lipka, "The Religious Divide on Views of Technologies That Would 'Enhance' Human Beings," *Pew Research*, https://bit.ly/2wzLxB9

66 Jayavardhana Gubbi, Rajkumar Buyya, Slaven Marusic, and Marimuthu Palaniswami, "Internet of Things (IoT): A Vision, Architectural Elements, and Future Directions," *Future Generation Computer Systems* 29, no. 7 (2013): 1645–60.

67 Rolf H. Weber, "Internet of Things-New Security and Privacy Challenges," *Computer Law & Security Review* 26, no. 1 (2010): 23–30.

68 Weheliye, *Habaeus Viscus*, 52, 130.

Chapter 5

1 Joe Feagin, *Systemic Racism: A Theory of Oppression* (Abington, PA: Routledge, 2013), 2.

2 Alison L. Kitson, "The Need for Systems Change: Reflections on Knowledge Translation and Organizational Change," *Journal of Advanced Nursing* 65, no. 1 (2009): 217–28.

3 Wynter, "Autopoietic Turn," 2007.

4 Calvin L. Warren, *Ontological Terror: Blackness, Nihilism, and Emancipation* (Durham, NC: Duke University Press, 2018).

5 Fred Moten, "Blackness and Nothingness (Mysticism in the Flesh)," *South Atlantic Quarterly* 112, no. 4 (2013): 737–80; Hortense Spillers, *Black, White, and in Color: Essays on American Literature and Culture* (Chicago, IL: University of Chicago Press, 2003), 406.

6 Tony Bradley, "Facebook AI Creates Its Own Language in Creepy Preview of Our Potential Future," *Forbes Magazine*, accessed April 4, 2019, http://bit.ly/2WLyLLh

7 Joel Z. Leibo, Vinicius Zambaldi, Marc Lanctot, Janusz Marecki, and Thore Graepel, "Multi-Agent Reinforcement Learning in Sequential Social Dilemmas," In *Proceedings of the 16th Conference on Autonomous Agents and MultiAgent Systems*, International Foundation for Autonomous Agents and Multiagent Systems, 2017, 464–73.

8 Narrow AI is AI that can only complete a narrow set of tasks. This is opposed to general and broad AI. General AI would be AI that spans many capacities. Broad AI has the capacity to cover a wider range of faculties than narrow AI, but cannot cover the expanse of general AI.

9 One could argue that oppression is the result of "the fall." But doesn't hierarchical means of existence precede the fall? Does God oppress creation, or, more specifically, God's people?

10 Reinhold Niebuhr, *The Children of Light and the Children of Darkness: A Vindication of Democracy and a Critique of Its Traditional Defense* (Chicago, IL: University of Chicago Press, 2011).

11 Warren, *Ontological Terror*, 170.

12 Venom is a symbiote from another planet. He attaches himself to a host (Eddie Brock), and he becomes an antihero in that he is not saint, but he also is not entirely a villain. He's a hero with no rules.

13 Fanon, *Wretched of the Earth*, 35.

14 Ibid., 70.

15 Ibid., 73.

16 Bessel A. Van der Kolk, *Psychological Trauma* (Washington, DC: American Psychiatric Pub, 2003); Etienne G. Krug, James A. Mercy, Linda L. Dahlberg, and Anthony B. Zwi, "The World Report on Violence and Health," *The Lancet* 360, no. 9339 (2002): 1083–88.

17 Here you can think about Achille Mbembe's "Necropolitics," CLR James' *Notes of Dialectics*, Frantz Fanon *Wretch of the Earth*, any of Sylvia Wynter's work, and Sadiya Hartman's *Scene's of Subjection*, just to name a few.

18 Ann Ulanov, "Jung and Religion: The Opposing Self," *The Cambridge Companion to Jung* (1997): 296–313; Angeliki Yiassemides, *Timelessness: Temporality in the Theory of Carl Jung* (Abbington: Routledge, 2013).

19 Kristen Bialik, "For the Fifth Time in a Row, the New Congress Is the Most Racially and Ethnically Diverse Ever," *Pew Research*, 2019, accessed April 7, 2019, http://bit.ly/2IevKiE

20 How many people are going to read this book? That is yet to be seen. Further, the language employed in these pages might be argued unsuitable for my intended audience. I might be too far removed from the Black people I purport to care enough about to write about. The list goes on.

21 Frank B. Wilderson III, Saidiya Hartman, Steve Martinot, J. Sexton, and Hortenese J. Spillers, *Afro-Pessimism: An Introduction* (Minneapolis, MN: Racked & Dispatched, 2017).

22 Fanon, *Wretched of the Earth*, 37.

23 Nipsey Hustle, "Ain't Hard Enough," *Slauson Boy 2*, Released August 15, 2016, ALL MONEY IN NO MONEY OUT, iTunes.

24 Nelson Maldonado-Torres, "Thinking through the Decolonial Turn: Post-Continental Interventions in Theory, Philosophy, and Critique—An Introduction," *Transmodernity: Journal of Peripheral Cultural Production of the Luso-Hispanic World* 1, no. 2 (2011).

25 Jidenna, *Long Live the Chief*, released February 17, 2017, Epic Records (a division of Sony Music Entertainment), iTunes; Herbert Aptheker, *American Negro Slave Revolts*, 50th Anniversary Edition (New York: International Publishers, 1993), 162.

26 Dick Gregory, *Dick Gregory's Political Primer* (Manhattan: Harper & Row, 1972), See Malcolm X on African Americans.

27 This may also be a conversation of the desire for inclusion or reform over freedom. Which raises an even larger question, What does it meant to be free? And from what?

28 Joy Buolamwini, "How I'm Fighting Bias in Algorithms" TEDxBeaconStreet, recorded November 2016, https://bit.ly/2wBKosM

29 Pinn, *The End of God-Talk*, 153.

30 A reference to a William Hinn sermon I heard once. Yes, he is Benny Hinn's brother.

31 Dirk Huyerbrouk has done some incredible scholarship on the mathematics of Central Africa. He outlines various number systems of Sub-Saharan Africans, how it was part of their art, built into their mating processes, and how the mathematician was considered an important role in the culture. He also recounts how the first mancala style game originated in Africa. His work does well to outline the African mathematical tradition which is an important epigenetic factor within Black biotechnology; Dirk Huylebrouck, "Mathematics in (Central) Africa Before Colonization," *Anthropologica et praehistorica* 117 (2006): 135–62.

32 Robert Fatton Jr., "Alex Dupuy: Haiti: From Revolutionary Slaves to Powerless Citizens: Essays on the Politics and Economics of Underdevelopment, 1804-2013," *New West Indian Guide* 89, no. 3–4 (2015): 358–60. *Academic OneFile*, accessed January 8, 2017, http://dx.doi.org/10.1163/22134360-08903024

33 Cone, *God of the Oppressed*; James H. Cone, *A Black Theology of Liberation* (Maryknoll, NY: Orbis Books, 1977); Alice Walker, *In Search of Our Mother's Gardens: Womanist Prose* (Boston, MA: Houghton Mifflin Harcourt, 2004); Jacquelyn Grant, *White Women's Christ and Black Women's Jesus: Feminist Christology and Womanist Response* No. 64 (Saarbrücken: Scholars Press, 1989); Coleman, *Making a Way Out of No Way: A Womanist Theology*; etc.

34 Marcuse, *One-Dimensional Man*, 83.

References

Adeofe, Leke. "Personal Identity in African Metaphysics." In *African Philosophy: New and Traditional Perspectives*. Lee M. Brown, ed. New York: Oxford University Press, 2004. Oxford Scholarship Online, 2006. doi: 10.1093/019511440X.003.0005.

Ahmad, Nahdatul Akma, F. Hanis, and A. Razak. "On the Emergence of Techno-Spiritual: The Concept and Current Issues." Quoted in *Computer and Mathematical Sciences Graduates National Colloquium 2013 (SISKOM2013)* (2013): 1–8.

Akiko, Kubo, Mayumi Kajimura, and Makoto Suematsu. "Matrix-Assisted Laser Desorption/Ionization (MALDI) Imaging Mass Spectrometry (IMS): A Challenge for Reliable Quantitative Analyses." *Mass Spectrometry* 1, no. 1 (2012): A0004. doi: 10.5702/massspectrometry.A0004.

Akrong, Abraham. "The Empowering Christ: A Post-Colonial African Christology," Unpublished Manuscript.

Albin, Roger and J. Greenamyre. "Alternative Excitotoxic Hypotheses." *Neurology* 42 (1992): 733–38.

Alexander, Michelle. *The New Jim Crow: Mass Incarceration in the Age of Colorblindness*. New York: The New Press, 2012.

Altman, Sam. "Moving Forward on Basic Income." *The Y-Combinator Blog*. May 31, 2016. https://web.archive.org/web/20161008005352/https://blog.ycombinator.com/moving-forward-on-basic-income.

Anderson, Victor. *Beyond Ontological Blackness: An Essay on African American Religious and Cultural Criticism*. New York: Continuum, 1995.

Appelhans, Bradley M. and Linda J. Luecken. "Heart Rate Variability as an Index of Regulated Emotional Responding." *Review of General Psychology* 10, no. 3 (2006): 229.

Aptheker, Herbert. *American Negro Slave Revolts*, 50th Anniversary Edition. New York: International Publishers, 1993.

Baron Short, E., Samet Kose, Qiwen Mu, et al. "Regional Brain Activation During Meditation Shows Time and Practice Effects: An Exploratory FMRI Study." *Evidence-Based Complementary and Alternative Medicine* 7, no. 1 (2010): 121–27.

Barraza, Jorge A., et al. "The Heart of the Story: Peripheral Physiology during Narrative Exposure Predicts Charitable Giving." *Biological Psychology* 105 (2015): 138–43.

Batiste, Stephanie L. "Dunham Possessed: Ethnographic Bodies, Movement, and Transnational Constructions of Blackness." *Journal of Haitian Studies* 13, no. 2 (2007): 8–22.

Beal, Frances M. "Double Jeopardy: To Be Black and Female." *Meridians: Feminism, Race, Transnationalism* 8, no. 2 (2008): 154.

Beattie, Tina. *Theology after Postmodernity: Divining the Void: A Lacanian Reading of Thomas Aquinas*. Oxford: Oxford University Press, 2013.

Beauregard, Mario and Vincent Paquette. "Neural Correlates of a Mystical Experience in Carmelite Nuns." *Neuroscience Letters* 405, no. 3 (2006): 186–90.

Beja-Pereira, A., G. Luikart, et al. "Gene-Culture Co-Evolution between Cattle Milk Protein Genes and Human Lactase Genes." *Nature Genetics* 35 (2003): 311–13.

Bender, Courtney. *The New Metaphysicals: Spirituality and the American Religious Imagination*. Chicago: University of Chicago Press, 2010.

Bhat, A. S. "Nanobots: The Future of Medicine." *International Journal of Engineering and Management Sciences* 5, no. 1 (2014): 44–49.

Bialik, Kristen. "For the Fifth Time in a Row, the New Congress is the Most Racially and Ethnically Diverse Ever." *Pew Research* (2019) (Accessed April 7, 2019). http://bit.ly/2IevKiE.

Bianconi, Eva, Allison Piovesan, Federica Facchin, Alina Beraudi, Raffaella Casadei, Flavia Frabetti, Lorenza Vitale, et al. "An Estimation of the Number of Cells in the Human Body." *Annals of Human Biology* 40, no. 6 (2013): 463–71.

Boggio, Kristin J., Emmanuel Obasuyi, Ken Sugino, Sacha B. Nelson, Nathalie Y. R. Agar, and Jeffrey N. Agar. "Recent Advances in Single-Cell MALDI Mass Spectrometry Imaging and Potential Clinical Impact." *Expert Review of Proteomics* 8, no. 5 (2011): 591–604.

Bonnet, Jerome, Subsoontorn, and Drew Endy. "Rewritable Digital Data Storage in Live Cells Via Engineered Control of Recombination Directionality." *Proceedings of the National Academy of Sciences* 109, no. 23 (2012): 8884–89.

Bostrom, Nick. "A History of Transhumanist Thought." In *Academic Writing Across the Disciplines*. Michael Rectenwald and Lisa Carl, eds. New York: Pearson Longman, 2011.

Bostrom, Nick. "Human Genetic Enhancements: A Transhumanist Perspective." *The Journal of Value Inquiry* 37, no. 4 (2003): 493–506.

Bostrom, Nick. "The Transhumanist FAQ: v 3.0." *Humanity+* 2018. https://web.archive.org/web/20180604232220/https://humanityplus.org/philosophy/transhumanist-faq/.

Boyatzis, Chris J. "A Critique of Models of Religious Experience." *International Journal for the Psychology of Religion* 4 (2001): 247–58.

Bradley, Tony. "Facebook AI Creates Its Own Language in Creepy Preview Of Our Potential Future." *Forbes Magazine* (Accessed April 4, 2019). http://bit.ly/2WLyLLh.

Braidotti, Rosi. *The Posthuman*. Cambridge: Polity Press, 2013.

Brandt, Allan M. "Racism and Research: The Case of the Tuskegee Syphilis Study." *The Hastings Center Report* 8, no. 6 (1978): 21–29.

Breeden, James O. "States-Rights Medicine in the Old South." *Bulletin of the New York Academy of Medicine* 52, no. 3 (1976): 348.

Brosnan, S. F. and R. Bshary. "Cooperation and Deception: From Evolution to Mechanisms." *Philosophical Transactions of the Royal Society B* 365 (2010): 2593–98.

Brouwer, Anne-Marie, Thorsten O. Zander, Jan BF Van Erp, Johannes E. Korteling, and Adelbert W. Bronkhorst. "Using Neurophysiological Signals That Reflect Cognitive or Affective State: Six Recommendations to Avoid Common Pitfalls." *Frontiers in Neuroscience* 9 (2015): 136. PMC. Web. April 18, 2016.

Brown, Norman W. "'What the Negro Thinks of God,' AME Church Review 51 (April–June 1935)." Quoted in *Social Protest Thought in the African Methodist Episcopal Churchy. 1862–1939*. Stephen Angell and Anthony B. Pinn, eds. Knoxville: The University of Tennessee Press, 2000.

Buckner, Randy L., Jessica R. Andrews-Hanna, and Daniel L. Schacter. "The Brain's Default Network." *Annals of the New York Academy of Sciences* 1124, no. 1 (2008): 1–38.

Bueya, Emmanuel. *Stability in Postcolonial African States*. Lanham: Lexington Books, 2017.

Buolamwini, Joy. "How I'm Fighting Bias in Algorithms." TEDxBeaconStreet. Recorded November 2016. https://bit.ly/2wBKosM.

Bureau of Labor Statistics. "Labor Force Statistics from the Current Population Survey" January 10, 2016. https://web.archive.org/web/20161008012804/http://www.bls.gov/cps/cpsaat11.htm.

Campbell, Heidi A. "Problematizing the Human-Technology Relationship Through Techno-Spiritual Myths Presented in The Machine, Transcendence and Her." *Journal of Religion & Film* 20, no. 1 (2016): 21.

Campbell, Heidi A., Brian Altenhofen, Wendi Bellar, and Kyong James Cho. "There's A Religious App for That! A Framework for Studying Religious Mobile Applications." *Mobile Media & Communication* 2, no. 2 (2014): 154–72.

Cannon, Walter B. "The James-Lange Theory of Emotions: A Critical Examination and an Alternative Theory." *The American Journal of Psychology* 39, no. 1/4 (1927): 106–24.

Carhart-Harris, Robin L., David Erritzoe, Tim Williams, et al. "Neural Correlates of the Psychedelic State as Determined by fMRI Studies with Psilocybin." *Proceedings of the National Academy of Sciences* 109, no. 6 (2012): 2138–43.

Carone, Benjamin R., Lucas Fauquier, Naomi Habib, Jeremy M. Shea, Caroline E. Hart, Ruowang Li, Christoph Bock, et al. "Paternally Induced Transgenerational Environmental Reprogramming of Metabolic Gene Expression in Mammals." *Cell* 143, no. 7 (2010): 1084–96.

Carter, Gregg Lee. "In the Narrows of the 1960s US Black Rioting." *Journal of Conflict Resolution* 30, no. 1 (1986): 115–27.

Cavalieri, Paola. *The Animal Question: Why Nonhuman Animals Deserve Human Rights*. Trans. Catherine Woollard. New York: Oxford University Press, 2001.

Chen, Min, Shiwen Mao, and Yunhao Liu. "Big Data: A Survey." *Mobile Networks and Applications* 19, no. 2 (2014): 171–209.

Chow, T. W. and J. L. Cummings. "Frontal Subcortical Circuits." In *The Human Frontal Lobes*. B. L. Miller and J. L. Cummings, eds. New York: Guilford Press, 1999.

Ciccariello-Maher, George. "Jumpstarting the Decolonial Engine: Symbolic Violence from Fanon to Chavez." *Theory & Event* 13, no. 1 (2010): doi:10.1353/tae.0.0120.

Clayton, Philip. *Mind and Emergence*. New York: Oxford University Press, 2005.

Clossy, Samuel. Samuel Clossy to George Cleghorn, August 1, 1764. Quoted in *Surgeon to Washington*. M. H. Saffron, ed. New York: Columbia University Press, 1977.

Clutton-Brock, T. H. and G. A. Parker. "Punishment in Animal Societies." *Nature* 373 (1995): 209–16.

Cocchi, Massimo, Fabio Gabrielli, Lucio Tonello, Mauro Delogu, Valentina Beghelli, et al. "Molecular Contiguity between Human and Animal Consciousness through Evolution: Some Considerations." *Journal of Phylogenetics & Evolutionary Biology* 1 (2013): 119. doi: 10.4172/2329-9002.1000119.

Coenen, V. A., et al. "Diffusion Tensor Imaging and Neuromodulation: DTI as Key Technology for Deep Brain Stimulation." *International Review of Neurobiology* 107 (2012): 207–34.

Coleman, Monica A. *Making a Way Out of No Way: A Womanist Theology*. Minneapolis: Fortress Press, 2008

Collins, William J. and Robert A. Margo. "The Economic Aftermath of the 1960s Riots in American Cities: Evidence from Property Values." *The Journal of Economic History* 67, no. 04 (2007): 849–83.

Cone, James H. *A Black Theology of Liberation*. Maryknoll: Orbis Books, 1977.

Cone, James H. *God of the Oppressed*. Maryknoll: Orbis Books, 1977.

Cone, James and Cornel West. "The Marty Forum: James H Cone SD." In *American Academy of Religion Annual Meeting, Montreal Quebec*. Published on June 26, 2015. Original recording Sunday November 8, 2009. Posted to American Academy of Religion Youtube Channel. 35:49. https://www.youtube.com/watch?v=28egmRya Inw.

Cornell, Jay. *Transcendence: The Disinformation Encyclopedia of Transhumanism and Singularity*. Newburyport: Red Wheel Weiser, 2015.

Date, Akira. "An Information Theoretic Analysis of 256-channel EEG Recordings: Mutual Information and Measurement Selection Problem." *Proceedings of the International Conference on Independent Component Analysis and Blind Signal Separation (ICA2001)* (2001): 85–188.

Daugherty, Alane. *From Mindfulness to Heartfulness*. Bloomington: Archway Publishing, 2014.

Daugherty, Alane. *The Power Within: From Neuroscience to Transformation*. Dubuque: Kendall Hunt Publishing Company, 2008.

Davies, E., C. J. Keyon, and R. Fraser. "The Role of Calcium Ions in the Mechanism of ACTH Stimulation of Cortisol Synthesis." *Steroids* 45 (1985): 551–60.

Davies, Paul and John Gribbin. *The Matter Myth: Beyond Chaos and Complexity*. London: Viking, 1991.

Davis, M. "The Role of the Amygdala in Fear and Anxiety." *Annual Review of Neuroscience* 15 (1992): 353–75.

De Dreu, K. W., L. L. Greer, M. J. Handgraaf, et al. "The Neuropeptide Oxytocin Regulates Parochial Altruism in Intergroup Conflict Among Humans." *Science* 328 (2010): 1408–11.

de Grey, Aubrey. "The Curate's Egg of Anti-Anti-Aging Bioethics." In *The Transhumanist Reader: Classical and Contemporary Essays on the Science, Technology, and Philosophy of the Human Future*. Max More and Natasha Vita-More, eds. West Sussex: Wiley-Blackwell, 2013.

De Mello, Anthony. *Sadhana*. Bournemouth: Image, 2011.

de Waal, Frans. *Chimpanzee Politics: Power and Sex Among Apes. 25th Anniversary Ed.* Baltimore: Johns Hopkins University Press, 1982.

de Waal, Frans. "The Integration of Dominance and Social Bonding in Primates." *Quarterly Review of Biology* 61, no. 4 (1986): 459–79.

Deane, G. "Technological Unemployment: Panacea or Poison?" Institute of Ethics and Emerging Technologies Blog, *March 5*. (Accessed October 7, 2016). http://ieet.org/index.php/IEET/more/deane20130305.

Deleuze, Gilles. *Pure Immanence*. New York: Zone Books, 2001.

Deuschl, Günther, Carmen Schade-Brittinger, Paul Krack, Jens Volkmann, Helmut Schäfer, Kai Bötzel, Christine Daniels, et al. "A Randomized Trial of Deep-brain Stimulation for Parkinson's Disease." *New England Journal of Medicine* 355, no. 9 (2006): 896–908.

Diehl, David J. and Samuel Gershon. "The Role of Dopamine in Mood Disorders." *Comprehensive Psychiatry* 33, no. 2 (1992): 115–20.

Douglass, Frederick. *Narrative of the Life of Frederick Douglass*. New York: Diversion Books, 1845.

Dvorsky, George. "Rights of Non-Human Persons." *The Institute for Ethics and Emerging Technologies (IEET)* (2011). https://ieet.org/index.php/IEET2/RNHP.

Dyson, Michael Eric. "'Searching for Black Jesus.'" Quoted in *Open Mike: Reflections on Philosophy, Race, Sex, Culture and Religion*. Michael Eric Dyson, ed. New York: Basic Civitas Books, 2003, 267–88.

Edwards, Stephen D. "HeartMath: A Positive Psychology Paradigm for Promoting Psychophysiological and Global Coherence." *Journal of Psychology in Africa* 25, no. 4 (2015): 367–74.

Einstein, Albert. *Sidelights on Relativity*. New York: E. P. Dutton, 1923.

Ernst, Aurélie and Jonas Frisén. "Adult Neurogenesis in Humans-Common and Unique Traits in Mammals." *PLoS Biology* 13, no. 1 (2015): e1002045. doi: 10.1371/ journal.pbio.1002045.

Eze, Michael Onyebuchi. "Humanitatis-Eco (Eco-Humanism): An African Environmental Theory." In *The Palgrave Handbook of African Philosophy*. Afolayan, Adeshina, and Toyin Falola, eds. New York: Palgrave Macmillan, 2017, 621–32.

Faber, Roland and Andrea M. Stephenson, eds. *Secrets of Becoming: Negotiating Whitehead, Deleuze, and Butler*. New York: Fordham University Press, 2011.

Falk, Emily B., Matthew Brook O'Donnell, Christopher N. Cascio, et al. "Self-Affirmation Alters the Brain's Response to Health Messages and Subsequent Behavior Change." *Proceedings of the National Academy of Sciences* 112, no. 7 (2015): 1977–82.

Fanon, Frantz. *Black Skin White Masks*. New York: Grove Press, 2008.

Fanon, Frantz. *The Wretched of the Earth*. New York: Grove Press, 1963.

Farra, Robert, Norman F. Sheppard, Laura McCabe, et al. "First-In-Human Testing of a Wirelessly Controlled Drug Delivery Microchip." *Science Translational Medicine* 4, no. 122 (2012): 122ra21. doi: 10.1126/scitranslmed.3003276.

Fatton, Robert Jr. "Alex Dupuy: Haiti: From Revolutionary Slaves to Powerless Citizens: Essays on the Politics and Economics of Underdevelopment, 1804–2013." *New West Indian Guide* 89, no. 3–4 (2015): 358–60. *Academic OneFile* (Accessed January 8, 2017). doi: 10.1163/22134360-08903024.

Feagin, Joe. *Systemic Racism: A Theory of Oppression*. Abington: Routledge, 2013.

Feinberg, Andrew P. "Phenotypic Plasticity and the Epigenetics of Human Disease." *Nature* 447, no. 7143 (2007): 433.

Fifer, Matthew S., Soumyadipta Acharya, Heather L. Benz, Mohsen Mollazadeh, et al. "Towards Electrocorticographic Control of a Dexterous Upper Limb Prosthesis." *IEEE Pulse* 3, no. 1 (2012): 38.

Fine, Cordelia. "Is There Neurosexism in Functional Neuroimaging Investigations of Sex Difference?" *Neuroethics* 6, no. 2 (2013): 369–409.

Fischer, Jörg Daniel. "The Braincon Platform Software-a Closed-loop Brain-Computer Interface Software for Research and Medical Applications." PhD Dissertation, University of Freiburg, Germany, 2015.

Fisher, Walter. "Physicians and Slavery in the Antebellum Southern Medical Journal." *Journal of the History of Medicine and Allied Sciences* 23, no. 1 (1968): 36–49.

Flanagan, Owen. *The Really Hard Problem: Meaning in a Material World*. Cambridge: MIT Press, 2007.

Flynn, Patrice. "Using an Autonomous Humanoid Robot as a Pedagogical Platform in the Business Classroom." *Journal of Social Science Studies* 4, no. 1 (2016): 178.

Fook, Jan and Gurid Aga Askeland. "Challenges of Critical Reflection:'Nothing Ventured, Nothing Gained.'" *Social Work Education* 26, no. 5 (2007): 520–33.

Foote, S. "Extrathalamic Modulation of Cortical Function." *Annual Review of Neuroscience* 10 (1987): 67–95.

Ford, M. *The Lights in the Tunnel*. Lexington: Acculant Publishing, 2009.

Forman, Sam and Dr. Joseph Warren. *The Boston Tea Party, Bunker Hill, and the Birth of American Liberty*. Gretna: Pelican Publishing Company, Inc, 2011.

Foucault, Michel. *The Order of Things: An Archaeology of the Human Sciences*. New York: Pantheon, 1971.

Fountain, Jane E. "On the Effects of e-Government on Political Institutions." In *Routledge Handbook of Science, Technology, and Society*. Daniel Lee Kleinman and Kelly Moore, eds. NewYork: Routledge, 2014, 471–88.

Froeliger, Brett, Eric L. Garland, and F. Joseph McClernon. "Yoga Meditation Practitioners Exhibit Greater Gray Matter Volume and Fewer Reported Cognitive Failures: Results of a Preliminary Voxel-Based Morphometric Analysis." *Evidence-Based Complementary and Alternative Medicine* 2012. Cairo: Hindawi Publishing Corporation, 2012. doi: 10.1155/2012/821307.

Fuentes, Agustín. *Race, Monogamy, and Other Lies They Told You: Busting Myths about Human Nature*. Berkeley: University of California Press, 2015.

Fukuyama, Francis. *Our Posthuman Future: Consequence of the Biotechnology Revolution*. New York: Farrar, Straus and Giroux, 2002.

Fuller, Steve and Veronika Lipińska. *The Proactionary Imperative: A Foundation for Transhumanism*. New York: Palgrave Macmillan, 2014.

Funk, Cary and Becka A. Alper. "Perception of Conflict Between Science and Religion." *Pew Research*. https://pewrsr.ch/1QXYU0B.

Galilei, Galileo and Sebastiano Timpanaro. *Opere. Il Saggiatore*. Milano: Rizzoli, 1936.

Gibson, A. St Clair and T. D. Noakes. "Evidence for Complex System Integration and Dynamic Neural Regulation of Skeletal Muscle Recruitment During Exercise in Humans." *British Journal of Sports Medicine* 38, no. 6 (2004): 797–806.

Gleick, James. *Chaos: Making a New Science*. London: Heinemann, 1988.

Glover, Jonathan. *What Sort of People Should There Be?* New York: Penguin, 1984.

Golden, Kristen Brown. *Nietzsche and Embodiment: Discerning Bodies and Non-dualism*. Albany: SUNY Press, 2012, 35.

Gordon, Lewis R. "Through the Hellish Zone of Nonbeing: Thinking Through Fanon, Disaster, and the Damned of the Earth." *Human Architecture: Journal of the Sociology of Self-Knowledge* 5, no. 3 (2007): 3.

Gover, Mark R. "The Embodied Mind: Cognitive Science and Human Experience." *Mind, Culture, and Activity* 3, no. 4 (1996): 295–99.

Grant, Jacquelyn. *White Women's Christ and Black Women's Jesus: Feminist Christology and Womanist Response* No. 64. Saarbrücken: Scholars Press, 1989.

Gregory, Dick. *Dick Gregory's Political Primer*. Manhattan: Harper & Row, 1972.

Gubbi, Jayavardhana, Rajkumar Buyya, Slaven Marusic, and Marimuthu Palaniswami. "Internet of Things (IoT): A Vision, Architectural Elements, and Future Directions." *Future Generation Computer Systems* 29, no. 7 (2013): 1645–60.

Guitchounts, Grigori, Jeffrey E. Markowitz, William A. Liberti, and Timothy J. Gardner. "A Carbon-Fiber Electrode Array for Long-Term Neural Recording." *Journal of Neural Engineering* 10, no. 4 (2013): 10.1088/1741-2560/10/4/046016.

Guleyupoglu, Berkan, Pedro Schestatsky, Felipe Fregni, and Marom Bikson. "Methods and Technologies for Low-Intensity Transcranial Electrical Stimulation: Waveforms, Terminology, and Historical Notes." In *Textbook of Neuromodulation*. Helena Knotkova and Dirk Rasche, eds. New York: Springer, 2015, 7–16.

Gurnard, D. A. and M. E. Raichle, "Searching for a Baseline: Functional Imaging and the Resting Human Brain." *Nature* 2 (2001): 685–94.

Hannaford, Blake and Allison M. Okamura. "Haptics." In *Springer Handbook of Robotics.* Bruno Siciliano and Oussama Khatib, eds. New York: Springer, 2016.

Haraway, Donna J. "A Cyborg Manifesto: Science, Technology, and Socialist-Feminism in the Late Twentieth Century." In *Simians, Cyborgs and Women: The Reinvention of Nature.* Penny Anthon, Green, ed. New York: Routledge, 1991, 117–58.

Haraway, Donna J. *When Species Meet.* Minnesota: University of Minnesota Press, 2008.

Harris, Sam, Sameer A. Sheth, and Mark S. Cohen. "Functional Neuroimaging of Belief, Disbelief, and Uncertainty." *Annals of Neurology* 63, no. 2 (2008): 141–47.

Hart, William David. *Afro-Eccentricity: Beyond the Standard Narrative of Black Religion.* Basingstoke: Palgrave Macmillan, 2011.

Hartman, Saidiya V. *Scenes of Subjection: Terror, Slavery, and Self-making in Nineteenth-century America.* New York: Oxford University Press on Demand, 1997.

Heifets, Boris D. and Robert C. Malenka. "MDMA as a Probe and Treatment for Social Behaviors." *Cell* 166, no. 2 (2016): 269–72.

Heller, Aaron S., et al. "Simultaneous Acquisition of Corrugator Electromyography and Functional Magnetic Resonance Imaging: A New Method for Objectively Measuring Affect and Neural Activity Concurrently." *Neuroimage* 58, no. 3 (2011): 930–34.

Herr, Hugh M. and Alena M. Grabowski. "Bionic Ankle–Foot Prosthesis Normalizes Walking Gait for Persons With Leg Amputation." *Proceedings of the Royal Society B* 279, no. 1728 (2012): 457–64.

Hofmann, Stefan G., Paul Grossman, and Devon E. Hinton. "Loving-Kindness and Compassion Meditation: Potential for Psychological Interventions." *Clinical Psychology Review* 31, no. 7 (2011): 1126–32.

Hogue, David A. "Sometimes It Causes Me To Tremble: Fear, Faith, and the Human Brain." *Pastoral Psychology* 63, no. 5–6 (2014): 659–71.

Hollingsworth, Andrea. "Implications of Interpersonal Neurobiology for a Spirituality of Compassion." *Zygon®* 43, no. 4 (2008): 837–60.

Holmes, Barbara Ann. *Joy Unspeakable: Contemplative Practices of the Black Church.* Minneapolis: Fortress Press, 2004.

Hopkins, Dwight N., ed. *Black Faith and Public Talk: Critical Essays on James H. Cone's Black Theology and Black Power.* Waco: Baylor University Press, 1999.

Howells, Annika, Itai Ivtzan, and Francisco Jose Eiroa-Orosa. "Putting the 'App' In Happiness: A Randomised Controlled Trial of a Smartphone-Based Mindfulness Intervention to Enhance Wellbeing." *Journal of Happiness Studies* 17, no. 1 (2016): 163–85.

Huettel, Scott A., Allen W. Song, and Gregory McCarthy. *Functional Magnetic Resonance Imaging* 1. Sunderland: Sinauer Associates, 2004.

Hull, Gloria T. *Soul Talk: The New Spirituality of African American Women.* Rochester: Inner Traditions, 2001.

Hume, David. *Essays Moral, Political and Literary*. Oxford: Oxford University Press, 1963.

Hustle, Nipsey. "Ain't Hard Enough," *Slauson Boy 2*. Released August 15, 2016. ALL MONEY IN NO MONEY OUT. iTunes.

Huxley, Julian. "America Revisited. III. The Negro Problem." *The Spectator* (November 29, 1924): 821.

Huxley, Julian. "America Revisited. V. 'The Quota.'" *The Spectator* (December 20, 1924): 980–82.

Huxley, Julian. "Knowledge, Morality, and Destiny: I." *Psychiatry* 14, no. 2 (1951): 129–40.

Huxley, Julian. "The Negro Mind" Typescript 1918. JSHP Box 58:6.

Huxley, Julian. "The Vital importance of Eugenics." *Harpers Monthly* 163 (1931): 324.

Huxley, Julian, Alfred Cort Haddon, and Alexander Morris Carr-Saunders. *We Europeans: A Survey of "Racial" Problems*. London: Harper, 1936, 122–28.

Huylebrouck, Dirk. "Mathematics in (Central) Africa Before Colonization." *Anthropologica et praehistorica* 117 (2006): 135–62.

Ibrahim, Fatima and Siti A. Ahmad. "Investigation of Electromyographic Activity During Salat and Stretching Exercise." *Biomedical Engineering and Sciences (IECBES). 2012 IEEE EMBS Conference* (IEEE, 2012): 335–38.

Imhotep, Asar. "Understanding Ase and Its Relation to Esu among the Yoruba and Ase. T in Ancient Egypt." *The MOCHA-Versity Institute of Philosophy and Research* (2012).

Irele, F. Abiola. *The African Experience in Literature and Ideology*. London: Heinemann, 1981.

Jacob, Pierre. "What Do Mirror Neurons Contribute to Human Social Cognition?" *Mind & Language* 23, no. 2 (2008): 190–223.

James, Cyril Lionel Robert. *Notes on Dialectics: Hegel, Marx, Lenin*. London: Allison & Busby, 1980.

James, George G. M. *Stolen Legacy*, Vol. 1. Sauk Village: Library of Alexandria, 1954.

Janal, M. E. Colt, W. Clark, et al. "Pain Sensitivity, Mood and Plasma Endocrine Levels in Man Following Long-Distance Running: Effects of Naxalone." *Pain* 19 (1984): 13–25.

Jenkins, George B. "The Legal Status of Dissecting." *The Anatomical Record* 7, no. 11 (1913): 387–99.

Jenkins, Trisha A., Jason C. D. Nguyen, Kate E. Polglaze, and Paul P. Bertrand. "Influence of Tryptophan and Serotonin on Mood and Cognition With a Possible Role of the Gut-Brain Axis." *Nutrients* 8, no. 1 (2016): 56.

Jidenna, *Long Live the Chief*. released February 17, 2017. Epic Records (a division of Sony Music Entertainment). iTunes.

Jobling, Mark, Matthew Hurles, and Chris Tyler-Smith. *Human Evolutionary Genetics: Origins, Peoples & Disease*. New York: Garland Science, 2014, 487.

Johnson, E. Patrick. "'Quare' Studies, or (Almost) Everything I Know About Queer Studies I Learned From My Grandmother." *Text and Performance Quarterly* 21, no. 1 (2001): 1–25.

Johnstone, Brick, et al. "Right Parietal Lobe-Related 'Selflessness' as the Neuropsychological Basis of Spiritual Transcendence." *International Journal for the Psychology of Religion* 22, no. 4 (2012): 267–84.

Johnstone, Brick, Angela Bodling, Dan Cohen, Shawn E. Christ, and Andrew Wegrzyn. "Right Parietal Lobe-Related 'Selflessness' as the Neuropsychological Basis of Spiritual Transcendence." *International Journal for the Psychology of Religion* 22, no. 4 (2012): 267–84.

Jones, Donna. Trans. "Ce Que L'homme Noir Apporte." In *L'Homme De Couleur*. Paris: Librairie Plon, 1939, 24.

Jones, Donna V. *The Racial Discourses of Life Philosophy: Negritude, Vitalism, and Modernity*, Vol. 45. New York: Columbia University Press, 2010.

Jung, S. H., Song W., Lee S. I., et al. "Synthesis of Graphene and Carbon Nanotubes Hybrid Nanostructures and their Electrical Properties." *Journal of Nanoscience and Nanotechnology* 13 (2013): 6730–34.

Kansaku, Kenji, Leonardo G. Cohen, and Niels Birbaumer, eds. *Clinical Systems Neuroscience*. Tokyo : Springer, 2015.

Kant, Immanuel. *Observations on the Feeling of the Beautiful and Sublime*. Cambridge: Cambridge University Press, 2006.

Kaphagawani, Didier N. "African Conceptions of a Person: A Critical Survey." In *A Companion to African Philosophy*. Kwasi Wiredu, ed. Malden: Blackwell Publishing, 2004, 332–42.

Kass, Leon. "Ageless Bodies, Happy Souls: Biotechnology and the Pursuit of Perfection." *New Atlantis* 1 (2003): 9–28.

Katz, Marion H. "The Study of Islamic Ritual and the Meaning of Wuḍūʾ." *Der Islam* 82, no. 1 (2005): 106–45.

Keeling, Kara. "I = Another: Digital Identity Politics." In *Strange Affinities: The Gender and Sexual Politics of Comparative Racialization*. Grace Kyungwon Hong and Roderick A. Ferguson, eds. Durham: Duke University Press, 2011, 53–75.

Keysers, Christian and Valeria Gazzola. "Social Neuroscience: Mirror Neurons Recorded in Humans." *Current Biology* 20, no. 8 (2010): R353–54.

Kim, Kyungmi and Marcia K. Johnson. "Activity in Ventromedial Prefrontal Cortex During Self-Related Processing: Positive Subjective Value Or Personal Significance?" *Social Cognitive and Affective Neuroscience* 10, no. 4 (2015): 494–500.

Kiss, József, Katalin Kocsis, Agnes Csaki, Tamás J. Görcs, and Béla Halász. "Metabotropic Glutamate Receptor in GHRH and b-Endorphin Neurons of the Hypothalamic Arcuate Nucleus." *Neuroreport* 8 (1997): 3703–7.

Kitson, Alison L. "The Need for Systems Change: Reflections on Knowledge Translation and Organizational Change." *Journal of Advanced Nursing* 65, no. 1 (2009): 217–28.

Kleingeld, Pauline. "Kant's Second Thoughts on Race." *The Philosophical Quarterly* 57, no. 229 (2007): 573–92.

Klingberg, Frank Joseph. *Anglican Humanitarianism in Colonial*. New York: Ayer Publishing, 1940.

Knierim, James J., Joshua P. Neunuebel, and Sachin S. Deshmukh. "Functional Correlates of the Lateral and Medial Entorhinal Cortex: Objects, Path Integration and Local–Global Reference Frames." *Philosophical Transactions of the Royal Society B* 369, no. 1635 (2014): 20130369. doi: 10.1098/rstb.2013.0369.

Kotrschal, Kurt. "Emotions Are at the Core of Individual Social Performance." In *Emotions of Animals and Humans: Comparative Perspectives.* Shigeru Watanabe and Stan A. Kuczaj, eds. Tokyo: Springer, 2013.

Kripal, Jeffrey J. *The Serpent's Gift: Gnostic Reflections on the Study of Religion.* Chicago: University of Chicago Press, 2008.

Krug, Etienne G., James A. Mercy, Linda L. Dahlberg, and Anthony B. Zwi. "The World Report on Violence and Health." *The Lancet* 360, no. 9339 (2002): 1083–88.

Kruis, Ayla, Heleen A. Slagter, David R. W. Bachhuber, Richard J. Davidson, and Antoine Lutz. "Effects of Meditation Practice on Spontaneous Eyeblink Rate." *Psychophysiology* (2016).

Kurthen, Martin. *White and Black Posthumanism: After Consciousness and the Unconscious.* Brooklyn: Springer, 2009.

Lajul, Wilfred. "African Metaphysics: Traditional and Modern Discussions." In *Themes, Issues and Problems in African Philosophy.* Ukpokolo, Isaac E., ed. New York: Palgrave Macmillan, 2017, 19–48.

Lan, F., and G. Li. "Direct Observation of Hole Transfer from Semiconducting Polymer to Carbon Nanotubes." *Nano Letters* 13 (2013): 2086–91.

Lazar, Sara W., Catherine E. Kerr, Rachel H. Wasserman, et al. "Meditation Experience is Associated with Increased Cortical Thickness." *Neuroreport* 16, no. 17 (2005): 1893.

Lehrer, Paul, Yuji Sasaki, and Yoshihiro Saito. "Zazen and Cardiac Variability." *Psychosomatic Medicine* 61, no. 6 (1999): 812–21.

Leibo, Joel Z., Vinicius Zambaldi, Marc Lanctot, Janusz Marecki, and Thore Graepel. "Multi-Agent Reinforcement Learning in Sequential Social Dilemmas." In *Proceedings of the 16th Conference on Autonomous Agents and MultiAgent Systems*, pp. 464–473. International Foundation for Autonomous Agents and Multiagent Systems, 2017.

Lemm, Vanessa. *Nietzsche's Animal Philosophy: Culture, Politics, and the Animality of the Human Being.* New York: Fordham University Press, 2009.

Lieberman, Harris R., William J. Tharion, Barbara Shukitt-Hale, Karen L. Speckman, and Richard Tulley. "Effects of Caffeine, Sleep Loss, and Stress on Cognitive Performance and Mood During US Navy SEAL Training." *Psychopharmacology* 164, no. 3 (2002): 250–61.

Lipka, Michael. "The Religious Divide on Views of Technologies that Would 'Enhance' Human Beings." *Pew Research.* https://bit.ly/2wzLxB9.

Lodish, James E. Darnell, Arnold Berk, Chris A. Kaiser, Monty Krieger, Matthew P. Scott, Anthony Bretscher, Hidde Ploegh, and Paul Matsudaira. *Molecular Cell Biology.* New York: Macmillan, 2008.

Lutz, Antoine, Julie Brefczynski-Lewis, Tom Johnstone, and Richard J. Davidson. "Regulation of the Neural Circuitry of Emotion by Compassion Meditation: Effects of Meditative Expertise." *PloS One* 3, no. 3 (2008): e1897. doi: 10.1098/rstb.2013.0369.

Lutz, Jacqueline, Uwe Herwig, Sarah Opialla, et al. "Mindfulness and Emotion Regulation—An fMRI Study." *Social Cognitive and Affective Neuroscience* 9, no. 6 (2014): 776–85.

MacCormack, Jennifer K. and Kristen A. Lindquist. "Bodily Contributions to Emotion: Schachter's Legacy for a Psychological Constructionist View on Emotion." *Emotion Review* 9, no. 1 (2017): 36–45.

MacCormack, Patricia. "Vitalistic Feminethics." In *Deleuze and Law: Forensic Futures.* Rosi Braidotti, Claire Colebrook, and Patrick Hanafin, eds. New York: Palgrave MacMillan, 2009, 73–95.

Maldonado-Torres, Nelson. "Thinking Through the Decolonial Turn: Post-continental Interventions in Theory, Philosophy, and Critique—An Introduction." *Transmodernity: Journal of Peripheral Cultural Production of the Luso-Hispanic World* 1, no. 2 (2011). https://escholarship.org/uc/item/59w8j02x

Marchant, Gary E., Yvonne A. Stevens, and James M. Hennessy. "Technology, Unemployment & Policy Options: Navigating the Transition to a Better World." *Technology* 24, no. (2014): 26–44.

Marcuse, Herbert. *One-Dimensional Man.* Boston: Beacon Press, 1964.

Marshall, Amanda C., Antje Gentsch, Valentina Jelinčić, and Simone Schütz-Bosbach. "Exteroceptive Expectations Modulate Interoceptive Processing: Repetition-suppression Effects for Visual and Heartbeat Evoked Potentials." *Scientific Reports* 7, no. 1 (2017): 16525.

Martin, Darnise C. "The Self Divine: Know Ye Not that Ye are Gods?" In *Esotericism in African American Religious Experience.* Stephen Finley, Margarita Guillory, and Hugh Page Jr., eds. Boston: Brill, 2014, 52–68.

Mazama, Mambo Ama. "Afrocentricity and African Spirituality." *Journal of Black Studies* 33, no. 2 (2002): 218–34.

Mbaegbu, Celestine Chukwuemeka. "The Mind Body Problem: The Hermeneutics of African Philosophy." *Journal of Religion and Human Relations* 8, no. 2 (2016): 2–18.

Mbembe, Achille. "Necropolitics." In *Foucault in an Age of Terror.* Morton, Stephen, and Stephen Bygrave, eds. London: Palgrave Macmillan, 2008, 152–82.

McAdam, Doug. "Tactical Innovation and the Pace of Insurgency." *American Sociological Review* 48, no. 6 (1983): 735–54.

McKibben, Bill. *Enough: Staying Human in an Engineered Age.* New York: Times Books, 2003.

Mehta, Pranjal H., Stefan M. Goetz, and Justin M. Carré. "Genetic, Hormonal, and Neural Underpinnings of Human Aggressive Behavior." In *Handbook of Neurosociology.* David D. Franks and Jonathan H. Turner, eds. New York: Springer, 2013, 47–65.

Mettler, S. and J. Soss. "The Consequences of Public Policy for Democratic Citizenship: Bridging Policy Studies and Mass Politics." *Perspectives on Politics* 2, no. 1 (2004): 60.

Meuleman, Ben, Agnes Moors, Johnny Fontaine, Olivier Renaud, and Klaus Scherer. "Interaction and Threshold Effects of Appraisal on Componential Patterns of Emotion: A Study Using Cross-cultural Semantic Data." *Emotion* 19, no. 3 (2019): 425

Mijares, Sharon G. *The Revelation of the Breath: A Tribute to Its Wisdom, Power, and Beauty*. Albany: SUNY Press, 2009.

Moors, Agnes. "Flavors of Appraisal Theories of Emotion." *Emotion Review* 6, no. 4 (2014): 303–7.

Moors, Agnes. "Theories of Emotion Causation: A Review." In *Cognition and Emotion: Reviews of Current Research and Theories*. Jan De Houwer and Dirk Hermans, eds. Florence: Psychology Press, 2010, 1–38.

Moors, Agnes, Phoebe C. Ellsworth, Klaus R. Scherer, and Nico H. Frijda. "Appraisal Theories of Emotion: State of the Art and Future Development." *Emotion Review* 5, no. 2 (2013): 119–24.

Moten, Fred. "Blackness and Nothingness (Mysticism in the Flesh)." *South Atlantic Quarterly* 112, no. 4 (2013): 737–80.

Mudimbe, Valentin Y. "African Gnosis Philosophy and the Order of Knowledge: An Introduction." *African Studies Review* 28, no. 2–3 (1985): 149–233.

Mujynya, E. N. C. *L'Homme dans l'Univers des Bantu*. Lubumbashi: Presses Universitairs du Zaire, 1972.

Mukamel, Roy, Arne D. Ekstrom, Jonas Kaplan, Marco Iacoboni, and Itzhak Fried. "Single-Neuron Responses in Humans During Execution and Observation of Actions." *Current Biology* 20, no. 8 (2010): 750–56.

Mulago, V. *Un Visage Africaine du Christianisme*. Paris: Presence Africaine, 1965.

Murphy, Nancey. "Nonreductive Physicalism." In *Encyclopedia of Sciences and Religions*. Dordrecht: Springer, 2013.

Nagoshi, Craig T. and Julie L. Nagoshi. "Being Human versus Being Transhuman: The Mind–Body Problem and Lived Experience." In *Beyond Humanism: Trans- and Posthumanism: Building Better Humans? Refocusing the Debate on Transhumanism*. Stefan Lorenz Sorgner, Hava Tirosh-Samuelson, and Kenneth L. Mossmaned, eds. Frankfurt: Peter Lang, 2011, 303–20.

Nasso, Selene, Marie-Anne Vanderhasselt, Ineke Demeyer, and Rudi De Raedt. "Autonomic Regulation in Response to Stress: The influence of Anticipatory Emotion Regulation Strategies and Trait Rumination." *Emotion* 19, no. 3 (2019): 443.

National Academy of Sciences. *Technology and Employment: Innovation and Growth in the U.S. Economy*. Washington DC: National Academy Press, 1987.

Newberg Andrew, B. and Eugene G. D'Aquili. *Mystical Mind*. Minneapolis: Fortress Press, 1999.

Newberg Andrew B. and Jeremy Iversen. "The Neural Basis of the Complex Mental Task of Meditation: Neurotransmitter and Neurochemical Considerations." *Medical Hypotheses* 61, no. 2 (2003): 282–91.

Newberg, Andrew B., Nancy A. Wintering, Donna Morgan, and Mark R. Waldman. "The Measurement of Regional Cerebral Blood Flow During Glossolalia: A Preliminary SPECT Study." *Psychiatry Research: Neuroimaging* 148, no. 1 (2006): 67–71.

Newman, J. and A. A. Grace, "Binding Across Time: The Selective Gating of Frontal and Hippocampal Systems Modulating Working Memory and Attentional States." *Consciousness and Cognition* 8 (1999): 196–212.

Niebuhr, Reinhold. *The Children of Light and the Children of Darkness: A Vindication of Democracy and a Critique of its Traditional Defense*. Chicago: University of Chicago Press, 2011.

Nietzsche, Friedrich. *Human, All Too Human: A Book for Free Spirits*. Lincoln: University of Nebraska Press, 1984.

Nozick, Robert. *Anarchy, State, and Utopia*. New York: Basic Books, 1974.

Nussbaum, Martha C. *Frontiers of Justice: Disability, Nationality, Species Membership*. Cambridge: Harvard University Press, 2006.

Osoegawa, Kazutoyo, Aaron G. Mammoser, Chenyan Wu, Eirik Frengen, Changjiang Zeng, Joseph J. Catanese, and Pieter J. de Jong. "A Bacterial Artificial Chromosome Library for Sequencing the Complete Human Genome." *Genome Research* 11, no. 3 (2001): 483–96.

Ostojic, Sergej M., Jelena Ostojic, Patrik Drid, and Milan Vranes. "Guanidinoacetic Acid Versus Creatine for Improved Brain and Muscle Creatine Levels: A Superiority Pilot Trial in Healthy Men." *Applied Physiology, Nutrition, and Metabolism* 41, no. 9 (2016): 1005–7.

Outhred, Tim, Brittany E. Hawkshead, Tor D. Wager, et al. "Acute Neural Effects of Selective Serotonin Reuptake Inhibitors Versus Noradrenaline Reuptake Inhibitors on Emotion Processing: Implications for Differential Treatment Efficacy." *Neuroscience & Biobehavioral Reviews* 37, no. 8 (2013): 1786–800.

Özdemir, Elif, Andrea Norton, and Gottfried Schlaug. "Shared and Distinct Neural Correlates of Singing and Speaking." *Neuroimage* 33, no. 2 (2006): 628–35.

Pagels, Elaine. *Beyond Belief: The Secret Gospel of Thomas*. New York: Random House, 2003.

Palma, Andy. "Meet Andrew Jones, The Bodybuilder Without a Pulse." *Futurism*. https://web.archive.org/web/20161012031029/http://futurism.com/meet-andrew-jones-the-bodybuilder-without-a-pulse/.

Pavlov, Ivan. *Conditioned Reflexes*. Mineola: Courier Dover Publications, 1927.

Payne, R. A., C. N. Symeonides, D. J. Webb, and S. R. J. Maxwell. "Pulse Transit Time Measured from the ECG: An Unreliable Marker of Beat-To-Beat Blood Pressure." *Journal of Applied Physiology* 100, no. 1 (2006): 136–41.

Pe, Madeline Lee, Filip Raes, and Peter Kuppens. "The Cognitive Building Blocks of Emotion Regulation: Ability to Update Working Memory Moderates the Efficacy of Rumination and Reappraisal on Emotion." *PloS One* 8, no. 7 (2013): e69071

Peat, David. *Einstein's Moon: Bell's Theorem and the Curious Quest for Quantum Reality*. Chicago: Contemporary Books, 1990.

Pepperell, Robert. *The Posthuman Condition: Consciousness Beyond the Brain*. Bristol: Intellect Books, 1995.

Pepperell, Robert. "The Posthuman Manifesto." *Kritikos* 2 (2005). http://intertheory.org/pepperell.htm.

Peterson, Christopher. "The Posthumanism to Come." *Angelaki: Journal of the Theoretical Humanities* 16, no. 2 (2011): 128.

Pfaus, James G. and Sherri L. Jones. "Central Nervous System Anatomy and Neurochemistry of Sexual Desire." In *Textbook of Female Sexual Function and Dysfunction: Diagnosis and Treatment*. Irwin Goldstein, Anita H. Clayton, Andrew T. Goldstein, Noel N. Kim, and Sheryl A. Kingsberg, eds. Oxford: Wiley-Blackwell, 2018, 25–51.

Philbeck, Thomas D. "Ontology" In *Post-and Transhumanism: An Introduction*. Robert Ranisch and Stefan Lorenz Sorgner, eds. Bern: Peter Lang Edition, 2014, 173–84.

Pietrowsky, R., et al. "Vasopressin and Oxytocin do not Influence Early Sensory Processing but Affect Mood and Activation in Man." *Peptides* 12 (1991): 1385–91.

Pinn, Anthony B., ed. *Black Religion and Aesthetics: Religious Thought and Life in Africa and the African Diaspora*. New York: Palgrave MacMillan, 2009.

Pinn, Anthony B. *Embodiment and the New Shape of Black Theological Thought*. New York: New York University Press, 2010.

Pinn, Anthony B. *The End of God-Talk: An African American Humanist Theology*. Cambridge: University Press, 2010.

Pinn, Anthony B. *Humanism: Essays on Race, Religion and Popular Culture*. New York: Bloomsbury, 2015.

Pinn, Anthony B. "Sweaty Bodies in a Circle: Thoughts on the Subtle Dimensions of Black Religion as Protest." *Black Theology* 4, no. 1 (2015): 11–26.

Pontin, Fabricio, Laura Dick Guerim, Camila Palhares Barbosa, and Bruna Fernandes Ternus. "Sexual Identity and Neurosexism: A Critique of Reductivist approaches of Sexual Behavior and Gender." *Revista Dissertatio de Filosofia* 5 (2017): 22–37.

Proctor, Darby and Sarah Brosnan. "Political Primates: What Other Primates Can Tell Us About the Evolutionary Roots of Our Own Political Behavior." In *Man Is by Nature a Political Animal: Evolution, Biology, and Politics*. Peter K. Hatemi and Rose McDermott, eds. Chicago: The University of Chicago Press, 2011, 47–71.

Rae, Caroline D. and Stefan Bröer. "Creatine as a Booster for Human Brain Function. How Might it Work?." *Neurochemistry International* 89 (2015): 249–59.

Rainie, Lee and Barry Wellman. *Networked: The New Social Operating System*. Cambridge: MIT Press. 2012.

Randell-Moon, Holly and Ryan Tippet, eds. *Security, Race, Biopower: Essays on Technology and Corporeality*. New York: Springer, 2016.

Reddie, Anthony G., ed. *Black Theology, Slavery and Contemporary Christianity: 200 Years and No Apology*. New York: Routledge, 2016.

Reddie, Anthony G. *Working Against the Grain: Re-Imaging Black Theology in the 21st Century*. New York: Routledge, 2014.

Reul, Johannes MHM, "Making Memories of Stressful Events: A Journey Along Epigenetic, Gene Transcription, and Signaling Pathways." *Frontiers in Psychiatry* 5 (2014): 5.

Ranisch, Robert and Stefan Lorenz Sorgner, eds. *Post-and Transhumanism: An Introduction*. Bern: Peter Lang Edition, 2014.

Rikowski, Glenn. "Education, Capital and the Transhuman." *Marxism Against Postmodernism in Educational Theory*. Dave Hill, Peter McLaren, Mike Cole, and Glenn Rikowski, eds. Lanham: Lexington Books, 2002, 111–43.

Roberts, Dorothy. "Black Women and the Pill." *Perspectives on Sexual and Reproductive Health* 32, no. 2 (2000): 92.

Rose Bird, Stephanie. *The Big Book of Soul: The Ultimate Guide to the African American Spirit*. Newburyport: Hampton Roads Publishing, 2010.

Rosenberg, Rosalind. *Jane Crow: The Life of Pauli Murray*. Oxdord: Oxford University Press, 2017.

Rothblatt, Martine. "Mind is Deeper Than Matter: Transgenderism, Transhumanism, and the Freedom of Form." In *The Transhumanist Reader: Classical and Contemporary Essays on the Science, Technology, and Philosophy of the Human Future*. Max More and Natasha Vita-More, eds. Oxford: Wiley-Blackwell, 2013.

Rubio-Araiz, Ana, Mercedes Perez-Hernandez, Andrés Urrutia, et al. "3, 4-Methylenedioxymethamphetamine (MDMA, Ecstasy) Disrupts Blood-Brain Barrier Integrity Through a Mechanism Involving P2X7 Receptors." *International Journal of Neuropsychopharmacology* 17, no. 8 (2014): 1243–55.

Rutsky, R. L. "Mutation, History, and Fantasy in the Posthuman." *Subject Matters: A Journal of Communications and the Self* (2007): 99–112.

Sanders, A. F. "Towards a Model of Stress and Human Performance." *Acta Psychologica* 53, no. 1 (1983): 61–97

Schachter, Stanley and Jerome Singer. "Cognitive, Social, and Physiological Determinants of Emotional State." *Psychological Review* 69, no. 5 (1962): 379.

Schacter, Daniel L. "Priming and Multiple Memory Systems: Perceptual Mechanisms of Implicit Memory." *Journal of Cognitive Neuroscience* 4, no. 3 (1992): 244–56.

Schaefer, Donovan. *Religious Affects: Animality, Evolution and Power*. Durham: Duke University Press, 2015.

Schjoedt, Uffe, Hans Stødkilde-Jørgensen, Armin W. Geertz, and Andreas Roepstorff. "Highly Religious Participants Recruit Areas of Social Cognition in Personal Prayer." *Social Cognitive and Affective Neuroscience* 4, no. 2 (2009): 199–207.

Schwanitz, Dietrich. "Systems Theory According to Niklas Luhmann—Its Environment and Conceptual Strategies." *Cultural Critique* 30 (Spring 1995): 146.

Searle, John. *The Rediscovery of the Mind*. Cambridge: MIT Press, 1992.

Senghor, Léopold Sédar. "Negritude: A Humanism of the Twentieth Century." In *Postcolonialisms: An Anthology of Cultural Theory and Criticism*. Gaurav Gajanan Desai and Supriya Nair, eds. New Brunswick: Rutgers University Press, 2005, 629–36.

Seung, Sebastian. *Connectome: How the Brain's Wiring Makes Us Who We Are*. New York: Houghton Mifflin Harcourt, 2012.

Shapiro, Michael H. "Performance Enhancement and Legal Theory." In *The Transhumanist Reader: Classical and Contemporary Essays on the Science, Technology, and Philosophy of the Human Future*. Max More and Natasha Vita-More, eds. West Sussex: Wiley-Blackwell, 2013, 279–81.

Sheriff, Michael J., Ben Dantzer, Oliver P. Love, and John L. Orrock. "Error Management Theory and the Adaptive Significance of Transgenerational Maternal-Stress Effects on Offspring Phenotype." *Ecology and Evolution* 8, no. 13 (2018): 6473–82.

Sherman, Rachel M., Juliet Forman, Valentin Antonescu, Daniela Puiu, Michelle Daya, Nicholas Rafaels, Meher Preethi Boorgula, et al. "Assembly of a Pan-genome from Deep Sequencing of 910 Humans of African Descent." *Nature Genetics* 51, no. 1 (2019): 30–35.

Short, Megan M., Dwight Mazmanian, Lana J. Ozen, and Michel Bédard. "Four Days of Mindfulness Meditation Training for Fraduate Students: A Pilot Study Examining Effects on Mindfulness, Self-Regulation, and Executive Function." *The Journal of Contemplative Inquiry* 2, no. 1 (2015). https://bit.ly/2ZIrTjd

Siegel, Daniel J. "Mindfulness Training and Neural Integration: Differentiation of Distinct Streams of Awareness and the Cultivation of Well-being." *Social Cognitive and Affective Neuroscience* 2, no. 4 (2007): 259–63.

Silver, Lee M. "Biotechnology in a World of Spiritual Beliefs." Quoted in *Biotechnology: Our Future as Human Beings and Citizens*. Sean D. Sutton, ed. Albany: State University of New York Press, 2009.

Silverthorn, Dee Unglaub, William C. Ober, Claire W. Garrison, Andrew C. Silverthorn, and Bruce R. Johnson, *Human Physiology: An Integrated Approach, Seventh Edition*. San Francisco: Pearson/Benjamin Cummings, 2016.

Sinyangwe, Samuel. "Mapping Police Violence." (Accessed January 5, 2017). https://web.archive.org/web/20170105072842/http://mappingpoliceviolence.org.

Slabodsky, Santiago. *Decolonial Judaism: Triumphal Failures of Barbaric Thinking*. New York: Springer, 2014.

Smith, Aaron. "Public Predictions for the Future of Workforce Automation." *Pew Research*. https://bit.ly/2wzLxB9.

Smith, Barbara Herrnstein and E. Roy Weintraub. *Emergence and Embodiment: New Essays on Second-Order Systems Theory*. Durham: Duke University Press, 2009.

Spillers, Hortense. *Black, White, and in Color: Essays on American Literature and Culture*. Chicago: University of Chicago Press, 2003.

Spillers, Hortense J. "Mama's Baby, Papa's Maybe: An American Grammar Book." *Diacritics* 17, no. 2 (1987): 65–81.

Srinivasan, Mandayam A. and Cagatay Basdogan. "Haptics in Virtual Environments: Taxonomy, Research Status, and Challenges." *Computers & Graphics* 21, no. 4 (1997): 393–404.

Stock, Gregory. "Germinal Choice Technology and the Human Future." *Reproductive Biomedicine Online* 10 (2005): 27–35.

Sweatt, J. David. "Epigenetic Regulation of Memory Formation and Maintenance." *Learning & Memory* 20, no. 2 (2013): 61–74.

Sweeney, Sean. "Apps to Get Them Chatting: A Mobile Device Doesn't Have to be a Conversation-Stopper. Some Apps Can Help Keep Your Clients' Conversation Flowing." *The ASHA Leader* 21, no. 11 (2016): online-only. doi: 10.1044/leader.APP.21112016.np.

Szyf, Moshe. "Nongenetic Inheritance and Transgenerational Epigenetics." *Trends in Molecular Medicine* 21, no. 2 (2015): 134–44.

Taddei, Francesco, Alessandro Bultrini, Donatella Spinelli, and Francesco Di Russo. "Neural Correlates of Attentional and Executive Processing in Middle-Age Fencers." *Medicine & Science in Sports & Exercise* 44, no. 6 (2012): 1057–66.

Tang, Yi-Yuan, Qilin Lu, Ming Fan, Yihong Yang, and Michael I. Posner. "Mechanisms of White Matter Changes Induced by Meditation." *Proceedings of the National Academy of Sciences* 109, no. 26 (2012): 10570–74.

Tao, Jing, Jiao Liu, Natalia Egorova, et al. "Increased Hippocampus–Medial Prefrontal Cortex Resting-State Functional Connectivity and Memory Function after Tai Chi Chuan Practice in Elder Adults." *Frontiers in Aging Neuroscience* 8 (2016): 25. doi: 10.3389/fnagi.2016.00025.

Taren, Adrienne A., J. David Creswell, and Peter J. Gianaros. "Dispositional Mindfulness Co-Varies with Smaller Amygdala and Caudate Volumes in Community Adults." *PLoS One* 8, no. 5 (2013): e64574. doi: 10.1371/journal.pone.0064574.

Taves, Ann. *Religious Experience Reconsidered: A Building-Block Approach to the Study of Religion and Other Special Things.* Princeton: Princeton University Press, 2009.

Taylor, John G. "The Perception-Conceptualisation-Knowledge Representation-Reasoning Representation-Action Cycle: The View from the Brain." In *Perception-Action Cycle.* Vassilis Cutsuridis, Amir Hussain, and John G. Taylor, eds. New York: Springer, 2011, 243–85.

Taziaux, Melanie, Annemieke S. Staphorsius, Mohammad A. Ghatei, Stephen R. Bloom, Dick F. Swaab, and Julie Bakker. "Kisspeptin Expression in the Human Infundibular Nucleus in Relation to Sex, Gender Identity, and Sexual Orientation." *The Journal of Clinical Endocrinology & Metabolism* 101, no. 6 (2016): 2380–89.

Tempels, Placide, A. Rubbens, and Colin King. *Bantu Philosophy.* Paris: Présence Africaine, 1959.

Teplan, Michal. "Fundamentals of EEG Measurement." *Measurement Science Review* 2, no. 2 (2002): 1–11.

"The Fitness Model Without a Pulse." *Great Big Story*. https://web.archive.org/web/20161012030340/http://www.greatbigstory.com/stories/living-on-an-artificial-heart.

Thimmapuram, Jayaram. Robert Pargament, Kedesha Sibliss, Rodney Grim, Rosana Risques, and Erik Toorens, "Effect of Heartfulness Meditation on Burnout, Emotional Wellness, and Telomere Length in Health Care Professionals." *Journal of Community Hospital Internal Medicine Perspectives* 7, no. 1 (2017): 21–27.

Torregrossa, Gianluca, Michiel Morshuis, Robin Varghese, et al. "Results with SynCardia Total Artificial Heart Beyond 1 Year." *ASAIO Journal* 60, no. 6 (2014): 626–34.

Tufekci, Zeynep. "Engineering the Public: Big Data, Surveillance and Computational Politics." *First Monday* 19, no. 7 (2014). doi: http://dx.doi.org/10.5210/fm.v19i7.4901.

Turman, Eboni Marshall. *Toward a Womanist Ethic of Incarnation: Black Bodies, the Black Church, and the Council of Chalcedon*. New York: Springer, 2013.

Ulanov, Ann. "Jung and Religion: The Opposing Self." *The Cambridge Companion to Jung*. Polly Young-Eisendrath, Terence Dawson, eds. Cambridge: Cambridge University Press, 1997, 296–313.

Van der Kolk, Bessel A. "The Body Keeps the Score: Memory and the Evolving Psychobiology of Posttraumatic Stress." *Harvard Review of Psychiatry* 1, no. 5 (1994): 253–65.

vanOyen Witvliet, Charlotte, Ross W. Knoll, Nova G. Hinman, and Paul A. DeYoung. "Compassion-focused Reappraisal, Benefit-focused Reappraisal, and Rumination After an Interpersonal Offense: Emotion-regulation Implications for Subjective Emotion, Linguistic Responses, and Physiology." *The Journal of Positive Psychology* 5, no. 3 (2010): 226–42.

Varu, Shailesh M. "Heart Based Meditation: Panacea for Today's Youth." *European Journal of Multidisciplinary Studies* 2, no. 6 (2017): 180–83.

Vollenweider, F. X., K. L. Leenders, C. Scharfetter, et al. "Metabolic Hyperfrontality and Psychopathology in the Ketamine Model of Psychosis Using Positron Emission Tomography (PET) and [18F]Fluorodeoxyglucose (FDG)." *Eur Neuropsychopharmacol* 7 (1997): 9–24.

Walker, Alice. *In Search of our Mother's Gardens: Womanist Prose*. Boston: Houghton Mifflin Harcourt, 2004.

Wallace, Jeff. *DH Lawrence, Science and the Posthuman*. New York: Palgrave MacMillan, 2005.

Walshe, Sadhbh. "How US Prison Labour Pads Corporate Profits at Taxpayers' Expense." *The Guardian*, July 6, 2012. (Accessed January 7, 2017). goo.gl/fElUje.

Ward, Benedicta. *The Sayings of the Desert Fathers: The Alphabetical Collection, No. 59*. Kalamazoo: Cistercian Publications, 1984.

Warren, Calvin L. *Ontological Terror: Blackness, Nihilism, and Emancipation*. Durham: Duke University Press, 2018.

Washington, Harriet A. *Medical Apartheid: The Dark History of Medical Experimentation on Black Americans from Colonial Times to the Present*. New York: Broadway, 2007.

Washington, Harriet A. "Tracking the Risks of Birth Control." *Heart and Soul* (February 1996).

Waters-Metenier, Sheena, Masud Husain, Tobias Wiestler, and Jörn Diedrichsen. "Bihemispheric Transcranial Direct Current Stimulation Enhances Effector-Independent Representations of Motor Synergy and Sequence Learning." *The Journal of Neuroscience* 34, no. 3 (2014): 1037–50.

Weber, Rolf H. "Internet of Things–New Security and Privacy Challenges." *Computer Law & Security Review* 26, no. 1 (2010): 23–30.

Weheliye, Alexander. mentions Stuart Hall. "Race, Articulation, and Societies Structured in Dominance." In *Sociological Theories: Race and Colonialism*. Paris: Unesco, 1980, 303–45. In *Habeas Viscus: Racializing Assemblages, Biopolitics, and Black Feminist Theories of the Human*. Durham: Duke University Press, 2014.

Wei, Gao-Xia, Ting Xu, Feng-Mei Fan, et al. "Can Tai Chi Reshape the Brain? A Brain Morphometry Study." *PLoS One* 8, no. 4 (2013): e61038. doi: 10.1371/journal.pone.0061038.

Wei, Gao-Xia, Hao-Ming Dong, Zhi Yang, et al. "Tai Chi Chuan Optimizes the Functional Organization of the Intrinsic Human Brain Architecture in Older Adults." *Frontiers in Aging Neuroscience* 6 (2014): 74. doi: 10.3389/fnagi.2014.00074.

Weindling, Paul. "Julian Huxley and the Continuity of Eugenics in Twentieth-Century Britain." *Journal of Modern European History = Zeitschrift fur Moderne Europaische Geschichte= Revue D'histoire Europeenne Contemporaine* 10, no. 4 (2012): 480–99.

Wernick, Miles N. and John N. Aarsvold. *Emission Tomography: the Fundamentals of PET and SPECT*. San Diego: Elsevier Academic Press, 2004.

West, Cornel. "Philosophy and the Afro-American Experience," In *A Companion to African-American Philosophy*. Tommy L. Lott and John P. Pittman, eds. Hoboken: Blackwell Publishing, 2003, 7–32.

West, Candace and Don H. Zimmerman. "Doing Gender." *Gender & Society* 1, no. 2 (1987): 125–51.

Whitehead, Alfred North. *Process and Reality*. New York: The Free Press, 1979.

Whitehead, Alfred North. *An Enquiry Concerning the Principles of Natural Knowledge*. Cambridge: Cambridge University Press, 2011.

Whitman, James Q. *Hitler's American Model: The United States and the Making of Nazi Race Law*. Princeton: Princeton University Press, 2017.

Wilderson III, Frank B., Saidiya Hartman, Steve Martinot, J. Sexton, and Hortenese J. Spillers. "*Afro-pessimism: An Introduction*." Minneapolis: Racked & Dispatched, 2017.

Wilker, Sarah, Thomas Elbert, and Iris-Tatjana Kolassa. "The Downside of Strong Emotional Memories: How Human Memory-Related Genes Influence the Risk for Posttraumatic Stress Disorder–A Selective Review." *Neurobiology of Learning and Memory* 112 (2014): 75–86.

Williams, Angel Kyodo. *Being Black: Zen and the Art of Living with Fearlessness and Grace*. London: Penguin, 2002.

Williams, E. Russ. "Slave Patrol Ordinances of St. Tammany Parish, Louisiana, 1835–1838." *Louisiana History: The Journal of the Louisiana Historical Association* 13, no. 4 (1972): 399–412. Stable URL: http://www.jstor.org/stable/4231289.

Wink, Paul and Michele Dillon. "Spiritual Development Across the Adult Life Course: Findings From a Longitudinal Study." *Journal of Adult Development* 9, no. 1 (2002): 79–94.

Witt, Karl J., Marvarene Oliver, and Christine McNichols. "Counseling Via Avatar: Professional Practice in Virtual Worlds." *International Journal for the Advancement of Counselling* 38, no. 3 (2016): 218–36.

Witte, P. "Exploratory Study: Use of Instant Messaging Tactics to Increase Loyalty." Master's Thesis, University of Twente. 2016.

Woiak, Joanne. "Designing a Brave New World: Eugenics, Politics, and Fiction." *The Public Historian* 29, no. 3 (2007): 105–29.

Wolfe, Cary. *What Is Posthumanism*. Minneapolis: University of Minnesota Press, 2009, xv.

Wolyniak, Joseph. "'The Relief of Man's Estate': Transhumanism, the Baconian Project, and the Theological Impetus for Material Salvation." In *Religion and Transhumanism: The Unknown Future of Human Enhancement*. C. Mercer, T. J. Trothen, eds. Santa Barbara: Praeger, 2014.

Wormald, Benjamin. "2014 Religious Landscape Study." In *Pew Research Centers Religion & Public Life Project*. (Accessed May 16, 2016). http://goo.gl/OIvdCx.

Wyche, Susan P. "Investigating Design For Global Techno-Spiritual Practices." In *Extended Abstracts, ACM SIGCHI Conf. on Computer Supported Cooperative Work (CSCW'08): ACM*. Dordrecht, Netherlands: Springer, 2008.

Wyche, Susan P., Gillian R. Hayes, Lonnie D. Harvel, and Rebecca E. Grinter. "Technology in Spiritual Formation: An Exploratory Study of Computer Mediated Religious Communications." In *Proceedings of the 2006 20th Anniversary Conference on Computer Supported Cooperative Work*. ACM. Dordrecht, Netherlands: Springer, 2006.

Wynter, Sylvia. "Human, 'Being as Noun? Or Being Human as Praxis? Towards the Autopoetic Turn/Overturn: A Manifesto" (2007). http://bit.ly/2I1A3Oj.

Yamagishi, T., et al. "The Private Rejection of Unfair Offers and Emotional Commitment." *Proceedings of the National Academy of Sciences* 106, no. 28 (2009): 11520–23.

Yang, Xiao, J. Richard Jennings, and Bruce H. Friedman. "Exteroceptive Stimuli Override Interoceptive State in Reaction Time Control." *Psychophysiology* 54, no. 12 (2017): 1940–50.

Yiassemides, Angeliki. *Time and Timelessness: Temporality In the Theory of Carl Jung*. Abbington: Routledge, 2013.

Zampin, Claudio, Roberta Ficacci, Miriam Checcacci, Fabio Franciolini, and Luigi Catacuzzeno. "Pain Control by Proprioceptive and Exteroceptive Stimulation at the Trigeminal Level." *Frontiers in Physiology* 9 (2018). doi: 10.3389/fphys.2018.01037

Zong, Chengzhi and Roozbeh Jafari. "Robust Heart Rate Estimation Using Wrist-Based PPG Signals in the Presence of Intense Physical Activities." In *2015 37th Annual International Conference of the IEEE Engineering in Medicine and Biology Society (EMBC)*. Milan: IEEE Conference Publications, 2015, 8078–82. doi: 10.1109/EMBC.2015.7320268.

Index